Table of Contents

Introduction

If you are using this book, you are among the three out of four car buyers who are purchasing a used, instead of new, car. No longer is buying a used car "buying someone else's troubles." In fact, more and more consumers consider it a smart choice. In addition, because year to year model changes are almost imperceptible, it is hard to tell a brand new car from a two- to three-year-old model. The simple bottom line is that used cars cost less to buy and operate. There's also an emotional benefit to driving a used car—that strange rumble or new scrape doesn't cause the same sinking feeling in your stomach as it does when it happens to a shiny, new model.

While used cars are less expensive, rising prices have turned them into major purchases. As the average price has gone up, right now it's around $13,000, so has the average age. Today's cars typically last more than eight years, so you'll be keeping this purchase longer than in the past. That's why it's more important to make a smart decision.

Even the process of buying a used car is getting better. Since the recent introduction of used car superstores, traditional dealers have been scrambling to change the way they treat consumers. And, of course, the Internet has become a powerful tool for car buyers.

Thanks to better reliability and the millions of previously leased vehicles hitting the used car market, there are more used cars available then ever before. *The Used Car Book* will get you started in the right direction by helping you separate the "peaches" from the "lemons."

To make the task as easy as possible, the book is divided into four parts:

✓ Finding Them and Checking Them Out
✓ Getting the Best Price and Selling Your Car
✓ Keeping Them Going
✓ How They Rate

Good luck in your search and safe driving!

Part One: Finding Them and Checking Them Out

The key to finding a good used car is being able to predict its future performance—and the best way to do that is to know how the car was treated and what problems it had in the past. That's why a trusted friend can be the best source for a used car. Among other things, you'll get an honest answer to the question, "Why are you selling it?"

Your chances of finding a good used car depend on where you look. There are five main sources: new car dealers, used car dealers, rental car companies, private sellers, and used car superstores.

New Car Dealers: Buying a used car from a new car dealer means that you will probably pay more for it. However, many dealers keep only the best cars for resale and generally have a wide selection, especially of the higher priced models. In addition, most new car dealers will give you a written warranty. But beware: These warranties are usually full of loopholes in the dealer's favor.

Another benefit of buying from new car dealers is that most have service facilities. This increases the chance that the car was inspected and repaired before being offered for sale. If you trust the dealership and know that it has serviced the car regularly, then a new car dealer can be a good source for a reliable car.

Tip: Used cars of the same brand as the new cars that the dealer sells are your best bets. Dealers can't get parts as easily and as inexpensively for cars from other manufacturers, and they are less likely to make repairs before reselling the car.

Used Car Dealers: You can usually get lower prices on an independent used car lot than from a new car dealer. However, the

5

majority of cars are sold in "as is" condition. Even if a used car dealer offers a warranty, it's often extremely difficult to get repair costs covered.

Another problem with buying from used car dealers is that they often get cast-offs, either from new car dealers or at auctions. In fact, they rarely know the history of the cars they're selling. Also, most used car dealerships do not have service facilities, so they have done little, if any, work on the cars. Many times used car dealers sell cars from lease fleets, taxi companies, or police departments—cars that have excessive wear.

Tip: The longer a dealer has been in the same location, the better your chances are of getting help should a problem arise. Because used car dealerships tend to be transient, it's best to find one that has been in business for at least five years at the same location.

Rental Car Companies: During the past few years, rental car companies have been reselling vehicles from their rental fleets to consumers. Contrary to popular belief, cars sold by the rental car companies haven't necessarily been "driven into the ground" by careless renters. For the most part, these cars are used by business people who simply drive from the airport to a meeting and then back again or by renters who use the cars on longer trips.

Many rental companies have facilities that resemble new car dealerships. They generally offer late models (12 to 18 months old) that have high mileage (an average of 23,000 miles). There are advantages to buying from a rental car company:

✓ You have access to the maintenance history of the car.
✓ Problem cars tend not to be sold through the rental dealerships.
✓ The cars have had regular maintenance work.
✓ There is generally a good selection.
✓ You don't negotiate the price.

On the other hand, buying from a rental car company means buying a late model car with high mileage. Also, these cars tend to be loaded with options, which adds to the overall price. (In general, prices at rental car companies tend to be slightly higher than a private seller's prices.)

Private Sales: One of the best and most common ways to buy a used car is from a private owner. The owner will often accept less than the car's retail value, because he or she doesn't have the overhead and expenses of a dealer. Also, buying from someone you know is the best way to get honest information about how well that car was cared for. On the other hand, buying a car from a private source usually requires a lot of running around in order to compare cars.

On a private sale, you should always call the seller before going to see the car. Asking the right questions over the phone can avoid some wasted trips. (See "Questions for the Owner" on page 10.)

One problem with buying through private sellers is determining whether the seller is truly an independent individual selling a single car or is actually a pro masquerading as a private seller. Don't be afraid to use your intuition, and, if you're in doubt, ask to see the title of the car. If the name on the title doesn't match the name of the seller, ask questions.

Tip: If you know someone who regularly trades in a car that they've taken good care of, contact them and ask if they'd be willing to sell it to you rather than trade it in. They can almost always get more by selling it to you than the wholesale price offered on the trade-in. And you will often pay less than the retail price that the dealer would charge.

Superstores: A relatively new way of buying a used car that avoids the hassles of negotiating the price with traditional dealers and private sellers. What is their appeal? They offer "no-haggle" pricing, an enormous selection, and salespeople who aren't on commission. At a superstore, your first stop will generally be a computer terminal where a salesperson will guide you through selecting a car based on your price range and desired features. The computer will identify the vehicles on the lot that meet your needs and tell you where they are located.

⚠ AUTOMOBILE AUCTIONS

Most newspapers carry ads for used car auctions. In general, cars sold at automobile auctions tend to be vehicles that would be difficult to sell in the regular marketplace. They've often been in accidents, have very high mileage, or have obvious wear and tear problems. Because automobile auctions can be intimidating for the average buyer and because there are better sources of used cars, we don't recommend them. However, as a source of entertainment, you might enjoy spending a few dollars to see what happens at one of these events.

Understanding the Classifieds

The easiest place to find privately sold cars is through the classified ads. While understanding classified ad "shorthand" won't guarantee that the cars you go to see are all that they claim to be, it will help you weed out the cars that you're interested in from those that won't meet your needs. For example, take the following ad:

> '97 Frd Taur: orig owr, 4 dr, lo mi, pw, air, cruise, am/fm, tlt str, snrf, mint, dk red, best offer.

Here's what it says: The original owner is selling a dark red, four-door 1997 Ford Taurus with low mileage, power windows, air conditioning, cruise control, am/fm radio, tilt steering wheel, sunroof, in like-new condition. Here is a list of frequently used abbreviations:

ABS = anti-lock brake system
a/c, air = air conditioning
a/t, at, auto = automatic trans.
am/fm = radio, no tape player
cass = cassette tape player
cd = compact disk player
cond = condition
conv = convertible
cpe = 2-door sporty coupe
cruise = cruise control
cu in = cubic inches
cyl = cylinders (3,4,5,6, or 8)
dk = dark (color)
dlr = dealer
dr = doors (2,4, or 5)
exc = excellent
full pwr = all power options
h/back, h/b = hatchback
hdtp = hardtop
hd = heavy duty
lk nw = like new
lo mi = low mileage

lt = light
man trans, mt = manual trans.
mint = superb, like-new
   condition
mpg = miles per gallon
orig owr = original owner
pb = power brakes
ps = power steering
pow seats = power seats
pw = power windows
rear dfg = rear defogger
rf = roof
sac = sacrifice
sed = sedan
spd = speed (3,4, or 5)
snrf = sunroof
t/d, tape = tape player
tlt str = tilt steering wheel
vnyl = vinyl top
wrnty = warranty
wgn = station wagon

Checking Them Out

There are literally millions of used cars in the marketplace. The key to finding a peach is to inspect the car very carefully before you buy. This section is designed to help you separate the peaches from the lemons. By following these guidelines, you'll find that checking out a used car is not as difficult as you may have imagined. In fact, you don't have to be a mechanical genius if you know what to look for.

Our checklist has seven sections. The first six will guide you through the inspection process—looking at the car from the inside, outside, and under the hood, as well as handling the test drive and safety checks. We've also included a special list of items you'll want a mechanic to check for you.

Before you hit the streets, you may want to take a few moments to read through the checklists. You'll get a general sense of the types of things that you should keep your eyes open for when you're looking for a good used car.

It's very important to take notes on the cars that you're considering. Not only is it easy to mix up the various features after you've looked at two or three cars, but it shows the seller that you're serious and will be looking very carefully for potential problems.

While these checklists will help prevent you from buying a lemon, the final step before signing on the dotted line is to have the car inspected by an independent mechanic. Don't forget that the car you are considering must meet certain safety and emissions requirements set forth by your state's Department of Motor Vehicles. Contact your DMV ahead of time to find out what the standards are. Some states require that the car be inspected before it can be registered. If that's a requirement in your state, make sure it has been inspected and that the seller has the documentation to prove it. If it is your responsibility to have the car inspected and/or the emission system checked, write into any contract the fact that the seller will pay for necessary repairs in the event that the car fails to pass inspection.

Shop in good weather, so you'll take the time to really look at the car. Get the names of the previous owners and give them a call. Ask the same questions (see next page) that you would ask the current owner.

Check all documentation carefully for words like "reassumed," which means the vehicle has been returned to the dealer because of recurring mechanical problems. Examine the title carefully; some states clearly identify on the title that the car has been reassumed and why. Most recycled lemons are cars that are one to three years old and have low mileage; they are often described as an "executive car" or a "demo."

If service history documents are available, check them carefully to see that it was well maintained. Service dates and locations will give you a clue as to whether the car was in normal use and who the owner was.

Finally, be sure to check on crash test performance, parts cost, insurance cost, fuel economy, theft rating, bumper performance, and recalls in the car listings in the back of this book.

Questions for the Owner

When responding to an ad for a used car, you should always make a call to the seller first to learn a little more about the car and find out who is selling it. If the seller sounds knowledgeable and forthcoming, that may be an indication that the car has received good care.

Curbstoners and used car dealers often place classified ads. To avoid them, tell the person who answers the phone that you're calling about the car for sale—but don't identify the car. If the person replies "Which one?" they are a professional used car dealer or a curbstoner. Also beware if there are a number of cars listed in the classified ads with the same telephone number.

Contact a previous owner if you're buying a car through a used car dealer. If the dealer can't or won't help you get in contact with the previous owner, the car may have come from an auction or another undesirable source.

If possible, ask the owner these questions:

✓ How long have you owned the car?
✓ Did you buy the car new?
✓ Has the car been in any accidents? What repairs were needed?
✓ What is the mileage?

✓ Generally, has the car been driven mainly around town or on long trips?

✓ Was this the only car in your family?

✓ What do you like best about the car?

✓ What major repair work has been done on the car? (If you assume that major repair work has been done on the car, the owner may be less defensive and possibly more truthful.)

✓ Have you ever had any problems with rust? Has the car ever been repainted?

✓ Why are you selling the car?

✓ Did you follow the manufacturer's maintenance schedule (found in the owner's manual)?

✓ Where did you generally get your service performed?

✓ What would I need to do to put the car into top shape?

✓ Are there any liens on the car? (If so, the owner owes money on the car.)

Inside Checklist

It's important to check the inside of the car carefully for several reasons. First, the interior of the car can give you a number of clues as to how well that car has been treated. If the car has been neglected on the inside, it is likely that it was neglected mechanically as well. A well-cared-for car is going to be a better buy than one that has not been maintained. A diligent inspection of the interior can help you tell the difference. Second, the cosmetic factor: If you're spending a lot of money on a car, you'll want it to look good. You'll also want to inspect it thoroughly to make sure that it has all of the features that are important to you.

The following ten spot checks will help you to evaluate the condition of the car's interior.

1 Study the seats. The upholstery and carpeting provide important clues as to the kind of care the previous owner gave the car. Check the car's seat cushions carefully. If they are weak, have broken springs, or are full of lumps, that's a sign that the car has had some pretty heavy use. If the rear seats show excessive wear, the car may have been used as a taxi. If they look clean and unused, that's an indication that the car was a one- or two-person car.

2 **Look under the mats and try the pedals.** If the car has floor mats or seat covers, check underneath them to find what kind of wear occurred before they were installed. Press on the gas, brake, and clutch pedals. They should all operate freely without any excessive play or binding.

3 **Examine the doors.** Look for heavy wear or discoloration on the upper part of the door panel where the driver's arm would rest. Also, check the inside handles to see if they are loose or worn. If there is a lot of wear and the odometer is relatively low, that's a sign that the odometer could have been turned back.

4 **Use your nose.** If the car smells musty or heavily deodorized, it probably leaks or, worse, was once underwater. Pull back the carpeting and check for rusted flooring. Also check under the seats for rust.

5 **Check the odometer.** The average car is driven about 12,000 miles per year. So compare the car's age with its total number of miles. For example, it's not unreasonable to expect a five-year-old car to have 60,000 miles on it. If the mileage is a lot less than the average (12,000 per year times the age of the car), you could have either a cream puff or a car with a rolled-back odometer. If the car has considerably more miles on it than the 12,000-mile average, don't give up on the car until you find out how those miles were put on. For example, 18,000 miles per year of highway driving can do less damage to a car than 6,000 miles per year of stop-and-go city traffic.

6 **Review the dash.** Take a minute to familiarize yourself with the dashboard layout and try every feature on the dashboard. Make sure everything works with the key turned on but without the engine running. Check the radio, windshield wipers, heater, air conditioner, cigarette lighter, clock, horn, parking brake, rear window defogger, fan, and all the air vents.

7 **Turn the ignition on.** With the key on but the engine off, make sure the alternator and oil pressure lights go on. If they don't, either the bulbs are burned out or the seller has disconnected the lights to ensure that they won't come on later while you're driving. This is something to put on your checklist for your mechanic to go over. When you turn the engine on, both of the lights should go

INSPECTING THE CAR: TOOLS OF THE TRADE

Be sure you wear some old clothes so you can peek underneath the car or open the hood and poke around a little bit. Here are some useful items to take along when you go out to inspect a used car:

Flashlight: for inspecting the wheel wells for signs of rust and for looking under the hood.

Rags: for checking the oil and other fluids and cleaning off your hands when you're done.

Magnet: for telling the difference between solid metal fender panels and those that have been filled with plastic body filler.

Screwdriver: for poking around the engine compartment.

Friend: for giving you practical and psychological support. Your friend can help you check the lights, exhaust, and back seat comfort while you're driving, as well as serve as a reminder to the seller that you're considering other cars by making comments like "The other car had more power."

Notebook and Pen: for taking notes. It's easy to forget the good and bad points of the cars you've looked at. Taking notes will prevent you from confusing details of one car with details of another. Using a notebook is also an effective negotiating technique. It shows the seller that you are serious about buying, that you've done your homework, and that you have other options.

off. If the oil pressure light stays on, turn the engine off and check the oil level. It may just be that the oil is low. However, if the oil level is okay, this light signals that the car could have major problems. If the alternator light stays on, it means the battery isn't charging, which could be a problem as simple as a loose fan belt or as serious as a bad alternator.

8 Try all the windows. Check to see that they slide smoothly and don't bind. Also, make sure that the front seats slide easily.

9 **Look in the glove compartment.** Look for the owner's manual and original warranty papers. If they are present (or if they are still available), and you're buying the car from a third party, you will have the opportunity to contact the previous owner to find out more about the condition of the car. If the warranty papers indicate that the original owner was from a distant area or another state, that's an indication that the car might have become available through an auction or an otherwise less desirable source for used cars. Also examine the original warranty and other papers to determine whether the serial numbers on these papers match the serial numbers on the car. If they don't match, either the car has been stolen or it is the product of two cars that have been welded together.

10 **Inspect convertible tops carefully.** To check a convertible, park the car in bright sunlight and carefully examine the roof from the inside for any holes or cracks in the fabric. Look for stains from leaks. Check the back window for clarity and test the top at least twice to make sure it goes up and down properly. If you have the opportunity, hose down the top or run it through a car wash to test for leaks.

Outside Checklist

There are three reasons to inspect the outside of the car carefully. First, it's one of your best clues as to whether the car has been in an accident. Second, it will help you avoid one of the most insidious of car repair problems—rust. Third, if the exterior shows signs of neglect, the owner may have also neglected the mechanical maintenance of the car.

Tip: Always shop in the daytime. Shopping at night or under the glare of lights in a used car lot can hide problems with the body work.

1 **Examine the glass and test the lights.** Front and back windows are expensive to replace, and problems with them can mean a safety hazard. Test the headlights, taillights, flashers, backup lights, brake lights, turn signals, and parking lights. (Bring a friend and this task will go a lot faster.)

2 **Look carefully for rust.** Repairing rust is far more expensive than most mechanical repairs, and rust does more to depreciate the value of a car than any other single item. Take special note of the following areas: wheel wells, rain gutters, window moldings, door frames (especially around the bottom), and the joints where the roof supports connect with the body. If the car has a vinyl top, look for bubbles and push on them with your finger. A crinkly, crunchy sound means there's rust under the vinyl that can be almost impossible to stop. Also check for bubbles or blisters around the trim, which indicate the beginning of rust under the paint.

Rust is a good reason to avoid a particular car, because there is no inexpensive way to repair rust problems.

3 **Examine the paint and body.** Beware of new paint jobs. A newly painted car may have had a severe rust problem or may have been in a major accident. Unless you know the person selling the car and know why it was repainted, stay away from cars with new paint jobs.

To determine whether a car has been repainted, check for telltale signs: the trim on the inside of the doors doesn't quite match the exterior trim; the color inside the hood and the trunk doesn't match the exterior; or little bits of paint on the rubber molding around the windows and doors or on the chrome.

A magnet can tell you if a fender is the original metal or filled with plastic body filler. Or you can check by tapping on suspect body areas with your knuckles. If the fender sounds hollow, it's probably okay. If it sounds solid, it may have been filled with body filler.

Tip: If the car is a sedan with a large engine, check the roof for holes that have been patched where lights or other equipment could have been mounted. Such a car may have been a cab or police car.

4 **Try all the doors, the hood, and the trunk.** Make sure the doors, trunk, and hood all open and close easily and tightly. Open the driver's side door and try to move it up and down. If it seems loose, then the car has probably had some heavy use. Also, if the door drops or falls out of place when you open it, again beware of heavy use. When the door is closed, check the gap between the door and the body. If it is uneven, the car may have been in an accident. The bumper can also provide a clue to a car's accident history. Both sides of the bumper should be evenly spaced from the car. If not, an accident could have knocked the bumper out of line.

5 **Look inside the trunk.** If it smells musty, it might leak. Check under the mat or carpeting for rust or other problems. Make sure you have all the jack equipment. Check the spare tire. If it's worn unevenly, it may have been changed with a front tire to hide a front-end problem.

6 **Check for leaks under the car.** A leaking black liquid may be oil from the engine or manual transmission; reddish fluid may be from an automatic transmission; greenish, watery liquid may be antifreeze. Clear water, usually from the air conditioner, is okay. Oily, odorous fluid may be brake fluid. You can recognize gasoline by its smell.

7 **Examine the tail pipe.** Make sure it's cool; then rub your finger inside the tail pipe. You should see a white or grey powder. If your finger is black and sooty, the car may simply need a tune-up. However, if it's black and gummy, the car probably has a problem with its rings or valves and is burning oil.

8 **Check the tires.** New tires may indicate that a serious alignment problem exists. Don't be afraid of old tires. They tell an important story about the car. Inspect them carefully for wear and scuffing. If they are worn irregularly (the middle seems balder than the sides or one side or the other seems to have less tread than the middle), the car has either bad shock absorbers, poor wheel alignment, or poor wheel balance. Don't forget to check the inside of the tires, the side of the tires facing the car. Sometimes, owners of tires that are badly scuffed will merely turn them around so that the good side faces out.

Tip: Check the inner side of the tires for evidence of leaking brake fluid.

9 **Test the shock absorbers.** Push up and down on each corner of the car until it starts bouncing. When you let go, the car should not bounce more than one time. If it does, you'll need to repair or replace the shock absorbers.

10 **Examine the car's overall alignment.** Park on a level surface and look at the car from a squatting position about 20 feet behind it. Are the front tires perfectly aligned with the rear tires? If not, the car has a severe frame problem and should be avoided. Also, you should check to see that the car is level. If one side dips lower than the other or if the front dips lower than the back, the car could have serious suspension or frame problems, and again you should avoid it.

11 **Remove the gas cap.** If a sign on the dash says to use only unleaded gasoline, look down the filler tube to the gas tank to see if the opening is small enough to prevent the larger, leaded gas fuel pump nozzles from fitting in it. If it looks like anything has been punched out, then the owner was probably using leaded gas, which can destroy the catalytic converter and will result in expensive repairs.

TIP

VEHICLE IDENTIFICATION NUMBER (VIN)

While you are inspecting the vehicle, write down the Vehicle Identification Number (VIN). You'll find it printed on a small strip of metal, either in the edge of the door or on the dashboard right beneath the windshield (look on the driver's side). Then, call the state's Department of Motor Vehicles (DMV) and ask them to look up the VIN in their records. They can tell you if the vehicle has been salvaged, totaled, or stolen.

Under the Hood

While many of us find the engine compartment to be a rather intimidating place, these simple checks can help you steer clear of lemons. Items 1 through 8 should be done before starting the car. Items 9 and 10, checking the oil and automatic transmission fluid, should be done after starting the engine.

Before you start the car:

1 Check the radiator. While the engine is cool, open the radiator cap to see if there is a shiny oil film on the top of the fluid in the radiator. If so, engine oil is probably leaking into your cooling system through a cracked head, cylinder block, or a leaky head gasket. All are expensive repairs. If the coolant mixture is rusty, you may need to replace the radiator. Stick your finger inside the filler neck and check for sludge. This usually means that somebody added a "stop leak" product to plug up holes in a leaky radiator.
Caution: Always make sure the radiator is cool before making these checks.

2 Examine the engine compartment. Check the overall cleanliness of the engine, but beware of perfectly clean engines. That's a possible indication that the engine has just been steam cleaned in order to prevent you from seeing various leaks. Inspect the engine carefully and look for leaking around the various components.

3 Look for maintenance stickers. Look around the engine compartment, air filter, underside of the hood, and door frames for any maintenance stickers put on by a service station. This may provide a clue to how frequently the car has been serviced. A key factor is frequent oil changes. If the owner regularly changed the oil, the chances of getting a well-running car increase dramatically.

4 Examine the belts. Check the fan belts for cracks or shredding and make sure that they are not too loose. When you push down on them, they should give only about half an inch. It's okay for the belts on a four- to five-year-old car to look as though they need to be replaced—they probably do. While you check the belts, wiggle the fan blade and other pulleys connected to the belts. If any are loose, the bearings may be gone, and they will have to be replaced.

5 **Check the wiring.** Check any wires for frayed or worn spots and cracks. If the car is more than two years old and all of the wiring looks new, the owner could have had a major problem. This isn't necessarily bad, but it's something that you should inquire about. The wires going to the spark plugs (known as the ignition wires) should have no cracks, burn marks, or wear. If so, they most likely will have to be replaced. This isn't a major repair. It's more an indication that the car has received poor preventive maintenance.

6 **Check all the fluids.** Inspect the brake fluid, power steering fluid, and windshield washer fluid. Low power steering or brake fluid could indicate a leak in either of those systems. If the windshield washer fluid is low, put some water in and test the system to see if it works. In general, low fluids may indicate that the car has been neglected overall.

7 **Look at the battery.** A brand new battery on a car that's less than two or three years old could mean electrical problems. If the car is four or five years old and you're convinced that it has the original battery (it bears a date), you can assume that the electrical system works fine.

8 **Check the air filter.** If it looks particularly dirty, then the owner probably did not do much preventive maintenance, because changing the air filter is one of the easiest things that can be done to keep a car in good shape.

After you start the car:
9 **Check the oil.** After the engine has been running, find the dipstick to check the oil level. If it's low, then the car is either an oil burner, has some kind of oil leak, or the owner has not replaced what was naturally lost. If the oil is fresh, it will be a clear, amber color; if it is dark, it usually indicates that the oil has been in the engine for some time. In older engines the oil will rapidly turn dark which is not necessarily a problem. Gritty or gummy oil is a sign of infrequent oil change, which could signal that the engine has not been very well maintained. If the oil is milky brown or grey or has

small bubbles in it, then water is present, and the car could have a cracked block. Very thin oil that smells like gasoline also indicates severe engine problems. Very thick oil could indicate that the owner is trying to quiet the noise from a failing valve lifter.

10 **Check the automatic transmission fluid.** The automatic transmission has a dipstick, which is usually located at the rear of the engine. Put the emergency brake on and, with the transmission in park, start the car and check the color of the fluid on the transmission dipstick. It should be reddish. If it's dark brown and sludgy, the transmission has been poorly maintained. If it has a burned smell, it means that the transmission has excessive wear and could quite possibly fail shortly. If you notice any metal flecks, actual parts of the gears are being ground up. If the fluid level is low, then the transmission leaks. (Note: This is a very important check. If you can't find the dipstick, put it on your mechanic's checklist.)

The Test Drive

Plan on taking every car you're considering for a good long test drive. You should map out two or three types of road ahead of time to include a highway, normal roads for around-town driving, and a bumpy road that will allow you to slow down and check for creaks and groans. If the owner does not allow you to test drive the car, then you have a simple solution: Don't buy it.

1 **Check the steering.** With the front wheels pointed straight ahead (and the engine on with the car in park for power steering), stick your head out the window and watch the front tire as you slowly turn the steering wheel. The tire should begin to move as you begin to turn the wheel. If the steering wheel has to turn more than two inches before the wheels start moving, the car's steering system could need some expensive repairs.

You can check the power steering when parked by turning the wheel all the way to the left and then all the way to the right. If the car screeches loudly or surges and bounces as you turn the wheel, the car might need a new power steering pump, or it may need repairs to the power steering system.

2 **Check the exhaust.** While you drive, check your rear-view mirror and note whether any exhaust smoke is coming from the tail pipe. Blue smoke indicates that the engine may need an expensive overhaul. If it's black, the car may simply need a tune-up or carburetor adjustment. If it's white as you start up but stops after a while, it could be water vapor that had built up in the engine and is nothing to worry about. If the white smoke continues throughout the drive, water from the radiator may be leaking into the engine.

3 **Check the brakes.** After the engine warms up, stop the car and push the brake pedal down as far as you can. It should go no more than an inch and a half to the floor. Keep the pedal down for at least a minute. If, during that period, the pedal seems to sink lower, the car could have serious brake problems.

When it's safe to do so, step on the brakes hard enough to slow down quickly without skidding. If the car dips forward excessively or pulls to one side, it probably needs brake or suspension work.

TIP

ENGINE STRESS TEST

Follow these steps to conduct an engine "stress" test for cars with automatic transmission and power steering: With the engine idling, air conditioner turned on full (whether you need it or not), lights on with high beams, radio on, and foot on the brake, put the engine in gear—automatic transmission only—and turn the wheel (if equipped with power steering) all the way to the left and right. Everything should continue running smoothly. Listen for screeches or howls in the power steering and feel for smoothness as you turn the wheel. There should be no surges or bouncing.

---

4 **Check the alignment.** When it's safe to do so, let go of the steering wheel on a level, straight road to see if the car pulls to either side. This pulling could mean something as simple as improper tire pressure or as serious as steering linkage out of alignment. Caution: Be careful in conducting this test, because, if the car is severely out of alignment, the wheels could turn sharply.

5 **Listen to the engine.** When you're on the highway at cruising speed, listen for unusual sounds of stress and strain. Even if the weather is very cold or very hot, drive with the window rolled all the way down in order to hear any clanks, groans, or other sounds that could signal expensive repairs down the road. As you accelerate, the engine should not feel as if it is laboring. Listen for a pinging or tapping from the engine. This sound may disappear by simply using a higher octane gas, or it may signal the need for a major engine overhaul. Have your mechanic check it out. Even if you can't identify the sounds, report anything unusual to the mechanic who inspects the car for you.

6 Listen to the engine idle. Pull over and let the engine idle while the transmission is in park. It should run smoothly. If you notice any acceleration, hesitation, or uneven performance, the problem could be something as simple as an idle adjustment or as serious as a carburetor overhaul. You shouldn't hear any loud tapping noises coming from the engine. If you do, the car may need expensive valve work. If you hear some light ticking or tapping noises, the car may simply need an adjustment. In either case, be sure to put these noises on your mechanic's checklist.

After you've listened to the engine for a while, turn off the key. The engine should stop immediately; if it continues to run for a few seconds, the car might need a carburetor overhaul, or it may simply require a tune-up.

7 Listen to the transmission. With your foot on the brake, move the shift lever from drive to reverse several times. If you hear a soft thump or no noise at all, the transmission is operating properly. However, if you hear a loud clank, that's a sign that the car may have a major transmission problem.

In general, the automatic transmission should shift smoothly from gear to gear. Any whining of the transmission, jumping, or irregular performance could indicate big transmission problems down the line. If it seems that the car drops temporarily into neutral while shifting from one gear to the next, your transmission is probably slipping and in need of repair. Don't forget to check the transmission while the car is in reverse. You should drive the car for at least fifty yards in reverse to make sure it runs smoothly and doesn't jump.

If the car has a manual transmission and the engine revs up when you step on the gas with your foot off the clutch and the car in gear, the clutch is slipping. You may have to replace it. If you hear a knocking sound from the transmission, press the clutch in. If the noise disappears, it's probably in the transmission; if it doesn't, there could be problems with the clutch.

Note: Any clanking sounds you hear when you're testing out your transmission could also indicate problems with the universal joint. For example, if you hear a clank each time you go down a hill, the car may have a worn universal joint.

8 **Listen for clunks.** Take the car out on a very bumpy road, roll down the windows, and drive slowly (five to ten miles per hour) to see if you can hear any unusual clanks or other sounds that may indicate you'll need to have some serious suspension work.

9 **Check the heater and air conditioner.** If it's winter, first check the heater by warming up the car. Then check the air conditioning system. To check the air conditioner, run it through all of its cycles. The air compressor should thump slightly as it kicks on and off. However, if you hear loud banging or rumbling, that's an indication that the air compressor may need replacing. Put your hands over the vents to check the pressure and temperature of the air coming out.

PURCHASE AGREEMENTS

Draft a purchase agreement to get in writing some of the things that may result in a legal dispute further down the line. Although this may seem to imply a distrust of the other person involved in the transaction, this document ensures that important points, such as when and how payment will occur, how any deposit that may be transferred will be handled, or how the lending of the car for inspection will be arranged, are clear to both parties. If these points are not clear, problems could result, and one of the involved parties could lose out in the end.

Be congenial when bringing up the subject of a purchase agreement. Be sure to point out that the purpose of such an agreement is to protect both parties and to avoid confusion.

10 **Check for inside leaks.** If it's handy on the test drive, try running the car through a car wash. For a few dollars, you'll find out whether the car has any obvious leaks. Otherwise, take the car to a place where you can hose it down vigorously. Directly spray the hose around the windows, vents, and trunk.

Avoiding Odometer Fraud

Each year, odometers get rolled back an average of 32,000 miles on three million used cars, and an estimated 50 percent of the leased cars on the used car market have odometers that have been rolled back.

Federal law makes it illegal to change a car's odometer. No one, not even the owner, is permitted to turn back or disconnect the odometer (except to perform necessary repairs). A new law also requires that the odometer reading be written on the vehicle title when the car is sold. All states require that the seller, or anyone transferring ownership of the vehicle, provide the buyer with a signed statement indicating the mileage on the odometer at the time of the transfer. Unfortunately, odometer fraud is so common that many buyers automatically assume that the mileage on a car's odometer is incorrect.

Be sure to make these checks before purchasing a used car to determine whether the odometer reading is correct:

1 Look for maintenance stickers on the door post or air filter cover, which may give the mileage at the date when last serviced.

2 Check the wear on the foot pedals and the ignition lock. If the odometer reads less than 20,000 miles, the pedals shouldn't show any excessive wear, and the lock shouldn't be heavily scratched.

3 Carefully check the dashboard for scratch marks or missing screws, which indicate that the odometer was tampered with.

4 See if all of the numbers on the odometer line up. Rolled-back odometers often have misaligned numbers.

5 Study the title carefully. All of the numbers should be clear and easy to read. Disreputable sellers may obscure the numbers with an official looking stamp or staple or fold the title right through the middle of the odometer reading, vehicle number, or other important information.

ODOMETER FRAUD

If you believe that you've been the victim of odometer fraud and that the car you purchased has a rolled-back odometer, the first thing to do is to contact the National Highway Traffic Safety Administration, Odometer Fraud Staff, 400 7th Street, SW, Washington, D.C. 20590, or call the Auto Safety Hotline at 800-424-9393 (202-366-0123 in Washington, D.C.). The agency will send you an odometer complaint form and a letter telling you what evidence you will need to get and what steps you'll need to take. The agency will not help you resolve your complaint; however, if you register the complaint with them, they can gather evidence on widespread problems and collect complaints from the same area or the same dealer.

If you are a victim of odometer fraud, you have the right to recover triple the difference between what you paid for the car and what it was actually worth or $1,500, whichever is greater.

In order to get action, you will have to file suit in your state or federal court. For the court to hear your case, you will need evidence indicating that the odometer has been rolled back. It can include such information as a previous owner's statement on the mileage of the car when it was sold or repair records from the dealer or service station that worked on the car that include the car's odometer reading.

Many states have an odometer enforcement unit within their state attorney general's office. Contact the office, in care of your state capitol, for suggestions on how to proceed with an investigation. In some cases, your state attorney general may bring suit against the seller on your behalf. If not, and you hire a private attorney, the fees are recoverable if you win.

6 If there is an odometer disclosure statement, check the number against the odometer, it should be close.

7 Check the name on the title. It should be either the seller's or, if you're buying from a used car dealer, the previous owner's or dealer's name. Be suspicious of titles with out-of-state addresses, post office box addresses, or auction company names.

8 Remember, half of all the leased cars for sale have rolled-back odometers. Compare the driver's seat and door with the passenger's seat and door for wear and tear. If the driver's side looks as though it received far heavier usage, it's a good indication that this was a company car with a single driver.

9 Have your mechanic check the engine compression and look for worn struts or ball joints and transmission problems—all signs of high use.

Mechanic's Checklist

The best "warranty" you can get with a used car is a $45 to $60 independent mechanic's inspection. One of the best places to get an inspection is your local office of the American Automobile Association (AAA). Because AAA inspection centers are not affiliated with repair facilities, they have no incentive to recommend unnecessary repairs. These diagnostic inspections are available to both members and non-members. If the seller will not allow you to take the car for a mechanic's inspection, don't buy it.

While AAA and most mechanics follow standard procedure when inspecting cars, make sure the following areas are included:

1 **Engine Compression:** This check will give you a good idea of the internal condition of the engine, including the valves and piston rings.

2 **Brakes:** The mechanic should take off at least one front and one rear wheel to inspect the condition of the brake disk or drum and brake pads. All the brake lines should be checked for rust or damage.

3 **Front Wheel Bearings and Suspension System:** The ball joint seals should be intact, the structural parts solid and straight, and the springs and shocks properly connected. Check shock absorbers for leakage and loose mountings.

4 **Frame:** Check the frame for rust, breaks, and signs of welding. If the frame or under-body has been welded, the car has either been in an accident or, worse, is actually two different cars welded together.

5 **Exhaust:** Inspect the muffler system and look for loose or missing brackets, rust, and holes.

6 **Cooling System:** Pressure test the radiator.

7 **Electrical:** Test the battery and charging system.

8 **Transmission:** Check the entire drive train.

9 **Road Test:** Ask if the mechanic will road test the car for you.

10 **Repair Estimate:** Have the mechanic give you an estimate for the cost of any repairs deemed necessary. This will be a big help when it's time to negotiate.

Safety Checklist

How do you buy for safety? While even a trained engineer would find it difficult to compare the safety of cars just by looking at them, here are some features to check in the used cars you consider.

1 **Recessed Knobs and Controls:** Are the items on the dashboard recessed below the surface of the dash?

2 **Steering Wheel:** Does the steering wheel have a large padded hub?

3 **Padding:** Are the dashboard, sun visors, and roof supports well padded?

4 **Doors:** Are the doors free of sharp and protruding objects?

5 **Headrests:** If adjustable, can they be set so the center of the headrest is just above the center of your head? If they are not adjustable, make sure they are high enough. Non-adjustable headrests will not slip out of place.

6 **Fuel Tank:** Is the fuel tank located forward or above the rear axle to prevent leakage in a rear-end collision?

7 **Visibility:** Is your vision free from obstructions or blind spots when you turn your head in either direction? Is there a right side rear-view mirror for better visibility?

8 **Brake Lights:** Does the car have a centrally mounted rear brake light? (These lights can cut rear-end collisions by 50 percent and are required in all models manufactured in 1986 or later. If you are buying an earlier model, they can be installed at a relatively low price.)

9 **Safety Belts:** Are the belts convenient and easy to use? If not, chances are you won't use them. Also check to see that they pull out and retract correctly and are not frayed.

10 **Special Features:** Some late model used cars have special safety features, such as anti-lacerative windshields, better seat belts, anti-lock brakes, and childproof locks. These can increase protection against injury.

Crash Tests

Most of the cars we rate have government crash test results. These crash tests show significant differences in the ability of various automobiles to protect belted occupants during frontal crashes. Our publication of the test results over the years has put pressure on manufacturers to improve the performance of their cars. For example, when the program began, Japanese cars were among the worst performers; now they are among the best.

An occupant's safety depends on the car's ability to absorb any force caused by impact. This is a function of the car's size, weight, and, most importantly, design. In the crash tests, engineers measure how much of the crash force is transferred to the head, chest, and thighs of the occupants.

The test consists of crashing an automobile into a concrete barrier at 35 mph. The effect is similar to that of two identical cars crashing head-on at 35 mph. In the test, each automobile contains electronically monitored dummies in the driver and passenger seats. This electronic data can then be analyzed in terms of the impact of such a collision on a human being.

We have analyzed the data and presented the results in the back of the book using a Very Good, Good, Average, Poor, or Very Poor performance rating. These ratings provide a means of comparing the overall results of one car with those of another. It is best to compare the test results of cars within the same weight class, such as compacts with compacts; the results should not be used to compare cars with vastly different weights. For example, you should not conclude that a subcompact that is rated "Good" is as safe as a minivan or large car with the same rating.

The results evaluate performance in frontal crashes, which cause about 50 percent of auto deaths and serious injuries. Remember that the results only measure protection for belted occupants. Buying a car equipped with airbags and using safety belts are the most effective means of protecting yourself in an accident.

Note: Not all cars are crash tested, and there is no absolute guarantee that a car that passed the government test will adequately protect you in an accident.

Safety Defects and Recalls

Over 17 million cars and trucks are recalled each year for inspection and safety-related defects. Safety recalls are an effort to reduce injuries and fatalities. When a safety recall occurs, manufacturers are required to notify individual car owners of the defect and to correct the defect quickly and at no cost to the consumer.

The effectiveness of a safety recall campaign is partly the responsibility of the car owner. The owner must bring the car to a dealer for inspection and repair.

If your car has been recalled, take it in for repair as soon as possible. A recalled automobile can be returned to any authorized dealer. The manufacturer, through the dealer, is responsible for fixing the defect, no matter how long ago the recall occurred.

The tables at the end of the book are a quick reference guide for determining whether your car, or the used car you are considering, has ever been recalled. In order to determine whether the defect has already been corrected, you need to find the vehicle identification number, which is located on the dashboard and can be seen by looking in through the windshield. The second step is to call the dealer. If the dealer can't tell you if your particular car has been fixed, then contact the manufacturer. If you still cannot get help, call the U.S. Department of Transportation's toll-free Auto Safety Hotline (800-424-9393; in Washington, D.C. call 202-366-0123) and register a complaint.

For information on defects and recalls that are not safety-related, contact the Federal Trade Commission or the Environmental Protection Agency.

⚠ PHONY INSPECTIONS

Beware of dealers who push you toward certain diagnostic centers or mechanics for your inspection. Sometimes mechanics and privately operated diagnostic centers have arrangements with certain used car dealers to ensure that the dealer's car checks out "just fine" in exchange for referrals to the mechanic or diagnostic center.

 MECHANICAL PROBLEMS

Don't automatically reject a car with a mechanical problem. The cost of repairing the problem may not be that great (have a mechanic give you an estimate), and you can use the problem and repair estimate to negotiate a lower price on the car.

Part Two: Getting the Best Price and Selling Your Car

The most difficult and intimidating part of buying a used car is negotiating the price. Most of us rarely bargain for the things we buy. So, it's no surprise that we feel uncomfortable negotiating, especially for an item whose value is so difficult to evaluate. This section will acquaint you with the process of negotiating and provide some tips for success. We will also provide some advice on warranties and service contracts.

First of all, the single most important thing you can do to negotiate a good price is to prepare yourself psychologically to get up and walk out. Always remember that you carry the highest trump card:

TIP · NEGOTIATING SHORTCUT

Some people get a thrill out of negotiating and will carry the process out to four, five, or even six counteroffers. Most of us, however, could do without the process altogether. One technique that you can try, especially if you've found three or four cars that you really like, involves no bargaining at all. It goes like this: After you have carefully determined a fair value for each of the cars that you are interested in, go to the seller(s) and state up front that you are only going to make one offer for the car. Be honest; simply say that you don't like negotiating and that you have determined what you believe is a very fair price for the car. Make your offer and be prepared to walk away and not listen to a counteroffer. If you have second thoughts later on, you can always call back with another offer. However, if your price is fair and your approach is reasonable, there's a good chance that the seller will respect your seriousness and sell you the car at the price you offered.

the 180-degree turn. If you are always prepared to walk out, you'll always maintain the upper hand in your negotiation.

Another important factor in successful negotiating is the attitude you bring to the process. Try to remain unemotional, detached, and deal in a straightforward manner. You should never exhibit a strong desire for the car. On the other hand, you should not be belligerent and exhibit an attitude that indicates you don't think the car is worth very much.

If you are bargaining with a professional, there will be times when you are waiting for him or her to respond. Professional salespeople often use silence to intimidate a buyer. Don't be intimidated. And don't let long periods of time in which the salesman is "talking with the sales manager" about your deal make you uncomfortable. That is simply a tactic to wear you down, make you nervous, and make you feel like you just want to "get this thing over with." Try not to be nervous. Instead, do something that indicates you are serious about looking other places. Bring the classified section of the newspaper with you and begin circling other cars that you want to check out. Or review your notes on the other cars that you've seen. Also, you should always give the salesperson a time limit. By sending the message that you have other options, you'll increase your bargaining power.

Here are some additional negotiating tips to help you to get the best price on a used car:

Find out how much the car is worth. You really can't begin to negotiate until you've determined the car's actual value. Like any other commodity, a used car will have a wholesale and a retail value; you need to determine both. The value of a car can be found in two basic ways. First, consult the *N.A.D.A. Official Used Car Guide* for the value of the car and the options that come with it. The range between the wholesale and retail value of the car is your bargaining range. And second, review the classified section in a large newspaper and see what people are asking for their cars. Prices in the classified section should be somewhere between the wholesale and retail values printed in the N.A.D.A. book.

Road test first. Never begin negotiating until you have road tested the car and checked it out mechanically.

Determine your maximum price. Before you begin negotiating, determine the most you would pay for the car. For most cars, this should be below the asking price.

Use a notebook. Keep a notebook with you and take notes. Don't hesitate to refer to notes on other cars while the seller is telling you about the current car under consideration. These notes will help you refresh your memory and indicate to the seller that you have other options.

Touch and comment. Use the same technique that new car dealers do when they inspect your trade-in. While you review the car, visibly point out, either to yourself or to a partner, the various problems that you note. An exaggerated touch of some loose part, or running your hand along body damage can put the seller in a defensive position. In addition to noting the problems audibly, write them down.

Start low. When you've determined that you like the car, your first offer should be 20 percent below the most you would pay for the car.

Prepare to counter. Most of the time (and nearly every time if you're dealing with a used car dealer), your first offer will not be accepted, and the seller will make a counteroffer. Your response, as a rule of thumb, should split the difference between your first offer and the most you're willing to pay for the car (not the counteroffer) unless, of course, the counteroffer is lower.

Take a second look. If the negotiation gets bogged down and you are not getting much movement toward your price, ask to take another look at the car. This indicates to the seller that you may have some second thoughts, and the seller may fear that you might see a problem you hadn't noticed the first time around.

The final offer. If the seller's second counteroffer is below the most you're willing to pay the car, consider accepting the offer. If it is not, your third offer (which should be your final offer) should be close to what you would be willing to pay for the car. At this point, you should make it very clear that you honestly believe you're offering a fair price and that your last offer is final.

Be ready to walk. You must be prepared to walk away if your third and final offer is not accepted. You'll be surprised at how many times you are called back. Remember, if you've determined the fair value of the car and it's not offered, you can probably find a better deal elsewhere.

Don't forget that there are items other than price to negotiate. The car may need repairs, or you may want more time on the warranty. Remember, if the seller agrees to any of these extras, make sure you get them in writing.

The "Blue Book" Value

The *N.A.D.A. Official Used Car Guide* is published monthly by the National Automobile Dealers Association and is generally recognized as one of the best sources of used car prices. (It is often called the "blue book," but it is actually orange.) The book is a compilation of average used car prices based on reports of actual transactions by dealers and wholesale auctions. Because car prices vary slightly by region, there are nine separate regional editions. Each guide includes the average trade-in or wholesale price, the average loan price, and the average retail price for nearly every car sold within the last seven years. Also included are mileage tables used to adjust the price of the car depending on how many miles it has been driven. The book is available in the reference section of many libraries.

There are other used car pricing guides available that tend to be more regional—for example, *Kelley Blue Book* is used quite frequently in the California area. While anyone can subscribe to these guides, they are generally not available in retail stores. What you will find in a bookstore is a publication called *Edmund's Used Car Prices*, which is published quarterly. Like the *N.A.D.A. Official Used Car Guide*, it includes the current average retail and wholesale prices. However, *Kelley Blue Book* is available online at www.kbb.com.

An important factor to remember when using these "blue books" is that local market conditions may not be reflected in the listed prices. That's why it's important to compare the book prices with those in used car ads and at local used car dealerships. Nevertheless, these books are probably the best source of general information in

Warranties

terms of determining the value of a used car.

Most used cars are sold "as is." This means you buy the car with any problems it may have, and the seller guarantees nothing at all, even if the seller will "guarantee the car as is."

With a few exceptions, a warranty that comes with a used car should be of little consequence to you. When used cars are sold in "as is" condition, warranties are difficult to enforce. There are, of course, some exceptions. Warranties from the major rental car companies are generally okay, although they may be rather limited. Also, the warranties that come with used cars that are sold by new car dealers (also limited) are usually backed by the dealer.

Federal law requires posting a buyer's guide on used cars. Anyone who sells six or more used cars in a period of less than 12 months is considered a used car dealer and must post this guide on every car for sale. The buyer's guide spells out what kind of warranty comes with the car, indicates the types of problems that could be present, and lists the name and phone number of the person to contact, should problems arise. If no warranty is applicable, the buyer's guide should read, "As is—no warranty." Information on the buyer's guide is incorporated into the final contract for sale.

If there is a warranty for the car, make sure you take the time to read and understand it. No two used car warranties are alike, so read them carefully. A dealer selling a used car will probably offer a 30-day or 1,000-mile warranty. Some dealers will want to split the cost of repairs with you, while others will cover 100 percent of the cost of repairs under warranty. Remember, you have the right to inspect the warranty before you buy the car. It's the law.

Claims made by the salesperson are considered expressed warranties, and you should have them put in writing if you consider them important. Do not confuse your warranty with a service con-

TIP
TRANSFERRING WARRANTIES

The original warranties of many cars can be transferred to the next owner. Unlike extended service contracts, which belong to the purchaser, the car's original warranty stays with the car. So, if the warranty is still in effect, then it is automatically transferred to the new owner. Be sure you get all the warranty documentation from the seller. Most warranties only last three years. However, be sure to also check the mileage limits on the warranty. Most limits only go up to 36,000 miles, so compare the mileage limit to the mileage on the car. If the car's mileage is under the mileage limit and the time limit has not expired, the warranty will transfer—but, both must still be valid.

tract. A service contract is purchased separately; the warranty is yours at no extra cost when you buy the car. If you find that the warranty is ambiguous or doesn't offer much coverage, you can use it to negotiate.

Known Defects Disclosure: If a dealer knows about a major defect prior to selling you a used car, the dealer is obligated, by law, to disclose it. If the dealer does not tell you about a defect prior to sale, you may be able to break the contract. You can find out the specific rules that apply in your state by contacting your state attorney general's office.

TRANSFERRING SERVICE CONTRACTS

If you buy a used car from a private individual who offers you the balance of the car's service contract along with the car, be sure to check it out carefully before you buy the car. Some contracts automatically cancel when the car is resold, and other companies require a hefty transfer fee before extending privileges to the new owner.

Selling Your Car

For most of us, buying a used car carries with it another task—selling our old one. There are three options: You can keep your car, trade it in on the newer car, or sell it yourself. If you decide not to keep your old car, you'll do better by selling it yourself, rather than trading it in. Why? Because even if you get a fair deal, the most a dealer will give you is the wholesale price of that car. If you sell it yourself, you can charge the full retail price.

To decide whether it's worth the effort to sell the car yourself, you need to know the difference between the retail price and the wholesale price. This difference is the money you make by selling the car yourself. For more information on determining the value of your car, see the first part of this section.

Determine the car's value. Pricing your car correctly is very important. In addition to checking the *N.A.D.A. Official Used Car*

Guide, take a look through your local newspaper for the prices of cars similar to yours. You may also want to take your car to a couple of used car lots and see how much they'll offer you.

Prepare the car for sale. Even if you decide not to sell it yourself and choose to trade it in, getting the car into the right condition can add more to its value than it will cost, and you'll come out ahead. Clean it thoroughly inside and out. You may want to have the engine steam cleaned to remove accumulated oil and dirt, and you should clean any corrosion from the battery.

Tip: When you clean the car, make sure you tighten anything that might be loose or rattling, such as the license plate or glove box door. Even a minor rattle may discourage a potential buyer.

Don't make major repairs. Any major mechanical repairs or body work will almost always cost more than the increase in price you'll get for the car. Instead of spending a lot of money, simply be honest and straightforward in your ad for the car. For example, if the right fender is crushed and rusted, say so in the ad:

> **FOR SALE:** 95 Ford Escort, runs like a dream, looks like an ugly duckling—Call...

Advertise. Once your car is ready for sale, it's time to advertise it. First, check neighborhood bulletin boards, community newspapers, and employee publications. There are generally many free or low cost places where you can place an ad. If you park in large lots, make a sign for the window and provide your telephone number. (Note: This may be illegal in some areas.) Check with your credit union or church and get your friends to spread the word.

When writing your ad, be honest. Skip the flowery phrases and stick to words that buyers will respond to, such as clean, low mileage, original owner, excellent fuel economy, regular service records available. Your ad should list the year, model, and body style, and you might want to include the number of miles, engine size, or color. If your car has any special features, let people know about them in your ad. The clearer and more honest your ad, the less hassle you'll have in selling.

Generally your ad should not include your address, only your telephone number and times when people may reach you. It's important to list when you'll be available, because, if you're not home, a frustrated caller may not call back.

If the free advertising sources aren't generating any buyers, then you should place an ad in your daily newspaper. Before you write your ad, look at how similar cars are written up. Try to make yours sound a little bit different and a little more special. Putting your asking price in the ad will save a lot of phone calls from people who aren't really interested or who can't afford the car.

Respond to the callers. Once prospective buyers start calling, be ready to answer questions. Prepare callers for what to expect when they see the car. If, at first glance, the car looks worse than they expected, the sale will be more difficult.

Make an appointment with each caller for a specific time, rather than allowing them to come "sometime this afternoon." This appointment will increase your chances of the buyers showing up, and, if they're late, you don't have to feel obligated to wait for them. But don't be surprised if some of these folks don't show.

Be honest and helpful. When prospective buyers come, make sure you go along with them on the test drive. This is not only for security but also to help the driver understand all the car's features and to answer any questions. If the buyers continue to show interest, help them arrange a mutually convenient time for a mechanic's appraisal, if they want one.

If possible, park the car in an inconspicuous place, especially if it has some dings and dents. By doing this, you will keep people who stop by from taking a quick look and moving on, rather than knocking on your door and giving you a chance to explain the car's good points.

It's important to prepare yourself psychologically for the sale. First of all, communicate honestly about the car. You'll obtain far more credibility and reduce buyer resistance much more effectively if you're honest about the car's problems. Most people realize that buying a used car means buying something less than perfect. By trying to hide some of the defects, you place the buyers in the position of being far more disappointed when they discover them.

It's equally important to be optimistic about the car. Don't hesitate to tell the buyer how much you enjoy driving the car and point out the special features that you particularly like.

Watch out for the pros! You may get calls from professionals trying to buy cars for resale. Often these people will put tremendous pressure on you to sell the car far below your asking price. A disreputable person may even squirt oil on parts of the car and tell you that it leaks, or they may fiddle with the engine while they're looking under the hood. If the car doesn't run properly during the test drive, they'll try to get you to lower the price. Fortunately, unscrupulous people like this are rare.

Price it right. As long as you've priced the car fairly, stay firm. Most buyers will have checked around and will realize that the car is fairly priced. If you really want to move the car, you may consider under-pricing it by a few hundred dollars. However, if you choose to do this, make sure that you stay firm on the final price. In a normal situation, you should add 10 to 15 percent to your rock bottom price to get the price you're advertising. That way, you have room to negotiate.

Be ready to negotiate. One technique for negotiating, when a buyer's offer is below your actual price, is to state cordially but firmly that you've already turned down an offer for "x" and can't possibly accept something lower. That will let the buyer know your rock bottom price, and the buyer will either have to match it or beat it in order to get the car. In all cases, get the name and telephone number of people that look at your car, and as a last resort you can call them back with a counteroffer.

Get cash. Make sure you always get either cash or a certified check.

Indicate that you are selling "as is," in writing. Remember when selling a car, you are selling it in "as is" condition. In order to prevent problems from coming back to haunt you, make sure you write on the buyer's receipt that the car is being sold in "as is" condition.

Check title transfer procedures. Consult your state Department of Motor Vehicles to determine what requirements you must follow to transfer the title to the new owner. This process usually consists of your signing and dating the title before you pass it on to the buyer and notifying the DMV of the transaction. Making sure that the title is correctly transferred and the DMV properly notified will prevent you from being liable for any accidents or tickets once the transfer is complete.

Finally, unless you live in a state where the license plates stay with the vehicle, keep them.

CURBSTONERS

Used car sellers who operate out of their homes are often called "curbstoners." These "semi-pros" avoid many of the state and local licensing requirements by representing themselves as private sellers when, in fact, they make a great deal of money selling used cars in their back yards.

There are some legitimate curbstoners. These are people who buy used cars at low prices and take the time to repair them for resale at a profit. A legitimate curbstoner can actually be a good source for a used car. Unfortunately, it's difficult to determine who is legitimate and who is not.

Tip: Ask to see the garage where repairs are done and always have an independent mechanic check the car out.

Many times, curbstoners are selling cars that they've picked up at auctions, stolen cars, or cars with rolled-back odometers. Curbstoners will claim they are simply selling their own cars. Most of them aren't. And if you question why the name on the title doesn't match theirs, they'll probably tell you they're selling the car for a friend or relative. Be cautious, because if it turns out that you purchased a stolen car, you can lose the car and have little or no recourse against the seller.

Following are warning signals which may indicate that you are dealing with an illegal curbstoner:

✔ The seller has several vehicles for sale.
✔ The same phone number appears in more than one ad.
✔ The seller evades questions about the vehicle's history.
✔ The vehicle has no license plates.
✔ The name on the title isn't the seller's name.
✔ The seller meets you at a location that's different from the the address on the title (such as a repair shop, gas station, or vacant lot).

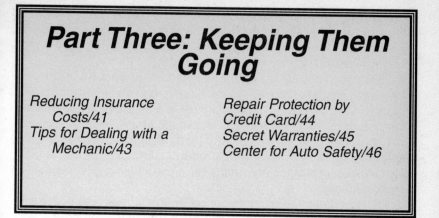

Part Three: Keeping Them Going

The reason why most of us buy a used car in the first place is because it is less expensive than a new car.

In order to make sure that your purchase is, in fact, one that will end up saving you money in the long run, this chapter includes important tips on keeping that car going both economically and safely. In this section, we will provide cost-saving tips on insurance, offer some important safety information that will make the operation of your car safe, give you some maintenance tips that will reduce your operating costs, explain how to get the best deal on tires, and give you some insight on how to resolve those inevitable problems down the road.

Reducing Insurance Costs

Insurance is a big part of ownership expenses, yet it's often forgotten in the showroom. As you shop, remember that the car's design and accident history may affect your insurance rates. Some cars cost less to insure because experience has shown that they are damaged less, less expensive to fix after a collision, or stolen less.

More and more consumers are saving hundreds of dollars by shopping around for insurance. In order to be a good comparison shopper, you need to know a few things about automobile insurance.

A number of factors determine what these coverages will cost you. A car's design can affect both the chances and severity of an accident. A car with a well-designed bumper may escape damage altogether in a low-speed crash. Some cars are easier to repair than others or may have less expensive parts. Cars with four doors tend to be damaged less than cars with two doors.

The reason one car may get a discount on insurance while another receives a surcharge also depends upon the way it is traditionally driven. Sports cars, for example, are usually surcharged due, in part, to the typical driving habits of their owners. Four-door sedans, minivans, and station wagons generally merit discounts. Insurance companies use this and other information to determine whether to offer a discount on insurance premiums for a particular car or whether to levy a surcharge.

Not all companies offer discounts or surcharges, and many cars receive neither. Some companies offer a discount or impose a surcharge on collision premiums only. Others apply discounts and surcharges on both collision and comprehensive coverage. Discounts and surcharges usually range from 10 to 30 percent. Allstate offers discounts of up to 35 percent on certain cars. Remember that one company may offer a discount on a particular vehicle while another may not.

Check with your insurance company to find out whether your company has a rating program.

Here are some of the most common insurance discounts:

Driver Education/Defensive Driving Courses: Many insurance companies offer (and in some cases mandate) discounts to young people who have successfully completed a state-approved driver education course. Typically, this can mean a $40 reduction in the cost of coverage. Also, a discount of 5 to 15 percent is available in some states to those who complete a defensive driving course.

Good Student Discounts: Many insurance companies offer discounts of up to 25 percent on insurance to full-time high school or college students who are in the upper 20 percent of their class, on the dean's list, or have a B or better average.

Mature Driver Credit: Drivers ages 50 and older may qualify for up to a 10 percent discount or a lower price bracket.

Sole Female Driver: Some companies offer discounts of 10 percent for females, ages 30 to 64, who are the only driver in a household, citing favorable claims experience.

Car Pooling: Commuters sharing driving may qualify for discounts of 5 to 25 percent or a lower price bracket.

Anti-Theft Device Credits: Discounts of 5 to 15 percent are offered in some states for cars equipped with a hood lock and an alarm or a disabling device (active or passive) that prevents the car from being started.

First Accident Allowance: Some insurers offer a "first accident allowance," which guarantees that if a customer achieves five accident-free years, his or her rates won't go up after the first at-fault accident.

Deductibles: Opting for the largest reasonable deductible is the obvious first step in reducing premiums. Increasing your deductible to $500 from $200 could cut your collision premium about 20 percent. Raising the deductible to $1,000 from $200 could lower your premium about 45 percent. The discounts may vary by company.

Collision Coverage: The older the car, the less the need for collision insurance. Consider dropping collision insurance entirely on an older car. Regardless of how much coverage you carry, the insurance company will only pay up to the car's "book value." For example, if your car requires $1,000 in repairs but its "book value" is only $500, the insurance company is required to pay only $500.

Tips for Dealing with a Mechanic

Call around. Don't choose a shop simply because it's nearby. Calling a few shops may turn up estimates cheaper by half.

Don't necessarily go for the lowest price. A good rule is to eliminate the highest and lowest estimates; the mechanic with the highest estimate is probably charging too much, and the lowest may be cutting too many corners.

Check the shop's reputation. Call your local consumer affairs agency and the Better Business Bureau. There aren't records on all shops, but unfavorable reports on a shop disqualify it.

Look for certification. Mechanics can be certified by the National Institute for Automotive Service Excellence, an industry-wide yardstick for competence. Certification is offered in eight areas of repair. However, make sure the mechanic working on your car is certified for the repair.

Take a look around. A well-kept shop reflects pride in workmanship. A skilled and efficient mechanic would probably not work in a messy shop.

Don't sign a blank check. The service order you sign should have specific instructions or describe your vehicle's symptoms. Avoid signing a vague work order. Be sure you are called for final approval before the shop does extra work.

Show interest. Ask about the repair but don't act like an expert if you don't really understand what's wrong. Express your satisfaction. If you're happy with the work, compliment the mechanic and ask for him or her the next time you come in. You will get to know each other, and the mechanic will get to know your vehicle.

Develop a "sider." If you know a mechanic, ask about work on the side, evenings or weekends. The labor will be cheaper.

Take a test drive. Before you pay for a major repair, you should take the car for a test drive. If you find that the problem still exists, there will be no question that the repair wasn't properly completed.

Repair Protection by Credit Card

Paying your auto repair bills by credit card can provide a much needed recourse if you are having problems with an auto mechanic. According to federal law, you have the right to withhold payment for sloppy or incorrect repairs. Of course, you may withhold no more than the amount of the repair in dispute.

In order to use this right, you must first try to work out the problem with the mechanic. Also, unless the credit card company owns the repair shop (this might be the case with gasoline credit cards used at gas stations), two other conditions must be met. First, the repair shop must be in your home state (or within 100 miles of your current address), and, second, the cost of repairs must be over $50. Until the problem is settled or resolved in court, the credit card company cannot charge you interest or penalties on the amount in dispute.

If you decide to take action, send a letter to the credit card company and a copy to the repair shop, explaining the details of the problem and what you want as settlement. Send the letter by certified mail with a return receipt requested.

Sometimes the credit card company or repair shop will attempt to put a "bad mark" on your credit record if you use this tactic. Legally, you can't be reported as delinquent if you've given the credit card company notice of your dispute, but a creditor can report that you are disputing your bill, which goes in your record. However, you have the right to challenge any incorrect information and add your side of the story to your file.

For more information, write to the Federal Trade Commission, Credit Practices Division, 601 Pennsylvania Avenue, NW, Washington, D.C. 20580, or visit their website at www.ftc.gov.

Secret Warranties

If dealers report a number of complaints about a certain part and the manufacturer determines that the problem is due to faulty design or assembly, the manufacturer may permit dealers to repair the problem at no charge to the customer even though the warranty has expired. In the past, this practice was often reserved for customers who made a big fuss. The availability of the free repair was never publicized, which is why we call these secret warranties.

Manufacturers deny the existence of secret warranties. They call these free repairs "policy adjustments" or "goodwill service." Whatever they are called, most consumers never hear about them.

Many secret warranties are disclosed in service bulletins that the manufacturers send to dealers. These bulletins outline free repair or reimbursement programs, as well as other problems and their possible causes and solutions.

Service bulletins from many manufacturers also may be on file at the National Highway Traffic Safety Administration. Visit www.nhtsa.dot.gov and look up your vehicle on NHTSA's technical bulletin search.

If you find that a secret warranty is in effect and repairs are being made at no charge after the warranty has expired, contact the Center for Auto Safety, 2001 S Street, NW, Washington, D.C. 20009. They will publish the information so others can benefit.

Disclosure Laws: Spurred by the proliferation of secret warranties and the failure of the FTC to take action, several states, including California, Connecticut, Virginia, and Wisconsin have passed legislation that requires consumers to be notified of secret warranties on their cars.

Typically, the laws require the following: Direct notice to consumers within a specified time after the adoption of a warranty adjustment policy; notice of the disclosure law to new car buyers; reimbursement, within a number of years after payment, to owners who paid for covered repairs before they learned of the extended warranty service; and dealers must inform consumers who complain about a covered defect that it is eligible for repair under warranty.

If you live in a state with a secret warranty law already in effect, write your state attorney general's office (in care of your state capitol) for information. To encourage passage of such a bill, contact your state representative (in care of your state capitol).

Center for Auto Safety

For over 25 years, the nonprofit Center for Auto Safety (CAS) has told the consumer's story to government agencies, to Congress, and to the courts. Its efforts focus on all consumers rather than only those with individual complaints.

CAS was established in 1970 by Ralph Nader and Consumers Union. As consumer concerns about auto safety issues expanded, so did the work of CAS. It became an independent group in 1972, and the original staff of two has grown to fourteen attorneys and researchers. CAS' activities include:

Representing the Consumer in Washington: CAS follows the activities of federal agencies and Congress to ensure that they carry out their responsibilities to the American taxpayer. CAS brings a consumer's point of view to vehicle safety policies and rulemaking. Since 1970, CAS has submitted more than 500 petitions and comments on federal safety standards.

Help CAS Help You: CAS depends on public support. Annual consumer membership is $30 with *The Lemon Book*. All contributions to this nonprofit organization are tax-deductible. Annual membership includes a quarterly newsletter called "Lemon Times." To join, send a check to: Center for Auto Safety, 1825 Connecticut Ave., NW, Suite #330, Washington, D.C. 20009–5708, www.autosafety.org

Part Four: How They Rate

With the huge number of used cars available, your chances of getting a good one are actually better than you may expect. To get you started in the right direction, on the following pages are some cars that we consider to be Best Bets. In developing this list, we sifted through a decade's worth of complaint statistics and safety defect information, as well as crash test results, insurance rates, theft ratings, repair costs, and safety features—all the information you need to make a smart choice. We've called the cars with the best overall ratings Best Bets and, on the next two pages, we've sorted them two ways: by size class and by price. Remember, there is no guarantee that every model of each car on the following lists will be a cream puff, so the mechanic's inspection is crucial before you buy. Nevertheless, if you find one of our Best Bets in good condition—go for it!

Registering Your Complaints: If you have a particular problem with your car, consider filing a complaint with the National Highway Traffic Safety Administration. Call the toll-free Auto Safety Hotline at 800-424-9393 (in Washington, DC, 202-366-0123), and ask for the Vehicle Owners Questionnaire.

Taking the time to complain will do two things—first, it will give the goverment an indication of which cars are causing consumers the most problems. Second, you will be adding your experience to the information we use to prepare the Complaint Index.

2001 COMPLAINT RATINGS

FEWEST COMPLAINTS	MOST COMPLAINTS
Lexus GS300/400 1998-2001	Audi A6 1998-2001
Ford F-Series Pickup 1997-2001	Mercury Cougar 1999-2001
Lexus LS400 1995-2001	Honda Passport 1998-2001
Infiniti G20 1999-2001	Lexus SC300/400 1992-2001
Lexus LX470 1999-2001	Kia Sportage 1995-2001

Best Bets by Price

$2-$4,000		
1995	Ford Aspire	Subcompact

$3-$5,000		
1992	Dodge Spirit	Compact

$4-$6,000		
1992	Olds Cutlass Supreme	Intermediate

$5-$7,000		
1995	Saturn SC/SL/SW	Subcompact

$6-$8,000		
1996	Buick Skylark	Compact
1994	Mercury Cougar	Large
1994	Oldsmobile 88	Large
1995	Olds Cutlass Ciera	Intermediate
1994	Pontiac Bonneville	Large
1996	Saturn SC/SL/SW	Subcompact

$7-$9,000		
1996	Buick Century	Intermediate
1994	Buick LeSabre	Large
1997	Buick Skylark	Compact
1996	Chevrolet Lumina	Large
1996	Chevrolet Lumina Minivan	Minivan
1995	Chrysler New Yorker	Intermediate
1996	Ford Taurus	Intermediate
1995	Mercury Cougar	Large

$8-$10,000		
1997	Chevrolet Lumina	Large
1996	Chevrolet Monte Carlo	Large
1997	Ford Taurus	Intermediate
1996	Pontiac Grand Prix	Intermediate
1997-98	Saturn SC/SL/SW	Subcompact

$9-$11,000		
1996	Chrysler Concorde	Intermediate
1995	Chrysler LHS	Large
1994	Lincoln Town Car	Large
1999	Mercury Tracer	Subcompact
1999	Saturn SC/SL/SW	Subcompact

$10-$12,000		
1996	Buick LeSabre	Large
1998	Chevrolet Lumina	Large
2000	Ford Escort	Subcompact
1998	Ford Taurus	Intermediate

$10-$12,000 (cont.)		
1997	Ford Windstar	Minivan
1998	Mercury Sable	Intermediate
1996	Oldsmobile 88	Large
1996	Pontiac Bonneville	Large
2000	Saturn SC/SL/SW	Subcompact

$11-$13,000		
1997	Buick Century	Intermediate
1998	Chevrolet Monte Carlo	Large
1997	Chrysler Concorde	Intermediate
1996	Chrysler LHS	Large
1999	Honda Civic	Subcompact
1997	Mercury Sable	Intermediate
1997	Oldsmobile 88	Large

$12-$14,000		
1999	Chevrolet Lumina	Large
1999	Chevrolet Monte Carlo	Large
2000	Ford Contour	Compact
2000	Honda Civic	Subcompact
1995	Isuzu Oasis	Minivan
1995	Lincoln Town Car	Large
1999	Oldsmobile Cutlass	Intermediate
1996	Subaru Legacy	Compact

$13-$15,000		
1998	Buick LeSabre	Large
2000	Chevrolet Lumina	Large
1998	Ford Crown Victoria	Large
2001	Honda Civic	Subcompact
1998	Oldsmobile 88	Large
2000	Oldsmobile Cutlass	Intermediate
1998	Pontiac Grand Prix	Intermediate
2001	Saturn SC/SL/SW	Subcompact

$14-$16,000		
1999	Buick Century	Intermediate
2001	Chevrolet Lumina	Large
2000	Mazda 626	Compact
1999	Oldsmobile 88	Large
1998	Pontiac Bonneville	Large
2000	Pontiac Grand Am	Compact

$15-$17,000		
1999	Buick LeSabre	Large
1999	Buick Regal	Intermediate
1998	Chrysler Concorde	Intermediate
1998	Chrysler LHS	Intermediate

Best Bets by Price

$15-$17,000 (cont.)

1999	Dodge Caravan	Minivan
1999	Ford Crown Victoria	Large
2000	Ford Taurus	Intermediate
2000	Mitsubishi Galant	Compact
1999	Pontiac Grand Prix	Intermediate

$16-$18,000

1999	Chrysler Concorde	Intermediate
2000	Dodge Caravan	Minivan
2000	Mercury Sable	Intermediate
2000	Bonneville	Large
2000	Pontiac Grand Prix	Intermediate

$17-$19,000

1998	Chrysler Town & Country	Minivan
2000	Buick Regal	Intermediate
2001	Mercury Sable	Intermediate

$18-$20,000

2000	Ford Crown Victoria	Large
2001	Ford Taurus	Intermediate

$19-$21,000

2000	Ford Windstar	Minivan

$20-$22,000

2001	Dodge Caravan	Minivan
2000	Subaru Legacy	Compact

$21-$23,000

2001	Subaru Legacy	Compact

$22-$24,000

1999	Buick Riviera	Large
2000	Chrysler LHS	Large
1999	Chrysler Town & Country	Minivan
2001	Ford Crown Victoria	Large
2000	Pontiac Bonneville	Large
2001	Pontiac Grand Prix	Intermediate

$23-$25,000

2001	Buick Regal	Intermediate
2000	Mercury Villager	Minivan
2000	Volkswagen Passat	Intermediate

$24-$26,000

1998	Lexus ES300	Intermediate

$25-$27,000

2001	Buick LeSabre	Large
2001	Pontiac Bonneville	Large

$27-$29,000

2000	Chrysler Town & Country	Minivan
2000	Lincoln Town Car	Large

$28-$30,000

2001	Acura TL	Large
2001	Chrysler Town & Country	Minivan
1999	Lexus ES300	Intermediate
1998	Volvo C70	Intermediate

$29-$31,000

1999	Volvo C70	Intermediate
1999	Volvo S80	Intermediate

>$30,000

1999-2001	Acura RL	Large
2000-2001	Lexus ES300	Intermediate
2001	Lincoln Town Car	Large
2001	Oldsmobile Aurora	Large
2000-2001	Volvo C70/S70/V70	Intermediate
2001	Volvo S80	Intermediate

CARS TO STAY AWAY FROM

The following is a list of cars that you may simply want to stay away from. These cars all received a "Very Poor" comparative rating, which is based on many factors, including crash tests, complaints, and repair costs. It is possible you owned one of these cars and had good luck with it. However, in general, we suggest you stay away from buying them because of their "Very Poor" overall rating. Also, avoid used cars with door-mounted belts. If the door pops open in a crash, you lose the protection of the belt.

1992-95 BMW 3 Series	1993 Jeep Grand Cherokee
1992-1994, 1995-96 Chev.	1992-95 Jeep Wrangler
Blazer, S10 Blazer	1994-95 Kia Sephia
1997-98 Chevrolet Tracker	1995-1997, 1999 Kia Sportage
1996 Chrysler Sebring	1995-96 Land Rover Discovery
1992, 1995 Eagle Talon	1994 Mazda 323
1992 Ford Explorer	1992-93 Mitsubishi Diamante
1992-93 Ford Probe	1992 Mitsubishi Galant
1992 Geo Prizm	1992, 1996-98 Mitsu. Montero
1992-95 Geo Tracker	1995, 1998 Nissan 240SX
1992-95 Hyundai Elantra	1993-94, 1998 NissanPathfinder
1992-93 Hyundai Sonata	1994 Saab 900
1992, 94-95, 98 Isuzu Rodeo	1993-95, 98 Toyota 4Runner
1992-93 Isuzu Trooper	1995 Volkswagen Golf
1993-94 Jeep Cherokee	1992-96 Volkswagen Passat

Ratings Explanation

The following tables rate hundreds of the most popular used cars. Each table contains information in a number of different categories. Blank spots in the tables mean that information is not available. Here's what you'll find on the tables:

Size/Type: The tables begin by giving the car's type: Subcompact, Compact, Intermediate, Large, Minivan, or Sport Utility.

Drive: This category shows whether the car is front-, rear-, or four-wheel drive.

Crash Test: This indicates how well the car performed in the U.S. government's 35 mph frontal crash test program. We have applied the results to those cars that were substantially unchanged from the model that was crash tested.

Airbags: Here we tell you which front seat occupants benefit from this life-saving device and who is left unprotected.

ABS: This safety feature comes in two-wheel and four-wheel versions. Two-wheel ABS is of little value.

Parts Cost: Very High, High, Average, Low, and Very Low ratings are based on nine typical repairs. We compare these costs with all other cars to determine the rating.

Complaints: These ratings are based on the number of complaints on file at the U.S. Department of Transportation. We developed the complaint index to give you a general idea of the experiences other owners have had with their cars.

Insurance: Insurance companies often use rating programs to determine whether or not a car should get a discount or a surcharge on its insurance prices. The ratings are partly based on each car's accident history. If the car is likely to receive neither a discount or surcharge, it is labeled as Regular.

MPG Rating: This is the EPA-rated fuel economy, in mpg, for city driving. We include the rating we believe represents the most popular engine/transmission combination for that model.

Theft Rating: This rating indicates if the car has a good or bad history of being stolen or broken into, according to statistics compiled by the Highway Loss Data Institute. While based on data collected during the three-year period following each model year, incidence of theft for these cars might vary slightly today.

Bumpers: Manufacturers no longer have to meet a rigid 5 mph crash test standard. Based on tests by the Insurance Institute for Highway Safety, we have categorized the bumpers as Strong, Fair, or Weak. A blank means that no data is available.

Recalls: These numbers indicate how many times each model was recalled for a safety problem. We have only included recalls in which the total number of cars recalled exceeded 500.

Turning Circle: The smaller a car's turning circle, the easier it will be for you to maneuver in and out of tight spaces. Different suspensions or braking systems found on varying models may cause the turning circle to vary.

Weight: This number gives you the weight of the automobile as it is measured by the manufacturer. Different transmissions, options, or trim levels may cause the weight to change.

Wheelbase: This measurement indicates the length from the center of the front wheel to the center of the rear wheel. The wheelbase usually changes when a truly new model is introduced.

Price ($): This column gives you a general idea of cost. This is to help you narrow down your choices within a price category, rather than serve as a predictor of what you should pay for the car. The actual value of the car is based on where you live, the condition of the car, and other unpredictable marketplace conditions.

Overall Rating: This column provides an overall evaluation of each model based on data we've collected since 1980. Each model year is rated Very Poor, Poor, Average, Good, Very Good, or Best Bet, based on crash tests, complaint histories, insurance premiums, theft ratings, repair costs, and safety features. Please note that model years without a crash test have no overall rating.

Note: If the car you are interested in does not appear on these tables, either it is available only in relatively small numbers or we did not have enough useful data to include it.

Note: You will note that there may be several footnotes per vehicle. We have tried to make these footnotes as consistent and concise as possible. Footnotes are placed on the bottom of the left-hand page and continue onto the right-hand page if necessary.

A QUICK CROSS REFERENCE GUIDE

We have combined the ratings of nearly identical cars that are sold under different names. To find information on the first car, look up the car written in italics.

Acura RL/*Acura Legend*
Acura TL/*Acura Vigor*
Audi 90/*Audi 80*
Audi 200/*Audi 100*
Audi A4/*Audi 80*
Audi A6/*Audi 100*
Audi S6/*Audi 100*
Cad. Fltwood 1990-92/*Cad. DeVille*
Cad. Fltwood 1993-96/*Cad. Brougham*
Chev. Blazer/*Chev. S-10 Blazer*
Chev. Corsica/*Chev. Beretta*
Chev. Impala/*Chev. Caprice*
Chev. Metro/*Geo Metro*
Chev. Monte Carlo/*Chev. Lumina*
Chev. Prizm/*Geo Prizm*
Chev. Tracker/*Geo Tracker*
Chev. Venture/*Chev. Lumina Minivan*
Chrys. LHS/*Chrys. New Yorker*
Dodge Avenger/*Chrys. Sebring*
Dodge Dynasty/*Chrys. New Yorker*
Dodge Intrepid/*Chrys. Concorde*
Dodge Stratus/*Chrys. Cirrus*
Eagle Summit/*Dodge Colt*
Eagle Summit Wagon/*Dodge Colt Vista*
Eagle Vision/*Chrys. Concorde*
Ford Aspire/*Ford Festiva*
Ford Expedition/*Ford Bronco*
GMC Jimmy/*Chev. S10 Blazer*
GMC Jimmy/*Chev. S10 Blazer*
GMC Safari/*Chev. Astro*
GMC Suburban/*Chev. Suburban*
Honda Passport/*Isuzu Rodeo*
Isuzu Oasis/*Honda Odyssey*
Isuzu Trooper II/*Isuzu Trooper*
Land Rover Discovery Series II/*Land Rover Discovery*
Lexus LS430/*Lexus LS400*
Lexus SC400/*Lexus SC300*

Lincoln Mark VIII/*Lincoln Mark VII*
Mazda Protegé/*Mazda 323*
Merc.-Benz E-Class/*Merc. Benz E*
Merc. Gr. Marquis/*Ford Crown Vic.*
Mercury Mystique/*Ford Contour*
Mercury Topaz/*Ford Tempo*
Mitsubishi Eclipse/*Eagle Talon*
Nissan Altima/*Nissan Stanza*
Nissan NX/*Nissan Pulsar*
Nissan Quest/*Mercury Villager*
Olds Bravada/*Chev. S10 Blazer*
Olds Cutlass/*Olds Cutlass Ciera*
Olds Silhouette/*Chev. Lumina*
Plym. Acclaim/*Dodge Spirit*
Plym. Breeze/*Chrys. Cirrus*
Plym. Colt/*Dodge Colt*
Plym. Colt Vista/*Dodge Colt Vista*
Plym. Laser/*Eagle Talon*
Plym. Neon/*Dodge Neon*
Plym. Sundance/*Dodge Shadow*
Plym. Voyager/*Dodge Caravan*
Pontiac Montana/*Chev. Lumina*
Pontiac Sunfire/*Pontiac Sunbird*
Pontiac Tr. Sport/*Chev. Lumina*
Saab 9-3/*Saab 900*
Saab 9-5/*Saab 9000*
Saturn SL/*Saturn SC*
Saturn SW/*Saturn SC*
Suzuki Sidekick/*Geo Tracker*
Suzuki Swift/*Geo Metro*
Toyota Avalon/*Toyota Cressida*
VW Jetta/*VW Golf*
Volvo C70/*Volvo 850*
Volvo S70/*Volvo 850*
Volvo S80/*Volvo 900 Series*
Volvo S90/*Volvo 900 Series*
Volvo V70/*Volvo 850*
Volvo V90/*Volvo 900 Series*

Acura CL 1997-2001

The Acura CL offers as standard, a more powerful 3.2 L V-6 as the base engine in 2001. A 2.3-liter 4-cylinder engine with the option of a more powerful 3.0-liter V6 was the standard in past

1997 Acura CL

years. The upgraded engine will cause a slight hit in fuel economy though. Standard safety features include dual airbags, 4-wheel ABS, rear headrests, front side window defoggers, keyless entry, and an anti-theft alarm. If that's not enough, the S version bumps you up to 260 hp. The options include perforated leather seating, an in-dash navigation system and heated seats. The navigation system comes with a DVD

	1992	1993	1994	1995	1996
Size Class					
Drive					
Crash Test					
Airbags					
ABS					
Parts Cost					
Complaints			No Model Produced		
Insurance					
Fuel Econ.					
Theft Rating					
Bumpers					
Recalls					
Trn. Cir. (ft.)					
Weight (lbs.)					
Whlbase (in.)					
Price					
OVERALL~					

~Cars without crash tests do not receive an overall rating.

2001 Acura CL

database that covers the entire U.S.

	1997	1998	1999	2000	2001
Size Class	Large	Large	Large	Large	Large
Drive	Front	Front	Front	Front	Front
Crash Test	N/A	N/A	N/A	N/A	N/A
Airbags	Dual	Dual	Dual	Dual	Dual/Side
ABS	4-Whl	4-Whl	4-Whl	4-Whl	4-Whl
Parts Cost	Average	Average	Average	Average	Average
Complaints	Good	Good	Vry. Gd.	Vry. Gd.	Average
Insurance	Discount	Discount	Discount	Discount	Regular
Fuel Econ.	20	20	24	24	19
Theft Rating	High	High	High	High	High
Bumpers			Strong	Strong	Strong
Recalls	0	0	0	0	0
Trn. Cir. (ft.)	39	39	39.04	39.04	37.4
Weight (lbs.)	3004	3004	3064	3483	3470
Whlbase (in.)	106.9	106.9	106.9	106.9	106.9
Price	13-15,000	16-18,000	19-21,000	20-22,000	28-30,000
OVERALL~					

Acura Integra 1992-2001

The most afford-able of Acura's mod-els, the Integra em-phasizes sportiness over luxury. Acura gave it thorough makeovers for 1990 and 1994, and the 1998 models have new front- and rear-end styling plus

1992 Acura Integra

new wheels. The Integra shares its chassis and some other components with the Honda Civic, which was redesigned for 1996. Watch out for all 1990-93 Integras which are equipped with unsafe, motorized shoul-der belts with separate lap belts. Dual airbags became standard with the 1994 redesign, while ABS became standard on the 1990-1993 GS and on later LS and GS-R models.

	1992	1993	1994	1995	1996
Size Class	Compact	Compact	Compact	Compact	Compact
Drive	Front	Front	Front	Front	Front
Crash Test	N/A	N/A	Average	Average	Average
Airbags	None	None	Dual	Dual	Dual
ABS	4-Whl*	4-Whl*	4-Whl*	4-Whl*	4-Whl*
Parts Cost	Average	Average	Average	High	High
Complaints	Good	Vry. Good	Vry. Good	Vry. Good	Vry. Good
Insurance	Surchg.	Surchg.	Surchg.	Surchg.	Surchg.
Fuel Econ.	24	23	25	25	24
Theft Rating	Average	Vry. High	Vry. High	Vry. High	Vry. High
Bumpers					
Recalls	0	0	0	1	
Trn. Cir. (ft.)	33.8	33.3	34.8	34.8	34.8
Weight (lbs.)	2608	2608	2703	2703	2703
Whlbase (in.)	102.4[1]	102.4[1]	103.1[1]	103.1[1]	103.1[1]
Price	6-8,000	7-9,000	8-10,000	10-12,000	11-13,000
OVERALL~			Poor	Average	Average

[1]Data given for sedan. Wheelbase for coupe for 1992-93 is 100.4; 1994-2001 is 101.2; *Optional; ~Cars without crash

2001 Acura Integra

The Integra's engines have twin overhead camshafts for maximum performance. Power ranges from 115 hp on early models up to 170 hp on the GS-R's 1.8-liter VTEC engine. Handling ranks equally well among the best small cars, and the ride is firm but certainly tolerable. Front seats, driver's controls, and instruments are fine, but the rear seat is cramped.

	1997	1998	1999	2000	2001
Size Class	Compact	Compact	Compact	Compact	Compact
Drive	Front	Front	Front	Front	Front
Crash Test	Average	Average	Average	Average	Average
Airbags	Dual	Dual	Dual	Dual	Dual
ABS	4-Whl*	4-Whl*	4-Whl	4-Whl	4-Whl
Parts Cost	Vry. High	High	High	High	High
Complaints	Vry. Good	Good	Vry. Gd.	Good	Vry. Gd.
Insurance	Surchg.	Surchg.	Surchg.	Surchg.	Surchg.
Fuel Econ.	25	25	25	25	25
Theft Rating	Vry. High	Vry. High	Vry. High**	Vry. High**	Vry. High**
Bumpers		Strong	Strong	Strong	
Recalls	0	0	0	0	0
Trn. Cir. (ft.)	34.8	34.8	34.8	34.8	34.8
Weight (lbs.)	2703	2703	2703	2703	2639
Whlbase (in.)	103.1[1]	103.1[1]	103.1[1]	103.1[1]	103.1[1]
Price	13-15,000	14-16,000	17-19,000	19-21,000	20-22,000
OVERALL~	Average	Poor	Good	Average	Good

tests do not receive an overall rating; **Estimate.

Acura Legend 1992-95, RL 1997-2001

The Legend, Acura's luxury flagship, was discontinued in 1996, replaced by the RL. A larger version of the Legend, the RL has improved upon its predecessor's ride and overall comfort. A driver's airbag is standard on all models. For 1991 came a new body and chassis, and LS models added a passenger airbag; other models (except base) had this option, and dual airbags eventually became standard on all 1993 Legends. ABS is standard on all models after 1990. For 1999, side airbags were added.

1992 Acura Legend

The Legend's V6 grew from 2.5 liters to 3.2 liters by 1994 but has

	1992	1993	1994	1995	1996
Size Class	Intermd.	Intermd.	Intermd.	Intermd.	
Drive	Front	Front	Front	Front	
Crash Test	Average	Average	Average	Average	
Airbags	Driver[#]	Dual	Dual	Dual	
ABS	4-Whl	4-Whl	4-Whl	4-Whl	
Parts Cost	High	Vry. High	Vry. High	Vry. High	
Complaints	Good	Vry. Gd.	Vry. Gd.	Vry. Gd.	No Model Produced
Insurance	Discount	Discount	Discount	Discount	
Fuel Econ.	19	19	19	18	
Theft Rating	High	Vry. High	Vry. High	Vry. High	
Bumpers					
Recalls					
Trn. Cir. (ft.)	34.8	34.8	34.8	34.8	
Weight (lbs.)	3479	3483	3583	3582	
Whlbase (in.)	114.6[1]	114.6[1]	114.6[1]	114.6[1]	
Price	13-15,000	14-16,000	15-17,000	17-19,000	
OVERALL~	Average	Good	Good	Good	

[1]Data given for sedan. Wheelbase for coupe for 1992-95 is 111.4; #Passenger Side Optional;**Estimate; ~Cars without

58

2001 Acura RL

since become a 3.5-liter V6; its power is ample. The manual transmission shifts gracefully, while the automatic is rough. Front seats are comfortable, and there's enough room in back for two to travel serenely. Instrument panel and controls are first-rate.

	1997	1998	1999	2000	2001
Size Class	Large	Large	Large	Large	Large
Drive	Front	Front	Front	Front	Front
Crash Test	Good	Good	Good	Good	Good
Airbags	Dual	Dual	Dual/Side	Dual/Side	Dual/Side
ABS	4-Whl	4-Whl	4-Whl	4-Whl	4-Whl
Parts Cost	High	Vry. High	Vry. High	Vry. High	Vry. Low
Complaints	Vry. Gd.	Vry. Gd.	Vry. Gd.	Vry. Gd.	Vry. Gd.
Insurance	Regular	Regular	Regular	Discount	Discount
Fuel Econ.	19	19	18	18	18
Theft Rating	Vry. High	Vry. High	Vry. High**	Vry. High**	Vry. High**
Bumpers			Strong	Strong	Strong
Recalls					
Trn. Cir. (ft.)	36.1	36.1	36.1	36.1	36.1
Weight (lbs.)	3660	3660	3840	3840	3840
Whlbase (in.)	114.6	114.6	114.6	114.6	114.6
Price	22-24,000	26-28,000	>30,000	>30,000	>30,000
OVERALL~	Good	Good	BEST BET	BEST BET	BEST BET

crash tests do not receive an overall rating.

Acura Vigor 1992-94, TL 1996-2001

The Vigor, introduced in the spring of 1991 as a 1992 model, and the TL are, in many ways, the ultimate Honda Accord, spiced up with impressive but seldom used extras. On the TL and the Vigor LS,

1992 Acura Vigor

you'll find leather seats and a wood-trimmed dash; if you don't mind cloth seats, you can save by getting a base TL or a Vigor GS. All Vigors have a driver's airbag and ABS; the 1993 model offers optional dual airbags, and the 1994 Vigor comes with standard dual airbags. All TLs come standard with dual airbags and 4-wheel ABS. For 2000, side airbags were added.

	1992	1993	1994	1995	1996
Size Class	Intermd.	Intermd.	Intermd.		Large
Drive	Front	Front	Front		Front
Crash Test	Poor	Poor	Poor		Good
Airbags	Driver#	Driver#	Dual		Dual
ABS	4-Whl	4-Whl	4-Whl		4-Whl
Parts Cost	Vry. High	Vry. High	Vry. High		Vry. High
Complaints	Average	Vry. Gd.	Average		Vry. Gd.
Insurance	Regular	Regular	Regular		Discount
Fuel Econ.	20	20	20		20
Theft Rating	Vry. High	Vry. High	Vry. High		Vry. High
Bumpers				No Model Produced	
Recalls	0	0	0		1
Trn. Cir. (ft.)	36.2	36.2	36.2		36.1
Weight (lbs.)	3150	3142	3197		3252
Whlbase (in.)	110.4	110.4	110.4		111.8
Price	7-9,000	8-10,000	9-11,000		15-17,000
OVERALL	Poor	Poor	Poor		Vry. Gd.

#Passenger Side Optional; **Estimate

2001 Acura TL

Vigors have a 2.5-liter engine with a nice 5-speed manual or a crude-shifting automatic overdrive. You have your choice of a 2.5-liter or a 3.2-liter engine on the TL. As with the Vigor, the TL's handling is quite good, but the ride is almost too firm. A shorter wheelbase model was introduced in 1999. Front seat riders have adequate comfort. Two will fit in the back, but three is a definite squeeze. The body doesn't filter out noise too well, which is surprising for such an expensive car. Good crash test results make the Acura TL a better choice than the Vigor.

	1997	1998	1999	2000	2001
Size Class	Large	Large	Large	Large	Large
Drive	Front	Front	Front	Front	Front
Crash Test	Good	Good	Good	Good	Good
Airbags	Dual	Dual	Dual	Dual/Side	Dual/Side
ABS	4-Whl	4-Whl	4-Whl	4-Whl	4-Whl
Parts Cost	Vry. High	Vry. High	High	High	Average
Complaints	Vry. Pr.	Vry. Gd.	Good	Average	Average
Insurance	Regular	Regular	Regular	Regular	Discount
Fuel Econ.	20	20	19	19	19
Theft Rating	Vry. High	Vry. High	Vry. High**	Vry. High**	Very Low
Bumpers			Strong	Strong	Strong
Recalls	1	1	0	0	0
Trn. Cir. (ft.)	36.1	36.8	36.8	36.8	36.8
Weight (lbs.)	3282	3446	3446	3446	3446
Whlbase (in.)	111.8	108.1	108.1	108.1	108.1
Price	16-18,000	20-22,000	24-26,000	27-29,000	28-30,000
OVERALL	Vry. Pr.	Good	Good	Good	BEST BET

Audi 100/200 1992-94, A6 1995-2001, S6 1995-2001

With a redesign of the 100 in 1995, Audi switched to an alphanumeric naming system, and the A6/S6 was born. This replacement for the 100 offers sleeker lines and a plusher interior. Other models are

1992 Audi 100

variations on the 100 - the 200 has a turbocharged engine and plusher trim; the Quattro has full-time 4-wheel drive; the S6 has sport suspension, turbocharger, and four-wheel drive; and wagon versions are available. In 1990, Audi's received an optional driver's airbag. Dual airbags became standard in 1994. ABS was offered in 1990 and became standard in 1992.

	1992	1993	1994	1995	1996
Size Class	Large	Large	Large	Large	Large
Drive	Front/All	Front/All	Front/All	Front/All	Front/All
Crash Test	N/A	N/A	N/A	Vry. Gd.	Vry. Gd.
Airbags	Driver	Dual	Dual	Dual	Dual
ABS	4-Whl	4-Whl	4-Whl	4-Whl	4-Whl
Parts Cost	Average	Average	Average	Vry. Gd.	Vry. Gd.
Complaints	Average	Good	Vry. Gd.	Vry. Gd.	Vry. Gd.
Insurance	Discount	Discount	Discount	Discount	Discount
Fuel Econ.	19	19	18	19	19
Theft Rating	Low	Low	Low	Low	Vry. Low
Bumpers			Weak	Strong	Strong
Recalls	2	1	2	2	2
Trn. Cir. (ft.)	34.8	34.8	34.8	34.8	34.8
Weight (lbs.)	3715	3329	3363	3363	3582
Whlbase (in.)	105.8	105.8	105.8	105.8	105.8
Price	10-12,000	11-13,000	12-14,000	14-16,000	17-19,000
OVERALL~				Vry. Gd.	Vry. Gd.

**Estimate; ~Cars without crash tests do not receive an overall rating.

2001 Audi A6

Cars before 1992 offered a standard 5-liter engine or a turbocharged 5-liter; 1992 and later models went to a V6 (except S6). Audi features the Quattro all-wheel drive system, which improves handling and wet weather traction. Inside, accommodations are fairly good for four. The controls on earlier models are inferior to many cheaper cars, but the gauges are fine. Unfortunately, the A6 has not been crash tested for the 1998-2001 model years.

	1997	1998	1999	2000	2001
Size Class	Large	Large	Large	Large	Large
Drive	Front/All	Front/All	Front/All	Front/All	Front/All
Crash Test	Vry. Gd.	N/A	N/A	N/A	N/A
Airbags	Dual	Dual/Side	Dual/Side	Dual/Side	Dual/Side
ABS	4-Whl	4-Whl	4-Whl	4-Whl	4-Whl
Parts Cost	Vry. Gd.	Average	Very High	Very High	Very High
Complaints	Vry. Gd.	Vry. Gd.	Vry. Pr.	Poor	Vry. Gd.
Insurance	Discount	Discount	Discount	Discount	Discount
Fuel Econ.	19	17	17	17	17
Theft Rating	Low	Low	Low**	Low**	Low**
Bumpers	Strong	Strong	Strong	Strong	Strong
Recalls	2	2	0	0	0
Trn. Cir. (ft.)	34.8	38.3	38.3	38.3	38.3
Weight (lbs.)	3428	3473	3473	3473	3473
Whlbase (in.)	105.8	108.7	108.7	108.7	108.7
Price	25-27,000	27-29,000	>30,000	>30,000	>30,000
OVERALL~	Vry. Gd.				

Audi 80/90 1992-95, A4 1996-2001

Audi not only re-designed the 90 for 1996 but renamed it too. In 1998, Audi introduced a wagon version of the same: the Avant. The Audi A4 comes standard with more features than ever before

1992 Audi 80

and a slick new look. The 90 was not available in 1992, as Audi prepared for the 1993 restyling; since 1993, only the up-level 90 has been available. ABS was originally an option on the 80 Quattro and standard on all 90s; all 80s got ABS for 1992. A driver's airbag first became available in 1990 and standard in 1991; dual airbags were added in 1994.

	1992	1993	1994	1995	1996
Size Class	Compact	Intermd.	Intermd.	Intermd.	Intermd.
Drive	Front/All	Front/All	Front/All	Front/All	Front/All
Crash Test	Vry. Gd.	N/A	N/A	N/A	Vry. Gd.
Airbags	Driver	Driver	Dual	Dual	Dual
ABS	4-Whl	4-Whl	4-Whl	4-Whl	4-Whl
Parts Cost	High	High	Vry. High	Vry. High	Vry. High
Complaints	Average	Average	Average	Average	Vry. Gd.
Insurance	Discount	Discount	Discount	Discount	Regular
Fuel Econ.	20	20	20	20	18
Theft Rating	Average	Average	Average	Average	Average
Bumpers					
Recalls	1	1	1	2	2
Trn. Cir. (ft.)	33	34	34.1	34.1	36.4
Weight (lbs.)	2906	3186	3197	3197	2976
Whlbase (in.)	100.2[1]	102.8[1]	102.8[1]	102.8[1]	103.0[1]
Price	9-11,000	10-12,000	11-13,000	12-14,000	21-23,000
OVERALL~	Good				Poor

[1]Wheelbase for Quattro for 1992 is 99.9; 1993-95 is 102.2; 1996-97 is 102.6; **Estimate; ~Cars without crash tests do not

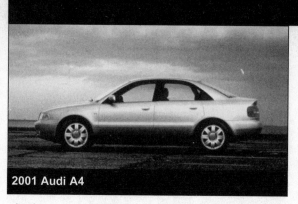

2001 Audi A4

The standard 2-liter 4-cylinder engine found on the base 80 through 1992 is only adequate; the in-line 5 found on the Quattro 80 and all 90s through 1992 is much more satisfying and still relatively economical. The A4 comes standard with a 1.8-liter four-cylinder and has recently been classified as an Ultra Low Emission Vehicle. The Quattro all-wheel drive system improves handling and traction on slick roads, especially on this surprisingly light car. There is also a sport package for the A4 which lowers the car, tightens the suspension, and adds some sporty wheels.

	1997	1998	1999	2000	2001
Size Class	Intermd.	Intermd.	Intermd.	Intermd.	Intermd.
Drive	Front/All	Front/All	Front/All	Front/All	Front/All
Crash Test	Vry. Gd.	Vry. Gd.	Vry. Gd.	Vry. Gd.	Vry. Gd.
Airbags	Dual	Dual/Side	Dual/Side	Dual/Side	Dual/Side
ABS	4-Whl	4-Whl	4-Whl	4-Whl	4-Whl
Parts Cost	Vry. High	Vry. High	Vry. High	Vry. High	Vry. High
Complaints	Vry. Gd.	Vry. Gd.	Vry. Pr.	Poor	Vry. Gd.
Insurance	Regular	Regular	Regular	Regular	Regular
Fuel Econ.	20	23	23	23	23
Theft Rating	Vry. Low	Average	Average	Very Low	Average**
Bumpers			Strong	Strong	Strong
Recalls	3	3	2	0	0
Trn. Cir. (ft.)	36.4	36.4	36.4	36.4	36.4
Weight (lbs.)	2877	2877	2877	2877	2998
Whlbase (in.)	103.0[1]	103	103	102.6	103
Price	22-24,000	23-25,000	24-26,000	25-27,000	26-28,000
OVERALL~	Good	Good	Average	Good	Good

receive an overall rating.

BMW 3-Series 1992-2001

For years, the 3-Series has been the cheapest BMW sold in the U.S., and with 8 variations of sedan, coupe and convertible there's a lot to choose from. The exterior styling on the 3-Series stayed the same through

1993 BMW 3-Series

1991, though convertibles carried on unchanged through 1993. The 1992 coupe and sedan and the 1994 convertibles received new, rounded styling. For 1996, BMW created an inexpensive (low $20,000s) hatchback version that revived the "ti" name from the '70s and should broaden the 3-Series appeal. The 1990-93 3-Series comes with a standard driver airbag, and later models add a passenger airbag.

	1992	1993	1994	1995	1996
Size Class	Compact	Compact	Compact	Compact	Compact
Drive	Rear	Rear	Rear	Rear	Rear
Crash Test	Good	Good	Good	Good	Good
Airbags	Driver	Driver	Dual	Dual	Dual
ABS	4-Whl	4-Whl	4-Whl	4-Whl	4-Whl
Parts Cost	High	Vry. High	Vry. High	High	High
Complaints	Average	Good	Poor	Poor	Good
Insurance	Surchg.	Surchg.	Surchg.	Surchg.	Surchg.
Fuel Econ.	20	20	26	22	20
Theft Rating	High	Vry. High	Vry. High	Vry. High	Vry. High
Bumpers					
Recalls	6	4	3	3	1
Trn. Cir. (ft.)	34.4	34.1	34.1	34.1	34.1
Weight (lbs.)	2867	2860	2866	2866	3086
Whlbase (in.)	106.3	106.3	106.3	106.3	106.3
Price	15-17,000	16-18,000	17-19,000	18-20,000	19-21,000
OVERALL~	Vry. Pr.	Vry. Pr.	Vry. Pr.	Vry. Pr.	Poor

**Estimate; ~Cars without a crash test do not receive an overall rating; *Optional.

The 318 has a 1.8-liter 4-cylinder engine through 1995; 1996 and later models have a 1.9-liter engine. The 318 disappeared after 1999 and the base models is now the much faster 325, which has a 2.5-liter 6-cylinder, and the 328 has a 2.8-liter 6-cylinder. Either engine can be teamed with a 5-speed manual or automatic overdrive. The 3-Series is a fine choice for precise response. Look for winter weather packages with limited slip differentials and traction control. The controls and gauges are outstanding.

2001 BMW 3-Series

	1997	1998	1999	2000	2001
Size Class	Compact	Compact	Compact	Compact	Compact
Drive	Rear	Rear	Rear	Rear	Rear
Crash Test	Good	Good	N/A	N/A	N/A
Airbags	Dual	Dual/Side*	Dual/Side*	Dual/Side*	Dual/Side*
ABS	4-Whl	4-Whl	4-Whl	4-Whl	4-Whl
Parts Cost	Vry. High	High	High	High	High
Complaints	Good	Average	Good	Poor	Average
Insurance	Surchg.	Surchg.	Surchg.	Surchg.	Reg
Fuel Econ.	23	23	20	23	21
Theft Rating	Vry. High	Vry. High	Vry. High**	Vry. High**	Vry. High**
Bumpers			Strong	Weak	
Recalls	1	0	0	0	1
Trn. Cir. (ft.)	34.1	34.1	34.4	34.4	34.4
Weight (lbs.)	3086	3075	3250	3250	3250
Whlbase (in.)	106.3	106.3	107.3	107.3	107.3
Price	24-26,000	25-27,000	28-30,000	29-31,000	>30,000
OVERALL~	Poor	Average			

BMW Z3 1998-2001

Ever since its splashy debut in a James Bond film, the Z3 has become a surefire way to turn heads on the road. The Z3 is a convertible based on the 3-Series platform. The original 1.9-liter 4-

1998 BMW Z3

cylinder engine was upgraded to the base 2.5-liter inline 6 engine and an optional 2.8-liter in-line 6 and beefier 3.2-liter in-line 6 are available. Dual and side airbags are standard as well as 4-wheel ABS. The Z3 is an attractive and popular sports car but, unfortunately, has yet to be crash-tested. This vehicle is extremely (many say too) fast, so be careful!

	1992	1993	1994	1995	1996
Size Class					
Drive					
Crash Test					
Airbags					
ABS					
Parts Cost					
Complaints					
Insurance					
Fuel Econ.					
Theft Rating		No Model Produced			
Bumpers					
Recalls					
Trn. Cir. (ft.)					
Weight (lbs.)					
Whlbase (in.)					
Price					
OVERALL~					

**Estimate; ~Cars without a crash test do not receive an overall rating.

2001 BMW Z3

	1997	1998	1999	2000	2001
Size Class		Compact	Compact	Compact	Compact
Drive		Rear	Rear	Rear	Rear
Crash Test		N/A	N/A	N/A	N/A
Airbags		Dual	Dual/Side	Dual/Side	Dual/Side
ABS		4-Whl	4-Whl	4-Whl	4-Whl
Parts Cost		High	High	Very High	Average
Complaints		Average	Vry. Gd.	Average	Good
Insurance		Discount	Discount	Discount	Discount
Fuel Econ.		23	19	19	21
Theft Rating		Average**	Average**	Average**	Average**
Bumpers		Weak	Weak	Weak	
Recalls		0	1	0	0
Trn. Cir. (ft.)		32.8	32.8	32.8	32.8
Weight (lbs.)		2723	2723	2723	2723
Whlbase (in.)		96.3	96.3	96.3	96.3
Price		28-30,000	>30,000	>30,000	>30,000
OVERALL~					

No Model Produced (spans 1997 column)

Buick Century 1992-2001

Few changes had taken place for the Buick Century until 1997 when the Century was redesigned, making it much sleeker and safer. The 1990-96 Centurys look exactly like what they are: an early 80s

1993 Buick Century

mid-size car. All models from 1990-1996 have GM's horrid door-mounted seat belts. Some 1993 models had an optional driver airbag; it became standard for 1994. ABS wasn't available until it became standard in 1994.

Typical of GM mid-size and large cars, the Century rides well on smooth roads, but it can become unsure over rough roads or bumps.

	1992	1993	1994	1995	1996
Size Class	Intermd.	Intermd.	Intermd.	Intermd.	Intermd.
Drive	Front	Front	Front	Front	Front
Crash Test	Average	Average[1]	Good	Good	Good
Airbags	None	Driver*	Driver	Driver	Driver
ABS	None	None	4-Whl	4-Whl	4-Whl
Parts Cost	Vry. Low	Vry. Low	Low	Vry. Low	Vry. Low
Complaints	Good	Good	Good	Average	Vry. Gd.
Insurance	Discount	Discount	Discount	Discount	Discount
Fuel Econ.	19	20	22	25	24
Theft Rating	Average	Average	Average	Low	Average
Bumpers	Weak	Weak	Weak	Weak	Weak
Recalls	4	3	7	2	1
Trn. Cir. (ft.)	38.5	38.5	38.5	38.5	38.5
Weight (lbs.)	2862	2949	2974	2986	2950
Whlbase (in.)	104.9	104.9	104.9	104.9	104.9
Price	3-5,000	3-5,000	4-6,000	5-7,000	7-9,000
OVERALL	Average	Vry. Gd.[2]	Vry. Gd.	Vry. Gd.	BEST BET

[1]Data given for model without airbags. Crash test for model with driver airbag is Good; [2]Data given for model without

2001 Buick Century

Wagons with the 4-cylinder engine lack reserve power; get the 3.8-liter V6 found on some Century models instead: it's powerful, but you'll pay for it with lower gas mileage. Room inside and comfort for four are passable, however, this improves for 1997. Driver's controls before 1997 are dated and inefficient. After the 1997 redesign, crash test performance became only average. However, traction control, ABS and daytime running lamps are standard.

	1997	1998	1999	2000	2001
Size Class	Intermd.	Intermd.	Intermd.	Intermd.	Intermd.
Drive	Front	Front	Front	Front	Front
Crash Test	Good	Average	Average	Average	Average
Airbags	Dual	Dual	Dual	Dual	Dual
ABS	4-Whl	4-Whl	4-Whl	4-Whl	4-Whl
Parts Cost	Low	Vry. Low	Low	Low	Low
Complaints	Good	Poor	Average	Good	Average
Insurance	Discount	Discount	Discount	Discount	Discount
Fuel Econ.	20	20	20	20	20
Theft Rating	Average	Low	Low	Very Low**	Very Low**
Bumpers			Strong	Strong	Strong
Recalls	1	1	0	4	2
Trn. Cir. (ft.)	36.5	37.5	37.5	37.5	37.5
Weight (lbs.)	3348	3335	3335	3335	3335
Whlbase (in.)	109	109	109	109	109
Price	11-13,000	12-14,000	14-16,000	16-18,000	20-22,000
OVERALL	BEST BET	Vry. Gd.	BEST BET	Good	Vry. Gd.

airbags. Overall rating for model with driver airbag may vary based on footnote; *Optional; **Estimate

Buick LeSabre 1992-2001

The LeSabre and its near-twins, the Olds 88 and the Pontiac Bonneville, have been consistent sellers for GM, and they show no sign of slowing down. The LeSabre's body changed slightly in 1992 on the same

1992 Buick LeSabre

front-wheel drive chassis, and there was a slight refreshing for 1997. In 1992, Buick replaced the belts with a driver's airbag and conventional, height-adjustable belts. Buick added a passenger airbag for 1994. In 1999, side airbags were added to the list of standard safety features. ABS was standard on the 1992 LeSabre Limited and all LeSabres beginning in 1993.

	1992	1993	1994	1995	1996
Size Class	Large	Large	Large	Large	Large
Drive	Front	Front	Front	Front	Front
Crash Test	Good	Good	Good	Good	Good
Airbags	Driver	Driver	Dual	Dual	Dual
ABS	4-Whl*	4-Whl	4-Whl	4-Whl	4-Whl
Parts Cost	Low	Average	Low	Average	Average
Complaints	Poor	Average	Good	Good	Vry. Gd.
Insurance	Discount	Discount	Discount	Discount	Discount
Fuel Econ.	18	18	19	19	19
Theft Rating	Low	Vry. Low	Vry. Low	Vry. Low	Vry. Low
Bumpers					
Recalls	3	2	0	1	2
Trn. Cir. (ft.)	40.7	40.7	40.7	40.7	40.7
Weight (lbs.)	3417	3433	3449	3442	3430
Whlbase (in.)	110.8	110.8	110.8	110.8	110.8
Price	5-7,000	6-8,000	7-9,000	8-10,000	10-12,000
OVERALL	Good	Good	BEST BET	Vry. Gd.	BEST BET

*Optional; **Estimate

72

2001 Buick LeSabre

There is only one engine choice, and, unfortunately, it's not as powerful as other GMs. With standard suspension, the LeSabre rides well on good roads, but the cornering is mediocre. To improve handling, look for LeSabres with T-Type or Grand Touring packages. Trunk space is generous. The LeSabre shares another unfortunate characteristic with the Olds 88: a flashy, badly designed dashboard. If you want a large GM car, consider a Bonneville.

	1997	1998	1999	2000	2001
Size Class	Large	Large	Large	Large	Large
Drive	Front	Front	Front	Front	Front
Crash Test	Good	Good	Good	Vry. Gd.	Vry. Gd.
Airbags	Dual	Dual	Dual	Dual	Dual/Side
ABS	4-Whl	4-Whl	4-Whl	4-Whl	4-Whl
Parts Cost	Average	Low	Low	Low	Average
Complaints	Poor	Average	Average	Vry. Pr.	Average
Insurance	Discount	Discount	Discount	Discount	Discount
Fuel Econ.	19	19	19	19	19
Theft Rating	Vry. Low	Vry. Low	Vry. Low**	Vry. Low**	Vry. Low**
Bumpers			Strong	Strong	Strong
Recalls	2	0	0	1	0
Trn. Cir. (ft.)	40.7	40.7	40.7	39.5	39.5
Weight (lbs.)	3441	3443	3443	3567	3567
Whlbase (in.)	110.8	110.8	110.8	112.2	112.2
Price	12-14,000	13-15,000	15-17,000	19-21,000	25-27,000
OVERALL	Good	BEST BET	BEST BET	Vry. Gd.	BEST BET

Buick Park Avenue 1992-2001

In 1991, Buick redesigned the Park Avenue and dropped the Electra name. Buick overhauled the Park Avenue one more time for 1997. The 1991 models featured regular belts with a standard driver

1992 Buick Park Avenue

airbag; 1994 models added a front passenger airbag. ABS was optional in 1990 and standard on all models beginning in 1991. In 1996 and 1997 models, you can drive 100,000 miles before your first tune-up.

Most cars have a 3.8-liter V6 with an optional supercharged version on Ultra models beginning in 1991. For 2001, a new Ultra Special Edition was added. A high-end audio system and Stabilitrak (all-weather

	1992	1993	1994	1995	1996
Size Class	Large	Large	Large	Large	Large
Drive	Front	Front	Front	Front	Front
Crash Test	N/A	N/A	N/A	Average	Average
Airbags	Driver	Driver	Dual	Dual	Dual
ABS	4-Whl	4-Whl	4-Whl	4-Whl	4-Whl
Parts Cost	Low	Low	Low	Low	Average
Complaints	Average	Good	Good	Poor	Vry. Gd.
Insurance	Discount	Discount	Discount	Discount	Discount
Fuel Econ.	18	19	19	19	19
Theft Rating	Low	Vry. Low	Vry. Low	Vry. Low	Vry. Low
Bumpers					
Recalls	4	2	0	1	3
Trn. Cir. (ft.)	39.4	39.4	40	40	39.4
Weight (lbs.)	3646	3536	3533	3532	3536
Whlbase (in.)	110.7	110.7	110.8	110.8	110.8
Price	6-8,000	7-9,000	8-10,000	11-13,000	13-15,000
OVERALL~				Vry. Gd.	Vry. Gd.

**Estimate; ~Cars without crash tests do not receive an overall rating.

2001 Buick Park Avenue

control) are available. The Park Avenue specializes in a soft, smooth ride at the expense of its handling ability. There's plenty of room for five and an ample-sized trunk (bigger on 1991-later models). The dashboard is more stylish than functional but improved after the 1991 makeover. Newer Park Avenues are expensive so consider the Olds 98 Touring Sedan, Buick LeSabre, or Pontiac Bonneville.

	1997	1998	1999	2000	2001
Size Class	Large	Large	Large	Large	Large
Drive	Front	Front	Front	Front	Front
Crash Test	Good	Good	Good	Good	Good
Airbags	Dual	Dual	Dual	Dual	Dual
ABS	4-Whl	4-Whl	4-Whl	4-Whl	4-Whl
Parts Cost	Average	Low	Low	Average	Low
Complaints	Poor	Poor	Good	Average	Average
Insurance	Discount	Discount	Discount	Discount	Discount
Fuel Econ.	19	19	19	19	19
Theft Rating	Vry. Low	Vry. Low	Vry. Low**	Vry. Low**	Vry. Low**
Bumpers			Strong	Strong	Strong
Recalls	2	0	0	2	0
Trn. Cir. (ft.)	40	39.4	39.4	39.7	39.7
Weight (lbs.)	3879	3740	3778	3778	3778
Whlbase (in.)	113.8	113.8	113.8	113.8	113.8
Price	16-18,000	18-20,000	20-22,000	24-26,000	>30,000
OVERALL~	Vry. Gd.	BEST BET	BEST BET	Vry. Gd.	BEST BET

Buick Regal 1992-2001

The Regal, unchanged from 1990-96, was redesigned for 1997. It is closely related to the Olds Cutlass Supreme and Pontiac Grand Prix. The first version of this vehicle, the 1987 model, had

1992 Buick Regal

squared-off styling and rear-wheel drive. For 1997, the Regal got a fresh, new look. All 1990-94 Regals have GM's deplorable door-mounted front belts; 1994 models added a standard driver's airbag. ABS was optional in 1990 and standard for 1995. The 1996 Regal meets the government's 1997 side impact standard.

The Regal's 2.8-liter V6 provides adequate power in this unusually

	1992	1993	1994	1995	1996
Size Class	Intermd.	Intermd.	Intermd.	Intermd.	Intermd.
Drive	Front	Front	Front	Front	Front
Crash Test	Good	Good	Vry. Pr.	Average	Average
Airbags	None	None	Driver	Dual	Dual
ABS	4-Whl*	4-Whl*	4-Whl*	4-Whl	4-Whl
Parts Cost	Vry. Low	Low	Low	Average	Average
Complaints	Poor	Average	Average	Average	Average
Insurance	Discount	Discount	Discount	Discount	Discount
Fuel Econ.	19	19	19	19	20
Theft Rating	Low	Vry. Low	Vry. Low	Vry. Low	Vry. Low
Bumpers					
Recalls	2	3	4	8	2
Trn. Cir. (ft.)	39	36.7	36.7	36.7	39
Weight (lbs.)	3320	3250	3240	3335	3232
Whlbase (in.)	107.5	107.5	107.5	107.5	107.5
Price	4-6,000	5-7,000	6-8,000	7-9,000	9-11,000
OVERALL~	Good	Good	Poor	Good	Good

*Optional; **Estimate;~Cars without crash tests do not receive an overall rating.

2001 Buick Regal

heavy mid-size car. Along with the LS and GS trim levels, a special Olympic version is available for 2001. You'll find more power in later models. Typical of Buicks, the Regal provides a good ride on good roads and low-grade handling; the heavy-duty suspension should help improve cornering ability. The controls and displays are awful, especially the digital instruments on the 1990 sedans; however, this improves for 1997. Interior space is reasonable, but comfort is no better than average. Trunk space is generous.

	1997	1998	1999	2000	2001
Size Class	Intermd.	Intermd.	Intermd.	Intermd.	Intermd.
Drive	Front	Front	Front	Front	Front
Crash Test	Good	Good	Good	Average	Average
Airbags	Dual	Dual	Dual	Dual	Dual
ABS	4-Whl	4-Whl	4-Whl	4-Whl	4-Whl
Parts Cost	Average	Average	Low	Low	Low
Complaints	Good	Poor	Good	Vry. Gd.	Average
Insurance	Discount	Discount	Discount	Discount	Discount
Fuel Econ.	20	19	18	18	18
Theft Rating	Vry. Low	Vry. Low	Vry. Low**	Vry. Low**	Vry. Low**
Bumpers			Strong	Strong	Strong
Recalls	2	1	0	4	2
Trn. Cir. (ft.)	39	37.5	37.5	37.5	37.5
Weight (lbs.)	3355	3562	3543	3543	3543
Whlbase (in.)	107.5	109	109	109	109
Price	13-15,000	14-16,000	15-17,000	17-19,000	23-25,000
OVERALL~	Vry. Gd.	Good	BEST BET	BEST BET	BEST BET

Buick Riviera 1992-93, 1995-99

1993 Buick Riviera

The Buick Riviera shares its body and chassis with the Cadillac Eldorado, Buick Park Avenue and Olds Aurora, yet it still maintains a look and feel of its own. The Riviera has undergone many changes over the years to boost sales, including a new 3.8 liter engine V8 engine for 1998. The Riviera continued without any major changes through the 1993 model year but was dropped for 1994. A new Riviera with bold, flowing lines was introduced in the fall of 1994 for 1995, and sales of this redesigned Riviera surpassed expectations. The 1990-93 Rivieras have a standard driver airbag; the 1995 Riviera added a pas-

	1992	1993	1994	1995	1996
Size Class	Large	Large		Large	Large
Drive	Front	Front		Front	Front
Crash Test	Good	Good		Average	Average
Airbags	Driver	Driver		Dual	Dual
ABS	4-Whl	4-Whl		4-Whl	4-Whl
Parts Cost	Average	Average		Low	Average
Complaints	Average	Average		Vry. Pr.	Average
Insurance	Discount	Discount		Regular	Discount
Fuel Econ.	18	19	No Model Produced	19	19
Theft Rating	Low	Low		Vry. Low	Vry. Low
Bumpers					
Recalls	2	1		0	2
Trn. Cir. (ft.)	39.4	39.4		39.1	39.1
Weight (lbs.)	3497	3504		3748	3690
Whlbase (in.)	108	108		113.8	113.8
Price	7-9,000	8-10,000		11-13,000	13-15,000
OVERALL	Good	Good		Average	Good

**Estimate

1999 Buick Riviera

senger airbag. ABS was optional in 1990, standard in 1991.

From 1990-1993, V6's were the only engine choice. With the redesign, Buick added a much more powerful V8 engine to the options list. Handling is better on T-Type and Grand Touring models, but the ride suffers. The 1995 model rides and handles much better and is much more comfortable than in previous years.

	1997	1998	1999	2000	2001
Size Class	Large	Large	Large		
Drive	Front	Front	Front		
Crash Test	Average	Average	Average		
Airbags	Dual	Dual	Dual		
ABS	4-Whl	4-Whl	4-Whl		
Parts Cost	High	Average	Low		
Complaints	Average	Good	Vry. Gd.		
Insurance	Discount	Discount	Discount		
Fuel Econ.	19	18	18		
Theft Rating	Vry. Low	Vry. Low**	Vry. Low**		
Bumpers					
Recalls	0	0	0		
Trn. Cir. (ft.)	39.1	39.1	39.1		
Weight (lbs.)	3720	3699	3713		
Whlbase (in.)	113.8	113.8	113.8		
Price	15-17,000	19-21,000	22-24,000		
OVERALL	Good	Vry. Gd.	BEST BET		

No Model Produced

Buick Roadmaster 1992-96

The Roadmaster bid farewell in 1996; it was the end of these rear-wheel drive cars, originally designed back in 1977. A restyled 1991 Estate Wagon became part of the new Roadmaster

1992 Buick Roadmaster

series, and featured standard ABS and driver's airbags. The 1994 Roadmaster added a passenger airbag. All versions are well-equipped.

The 5-liter V8 provides adequate power, but gas mileage is dismal and transmissions are vulnerable. With the standard suspension, the Roadmaster is a handful in turns, and severe bumps can be unsettling. There's room for up to six (eight with the third seat option), but the car

	1992	1993	1994	1995	1996
Size Class	Large	Large	Large	Large	Large
Drive	Rear	Rear	Rear	Rear	Rear
Crash Test	Average	Average	Poor	Poor	Poor
Airbags	Driver	Driver	Dual	Dual	Dual
ABS	4-Whl	4-Whl	4-Whl	4-Whl	4-Whl
Parts Cost	Vry. Low	Vry. Low	Vry. Low	Vry. Low	Vry. Low
Complaints	Vry. Pr.	Poor	Average	Average	Poor
Insurance	Discount	Discount	Discount	Discount	Discount
Fuel Econ.	16	16	17	17	17
Theft Rating	Low	Vry. Low	Vry. Low	Average	Vry. Low
Bumpers					
Recalls	3	0	5	6	3
Trn. Cir. (ft.)	39.9	39	39.5	39.5	38.6
Weight (lbs.)	4073	3973	4191	4211	4563
Whlbase (in.)	115.9	115.9	115.9	115.9	115.9
Price	6-8,000	7-9,000	8-10,000	10-12,000	13-15,000
OVERALL	Average	Good	Good	Good	Good

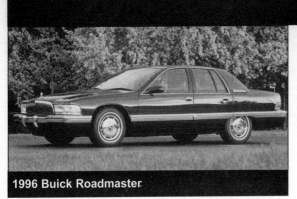

1996 Buick Roadmaster

is most comfortable for four. The cargo area is large and well-shaped. The dashboard empha-sizes form over function.

	1997	1998	1999	2000	2001
Size Class					
Drive					
Crash Test					
Airbags					
ABS					
Parts Cost					
Complaints					
Insurance					
Fuel Econ.					
Theft Rating					
Bumpers					
Recalls					
Trn. Cir. (ft.)					
Weight (lbs.)					
Whlbase (in.)					
Price					
OVERALL					

No Models Produced

Buick Skylark 1992-97

1992 Buick Skylark

The Skylark received new sheet metal for 1992, and grew a lot—nine inches—though the chassis and wheelbase remained unchanged. Finally, Buick redesigned the Skylark inside and out for 1996, resulting in a fresher, sleeker look. These cars pioneered the use of GM's notorious door-mounted belts midway through 1987. Though all Skylarks got a driver's airbag for 1994, they kept door-mounted belts until the redesign in 1996, when dual airbags became standard. From 1992, ABS has been standard on all Skylarks.

These cars offer several 4-cylinder and V6 engines. The Quad 4 is

	1992	1993	1994	1995	1996
Size Class	Compact	Compact	Compact	Compact	Compact
Drive	Front	Front	Front	Front	Front
Crash Test	Vry. Pr.[1]	Vry. Pr.[1]	Average[1]	Average[1]	Vry. Gd.
Airbags	None	None	Driver	Driver	Dual
ABS	4-Whl	4-Whl	4-Whl	4-Whl	4-Whl
Parts Cost	Vry. Low	Low	Low	Vry. Low	Low
Complaints	Good	Good	Good	Poor	Average
Insurance	Regular	Regular	Regular	Regular	Discount
Fuel Econ.	19	22	22	22	22
Theft Rating	Low	Vry. Low	Vry. Low	Vry. Low	Vry. Low
Bumpers					
Recalls	4	1	1	0	7
Trn. Cir. (ft.)	35.3	35.3	35.3	35.3	35.3
Weight (lbs.)	2782	2846	2791	2888	2917
Whlbase (in.)	103.4	103.4	103.4	103.4	103.4
Price	2-4,000	3-5,000	4-6,000	5-7,000	6-8,000
OVERALL~	Poor	Poor	Good	Good	BEST BET

[1]Data given for coupe. Crash test for sedan from 1992-93 is Poor; 1994-95 is Good.

1996 Buick Skylark

quick but rough and unreliable. Most models have only a 3-speed automatic. Automatic overdrive became optional in 1994; it improves performance and fuel economy. Seating for four adults is average; try to squeeze in five and it becomes very snug. Avoid the adjustable ride control but consider the Grand Touring suspension for better handling.

	1997	1998	1999	2000	2001
Size Class	Compact				
Drive	Front				
Crash Test	Vry. Gd.				
Airbags	Dual				
ABS	4-Whl				
Parts Cost	Average				
Complaints	Good				
Insurance	Discount				
Fuel Econ.	22				
Theft Rating	Vry. Low				
Bumpers			No Models Produced		
Recalls	2				
Trn. Cir. (ft.)	35.3				
Weight (lbs.)	2985				
Whlbase (in.)	103.4				
Price	7-9,000				
OVERALL~	BEST BET				

Cadillac Brougham 1992, Fleetwood 1993-96

This Cadillac is the longest car you can buy (the Lincoln Town Car is a close second), if that's what you're looking for. In essence, it's a plusher version of the Chevy Caprice and Buick Road-

1992 Cadillac Brougham

master. The Cadillac didn't change much from the late >70s through 1992-it just got a little longer and heavier. For 1993, it got a new body on the same chassis. These Cadillacs offer expensive options, such as a vinyl roof and heated, leather seats. The 1990-92 models have GM's door mounted belts, a disgrace on a car of this price. A driver's airbag has been standard since 1990; fortunately, in 1995, Cadillac put dual

	1992	1993	1994	1995	1996
Size Class	Large	Large	Large	Large	Large
Drive	Rear	Rear	Rear	Rear	Rear
Crash Test	N/A	N/A	N/A	N/A	N/A
Airbags	Driver	Driver	Driver	Dual	Dual
ABS	4-Whl	4-Whl	4-Whl	4-Whl	4-Whl
Parts Cost	Vry. Low	Vry. Low	Average	High	High
Complaints	Poor	Average	Good	Vry. Gd.	Good
Insurance	Discount	Discount	Discount	Discount	Discount
Fuel Econ.	16	16	16	17	17
Theft Rating	High	Average	Average	Average	Average
Bumpers					
Recalls	0	2	5	7	4
Trn. Cir. (ft.)	40.5	40.5	40.5	40.4	44.5
Weight (lbs.)	4277	4418	4477	4478	4448
Whlbase (in.)	121.5	121.5	121.5	121.5	121.5
Price	7-9,000	9-11,000	11-13,000	15-17,000	18-20,000
OVERALL~					

~Cars without crash tests do not receive an overall rating.

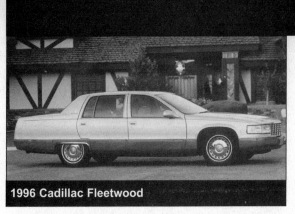
1996 Cadillac Fleetwood

airbags with conventional belts on all models. ABS was been standard since 1990.

These Cadillacs use V8 engines of various displacements, none of which provides good fuel economy. The car plows through turns, and severe bumps can upset the ride. The trailer package has a heavier-duty suspension, which will allow you to tow 7,000 lbs., but you won't gain much improvement in handling.

	1997	1998	1999	2000	2001
Size Class					
Drive					
Crash Test					
Airbags					
ABS					
Parts Cost					
Complaints					
Insurance					
Fuel Econ.					
Theft Rating					
Bumpers					
Recalls					
Trn. Cir. (ft.)					
Weight (lbs.)					
Whlbase (in.)					
Price					
OVERALL~					

No Model Produced

Cadillac DeVille 1992-2001, Fleetwood 1992

These large luxury vehicles have shared a body and chassis with the Buick Electra/Park Avenue and Olds 98 for years, although the Fleetwood and DeVille received longer wheelbases and bodies during the late 1980s. Changes beginning with 1997s included a new interior and a restyled exterior along with improved handling. The DeVille/Concours was new for 1994 and is now based on the Seville/Eldorado chassis; the coupe model disappeared after 1993. These Cadillacs come with a standard driver's airbag for 1990, and dual airbags are standard from 1995 on. ABS is standard on Fleetwood as

1992 Cadillac DeVille

	1992	1993	1994	1995	1996
Size Class	Large	Large	Large	Large	Large
Drive	Front	Front	Front	Front	Front
Crash Test	N/A	N/A	N/A	N/A	N/A
Airbags	Driver	Driver	Driver	Dual	Dual
ABS	4-Whl	4-Whl	4-Whl	4-Whl	4-Whl
Parts Cost	Low	Low	Low	High	Vry. High
Complaints	Average	Good	Good	Vry. Gd.	Average
Insurance	Discount	Discount	Discount	Discount	Discount
Fuel Econ.	16	16	16	16	17
Theft Rating	Average	Average	Low	Low	Vry. Low
Bumpers					
Recalls	1	1	1	1	1
Trn. Cir. (ft.)	41	41	41	41	41.6
Weight (lbs.)	3653	3605	3757	3758	3981
Whlbase (in.)	110.8[1]	110.8[1]	113.8	113.8	113.8
Price	8-10,000	9-11,000	10-12,000	14-16,000	15-17,000
OVERALL~					

[1]Data given for coupe. Wheelbase for sedan for 1992-93 is 113.8; **Estimate; ~Cars without crash tests do not receive an

2001 Cadillac DeVille

far as back as 1990 and on the rest of the lineup soon after in 1991.

The Concours after 1993 and the 1996 DeVille have Cadillac's powerful but thirsty NorthStar V8. On later models, you have your pick of safety features, including daytime running lamps, traction control, and even side airbags, and the added security of good crash test results in models before 2000. For 2000, the DeVille received a major redesign and crash tests became poor.

	1997	1998	1999	2000	2001
Size Class	Large	Large	Large	Large	Large
Drive	Front	Front	Front	Front	Front
Crash Test	Vry. Gd.	Vry. Gd.	Vry. Gd.	Poor	Poor
Airbags	Dual/Side	Dual/Side	Dual/Side	Dual/Side	Dual/Side
ABS	4-Whl	4-Whl	4-Whl	4-Whl	4-Whl
Parts Cost	Vry. High	Vry. High	Vry. High	Vry. High	Vry. High
Complaints	Average	Poor	Average	Good	Average
Insurance	Discount	Discount	Discount	Discount	Discount
Fuel Econ.	17	17	17	17	17
Theft Rating	Vry. Low	Vry. Low	Vry. Low	Vry. Low**	Vry. Low**
Bumpers			Weak	Weak	Weak
Recalls	1	2	0	1	0
Trn. Cir. (ft.)	40.7	41	41	40.2	40.2
Weight (lbs.)	4009	4012	4012	4012	4012
Whlbase (in.)	113.8	113.8	113.8	115.3	115.3
Price	19-21,000	22-24,000	25-27,000	>30,000	>30,000
OVERALL~	Vry. Gd.	Good	Vry. Gd.	Good	Good

overall rating.

Cadillac Eldorado 1992-2001

In 1992, Cadillac unveiled a successful, new, sleeker version of the Eldorado. The 1992 has a driver airbag and all models, from 1993 on, also have a passenger airbag. ABS became standard in 1991.

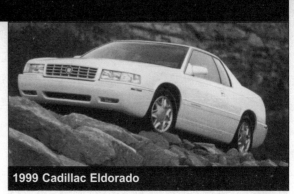

1999 Cadillac Eldorado

The 1993 models offer Cadillac's sophisticated NorthStar V8; it's powerful but delivers poor gas mileage. For 1994, all models received the more modern rear suspension. Base Eldorados have plenty of features, but avoid the digital gauges. Handling improves on Touring and STS models, but the ride still suffers. Room is okay in front, somewhat tighter in back. The seats are as comfortable and roomy as you'd expect

	1992	1993	1994	1995	1996
Size Class	Large	Large	Large	Large	Large
Drive	Front	Front	Front	Front	Front
Crash Test	Good	Average	Average	Average	Average
Airbags	Driver	Dual	Dual	Dual	Dual
ABS	4-Whl	4-Whl	4-Whl	4-Whl	4-Whl
Parts Cost	Average	Average	Vry. High	High	Vry. High
Complaints	Average	Poor	Average	Good	Poor
Insurance	Discount	Discount	Discount	Discount	Discount
Fuel Econ.	16	16	16	16	17
Theft Rating	High	Vry. High	Average	Low	Vry. High
Bumpers					
Recalls	1	2	2	1	1
Trn. Cir. (ft.)	39.4	40.2	40.2	40.2	40.4
Weight (lbs.)	3604	3604	3773	3774	3765
Whlbase (in.)	108	108	108	108	108
Price	9-11,000	11-13,000	13-15,000	15-17,000	19-21,000
OVERALL	Good	Average	Average	Good	Poor

**Estimate

2001 Cadillac Eldorado

from a car priced this high. An upgraded chassis control system which greatly improves traction and stability can be found on the 1997 models. The 2000 and 2001 models come in two trim levels: base and touring coupe. Some later models will have the OnStar GPS System.

	1997	1998	1999	2000	2001
Size Class	Large	Large	Large	Large	Large
Drive	0Front	Front	Front	Front	Front
Crash Test	Average	N/A	N/A	N/A	Vry. Gd.
Airbags	Dual	Dual/Side	Dual/Side	Dual/Side	Dual/Side
ABS	4-Whl	4-Whl	4-Whl	4-Whl	4-Whl
Parts Cost	Vry. High	Vry. High	Vry. High	Vry. High	Vry. High
Complaints	Average	Poor	Good	Good	Good
Insurance	Discount	Discount	Discount	Discount	Discount
Fuel Econ.	17	17	17	17	17
Theft Rating	Vry. High	Vry. High	Vry. High**	Vry. High**	Vry. High**
Bumpers	Weak	Weak	Weak	Weak	Weak
Recalls	1	1	0	0	0
Trn. Cir. (ft.)	40.4	40.4	40.4	40.4	40.4
Weight (lbs.)	3900	3843	3876	3876	3876
Whlbase (in.)	108	108	108	108	108
Price	23-25,000	22-27,000	>30,000	>30,000	>30,000
OVERALL	Average				Poor

Chevrolet Astro/GMC Safari 1992-2001

GM's response to Chrysler's mini-vans was the Chevy Astro and the GMC Safari. They were poor competitors at first; however they have done well enough to stick

1992 Chevrolet Astro

around. Following their introduction in the mid-1980's, the addition of extended-length models and a 4-wheel drive option were the Astro/Safari's only major changes until 1996, when they received fresh new interior designs, making them more like GM's other minivans. In the 1994 model year, a driver's airbag became standard, but crash test results remained abysmal. They improved a bit in 1998 - they were aver-

	1992	1993	1994	1995	1996
Size Class	Minivan	Minivan	Minivan	Minivan	Minivan
Drive	Rear/4	Rear/4	Rear/4	Rear/4	Rear/4
Crash Test	Vry. Pr.	Vry. Pr.	Vry. Pr.	Vry. Pr.	Poor
Airbags	None	None	Driver	Driver	Dual
ABS	4-Whl*	4-Whl	4-Whl	4-Whl	4-Whl
Parts Cost	Vry. Low	Vry. Low	Vry. Low	Vry. Low	Low
Complaints	Average[1]	Average	Poor	Vry. Pr.	Average[1]
Insurance	Discount	Discount	Discount	Discount	Discount
Fuel Econ.	15	16	16	16	16
Theft Rating	Average	Vry. Low	Vry. Low	Low	Low
Bumpers					
Recalls	1	2	2	2	1
Trn. Cir. (ft.)	39.5	39.5	40.5	39.5	39.5
Weight (lbs.)	3554	4160	3653	3998	3998
Whlbase (in.)	111	111	111	111	111
Price	4-6,000	5-7,000	6-8,000	7-9,000	9-11,000
OVERALL	Average	Average	Average	Poor	Good

[1]Data given for Astro. Complaint rating for Safari in 1992 is Poor; 1996 is Poor; 1999 is Poor.; [2]Data given for Astro.

2001 Chevrolet Astro

age from then to now. The 1996 model comes with dual airbags. For 1991 and 1992 models, 4-wheel ABS is optional; from 1993 on, it's standard.

The 4.3-liter V6, the standard engine from 1990 on, has enough power for heavy use, but it delivers poor gas mileage. Handling is sloppy, even with 4-wheel drive. The ride is unsettling, and getting in and out of the front seats is tricky. Beyond just basic towing and hauling, the Astro/Safari lacks the personal touches that make the Chrysler and newer GM minivans so popular.

	1997	1998	1999	2000	2001
Size Class	Minivan	Minivan	Minivan	Minivan	Minivan
Drive	Rear/4	Rear/4	Rear/4	Rear/4	Rear/4
Crash Test	Poor	Poor	Poor	Poor	Poor
Airbags	Dual	Dual	Dual	Dual	Dual
ABS	4-Whl	4-Whl	4-Whl	4-Whl	4-Whl
Parts Cost	Low	Low	Low	Low	Low
Complaints	Poor	Vry. Pr.	Average[1]	Poor	Good
Insurance	Discount	Discount	Discount	Discount	Discount
Fuel Econ.	17	16	16	16	16
Theft Rating	Low	Low	Low	Very Low**	Very Low**
Bumpers	Weak	Weak	Strong	Strong	Strong
Recalls	2	1	0	0	0
Trn. Cir. (ft.)	39.5	39.5	38.3	38.3	38.3
Weight (lbs.)	4197	4197	4186	4186	4186
Whlbase (in.)	111	111.2	111.2	111.2	111.2
Price	10-12,000	12-14,000	14-16,000	16-18,000	23-25,000
OVERALL	Average	Average	Vry. Gd.	Good	Vry. Gd.

Overall rating for Safari may vary based on footnotes.; *Optional; **Estimate

Chevrolet Beretta/Corsica 1992-96

The Beretta and Corsica share the same chassis and are distant cousins to GM's other compacts. The 1991-93 models have a driver's airbag and conventional front belts; 1994 models regressed to door-mounted belts in front with a driver airbag. Door-mounted belts don't work if the door pops open. ABS became standard in 1992. Unfortunately, the Beretta/Corsica remained one of the few 1996 models with only one airbag. For 1997, the Beretta/Corsica was replaced by the flashier, all-new Malibu.

1992 Chevrolet Corsica

The early 2-liter 4-cylinder engine is a slowpoke; the 2.2-liter 4-

	1992	1993	1994	1995	1996
Size Class	Compact	Compact	Compact	Compact	Compact
Drive	Front	Front	Front	Front	Front
Crash Test	Good[1]	Good[1]	Poor[1]	Poor[1]	Poor[1]
Airbags	Driver	Driver	Driver	Driver	Driver
ABS	4-Whl	4-Whl	4-Whl	4-Whl	4-Whl
Parts Cost	Vry. Low	Low	Low	Low	Low
Complaints	Poor	Good	Average	Poor	Average
Insurance	Regular[2]	Regular[2]	Regular[2]	Surchg.	Surchg.
Fuel Econ.	20	21	21	24	25
Theft Rating	Low	Low	Average	Average	Vry. Low
Bumpers	Weak	Weak	Weak	Weak	Weak
Recalls	2	1	2	1	2
Trn. Cir. (ft.)	35.5	35.5	37.8	35.3	35.3
Weight (lbs.)	2638	2665	2715	2756	2756
Whlbase (in.)	103.4	103.4	103.4	103.4	103.4
Price	2-4,000	2-4,000	3-5,000	4-6,000	5-7,000
OVERALL	Average	Good	Poor	Poor	Average

[1]Data given for Corsica. Crash test for Beretta is Vry. Good; [2]Data given for Corsica. Insurance rating for Beretta is Sur-

1996 Chevrolet Beretta

cylinder on later models is better. For more power, you can pick from two V6s. The 5-speed isn't much fun to shift, and the unreliable automatic on pre-1994 models has only 3 speeds. The 1994 V6 models have automatic overdrive, which helps acceleration and fuel economy. Cornering on base Berettas and Corsicas is sluggish; look for the Beretta GT or models with F-41 suspension or sport handling package. When properly equipped, the 1991-93 Beretta/Corsica is one of GM's best compacts.

	1997	1998	1999	2000	2001
Size Class					
Drive					
Crash Test					
Airbags					
ABS					
Parts Cost					
Complaints					
Insurance					
Fuel Econ.					
Theft Rating					
Bumpers					
Recalls					
Trn. Cir. (ft.)					
Weight (lbs.)					
Whlbase (in.)					
Price					
OVERALL					

No Model Produced

charge.

Chevrolet Camaro 1992-2001

The Camaro and its close cousin, the Pontiac Firebird, went through a major redesign in the early 80's and didn't change much for the next 11 years. Both have consistently been good performers in

1992 Chevrolet Camaro

the government's crash test program. The Camaro is available as a hatchback coupe or as a sportier convertible. In the spring of 1993, Chevrolet redesigned the Camaro with plastic external body panels. A driver airbag was added in 1990, and a passenger's airbag was available starting in 1993. ABS became standard in 1993.

New for 1996 is a more powerful standard 3.8-liter V6 with more

	1992	1993	1994	1995	1996
Size Class	Intermd.	Intermd.	Intermd.	Intermd.	Intermd.
Drive	Rear	Rear	Rear	Rear	Rear
Crash Test	Vry. Gd.	Vry. Gd.	Vry. Gd.	Vry. Gd.	Vry. Gd.
Airbags	Driver	Dual	Dual	Dual	Dual
ABS	None	4-Whl	4-Whl	4-Whl	4-Whl
Parts Cost	Low	Low	Average	Low	Average
Complaints	Poor	Poor	Poor	Poor	Average
Insurance	Surchg.	Surchg.	Surchg.	Surchg.	Surchg.
Fuel Econ.	18	19	17	19	19
Theft Rating	High	Low	Average	Average	Average
Bumpers					
Recalls	2	1	1	1	0
Trn. Cir. (ft.)	38.5	40.3	39.3	40.7	40.7
Weight (lbs.)	3105	3241	3324	3342	3306
Whlbase (in.)	101	101.1	101.1	101.1	101.1
Price	5-7,000	6-8,000	7-9,000	8-10,000	11-13,000
OVERALL	Average	Average	Average	Average	Average

**Estimate

2001 Chevrolet Camaro

horsepower than in years past. The IROC and Z-28 models have a powerful 5.7-liter V8. Automatics have been troublesome, but sports car enthusiasts will prefer the manual transmission anyway. The Camaro delivers a firm ride and good handling with either engine choice. The dashboard has all the needed gauges, though some of the smaller controls are hard to operate. The Camaro is roomy for the driver and front seat passenger, but the rear seat is very small, even for young children - but this is not your typical family car.

	1997	1998	1999	2000	2001
Size Class	Intermd.	Intermd.	Intermd.	Intermd.	Intermd.
Drive	Rear	Rear	Rear	Rear	Rear
Crash Test	Vry. Gd.	Vry. Gd.	Vry. Gd.	Vry. Gd.	Vry. Gd.
Airbags	Dual	Dual	Dual	Dual	Dual
ABS	4-Whl	4-Whl	4-Whl	4-Whl	4-Whl
Parts Cost	Average	High	High	High	High
Complaints	Good	Vry. Pr.	Poor	Average	Poor
Insurance	Surchg.	Surchg.	Surchg.	Surchg.	Surchg.
Fuel Econ.	19	18	19	19	19
Theft Rating	Average	Average	Average	High**	Very High**
Bumpers			Strong	Strong	Strong
Recalls	1	0	0	0	0
Trn. Cir. (ft.)	40.7	40.7	40.8	40.8	40.8
Weight (lbs.)	3307	3331	3306	3306	3306
Whlbase (in.)	101.1	101.1	101.1	101.1	101.1
Price	13-15,000	15-17,000	17-19,000	19-21,000	23-25,000
OVERALL	Good	Poor	Average	Average	Average

Chevrolet Caprice 1992-96, Impala 1994-96

The Caprice is the cheapest of GM's full-size rear-wheel drive cars. For 1991, the Caprice received a new, aerodynamic but unappealing body, which kept buyers away. The Impala reappeared in 1994, after an

1993 Chevrolet Caprice

unsuccessful reincarnation in the mid 1980's, as the Impala SS, a sportier, more powerful Caprice. The 1991 and later models have a standard driver airbag, joined by a passenger airbag for 1994. Starting in 1991, ABS is standard. The Impala SS also gets standard traction control, giving it more powerful handling and control.

The Caprice's standard V6 performs adequately, but not if you load

	1992	1993	1994	1995	1996
Size Class	Large	Large	Large	Large	Large
Drive	Rear	Rear	Rear	Rear	Rear
Crash Test	Average	Average	Poor	Poor	Poor
Airbags	Driver	Driver	Dual	Dual	Dual
ABS	4-Whl	4-Whl	4-Whl	4-Whl	4-Whl
Parts Cost	Vry. Low	Vry. Low	Vry. Low	Vry. Low	Vry. Low
Complaints	Vry. Gd.	Poor	Vry. Pr.	Poor	Good
Insurance	Discount	Discount	Discount	Discount	Discount
Fuel Econ.	18	18	17	18	18
Theft Rating	Average	Vry. Low	Low	Average	Average
Bumpers					
Recalls	6	1	6	9	6
Trn. Cir. (ft.)	38.9	38.9	38.9	39.9	39.9
Weight (lbs.)	3907	4202	4045	4061	4061
Whlbase (in.)	115.9	115.9	115.9	115.9	115.9
Price	4-6,000	5-7,000	7-9,000	9-11,000	12-14,000
OVERALL	Average	Vry. Gd.	Average	Average	Good

1996 Chevrolet Impala

up with passengers or cargo. The V8 delivers more power at the expense of gas mileage. Some transmission problems have been common, but later cars seem to fare better. You'll find the Caprice likes straight, smooth roads, wallows in severe turns and does not handle severe bumps well. The F-41 suspension, standard on Impala SS and LTZ, improves handling with little sacrifice in ride; look for the F-41 lettering near the trunk. The interior is roomy and the trunk is huge. Overall, they are among the better of GM's "living rooms on wheels".

	1997	1998	1999	2000	2001
Size Class					
Drive					
Crash Test					
Airbags					
ABS					
Parts Cost					
Complaints					
Insurance					
Fuel Econ.			No Model Produced		
Theft Rating					
Bumpers					
Recalls					
Trn. Cir. (ft.)					
Weight (lbs.)					
Whlbase (in.)					
Price					
OVERALL					

Chevrolet Cavalier 1992-2001

The Cavalier received some mild exterior changes in 1991. In 1995, the Cavalier received all-new styling, which received high praise. Cavaliers come in a coupe, sedan, wagon, or convertible, though a wagon

1992 Chevrolet Cavalier

version is not offered after 1994. The 1990-94 models have door-mounted seat belts in front. ABS became standard in 1992, but airbags were not offered until the 1995 redesign added two.

The 4-cylinder engines in Cavaliers perform adequately. If you want an automatic, you're stuck with a 3-speed and inferior gas mileage, unless you get a 1996 or 1997 model with the optional 4-speed automat-

	1992	1993	1994	1995	1996
Size Class	Compact	Compact	Compact	Compact	Compact
Drive	Front	Front	Front	Front	Front
Crash Test	Good	Good	Good	Good	Good
Airbags	None	None	None	Dual	Dual
ABS	4-Whl	4-Whl	4-Whl	4-Whl	4-Whl
Parts Cost	Vry. Low	Low	Low	Average	Low
Complaints	Good	Good	Average	Good	Average
Insurance	Surchg.	Regular	Discount	Discount	Surchg.
Fuel Econ.	23	23	23	25	26
Theft Rating	Low	Vry. Low	Vry. Low	Vry. Low	Vry. Low
Bumpers	Weak	Weak	Weak	Weak	Weak
Recalls	1	2	2	3	5
Trn. Cir. (ft.)	37.2	34.3	34.3	35.6	35.6
Weight (lbs.)	2520	2678	2520	2537	2617
Whlbase (in.)	101.3	101.3	101.3	104.1	104.1
Price	2-4,000	3-5,000	3-5,000	5-7,000	6-8,000
OVERALL	Good	Good	Good	Vry. Gd.	Average

**Estimate

98

2001 Chevrolet Cavalier

ic. The early 5-speed transmission isn't too smooth, but did improve around 1988. A 2.2-liter engine comes standard on the base coupe and sedan models; on the LS and Z24 trim levels, a more powerful 2.4-liter engine is available. In earlier models, the controls and dashboard feel old fashioned. The 1995 redesign helped driver visibility and improved trunk access. Accommodations for four in any Cavalier are tight, but the wagon's cargo area is a practical shape.

	1997	1998	1999	2000	2001
Size Class	Compact	Compact	Compact	Compact	Compact
Drive	Front	Front	Front	Front	Front
Crash Test	Good	Good	Good	Good	Good
Airbags	Dual	Dual	Dual	Dual	Dual
ABS	4-Whl	4-Whl	4-Whl	4-Whl	4-Whl
Parts Cost	High	Average	Low	Low	Low
Complaints	Good	Good	Good	Average	Good
Insurance	Surchg.	Surchg.	Surchg.	Surchg.	Surchg.
Fuel Econ.	25	25	24	24	24
Theft Rating	Vry. Low	Vry. Low	Vry. Low	Vry. Low**	Vry. Low**
Bumpers	Weak	Weak	Strong	Strong	Strong
Recalls	4	1	0	0	0
Trn. Cir. (ft.)	35.6	35.6	35.6	35.6	35.6
Weight (lbs.)	2617	2630	2617	2617	2617
Whlbase (in.)	104.1	104.1	104.1	104.1	104.1
Price	7-9,000	8-10,000	10-12,000	11-13,000	14-16,000
OVERALL	Average	Good	Good	Good	Vry. Gd.

Chevrolet Lumina 1992-2001, Monte Carlo 1995-2001

The Chevrolet Lumina shared its structure with the Buick Regal, Pontiac Grand Prix, and Olds Cutlass Supreme. A new, more luxurious Lumina appeared in the spring of 1994 as a 1995 model,

1992 Chevrolet Lumina

and the Monte Carlo name was revived for the new 1995 coupe. All Luminas through 1994 have door-mounted seat belts. ABS is optional after 1992, standard on the Monte Carlo from 1996 on. But, you won't find airbags before 1995, when standard dual airbags were introduced.

The original Monte Carlo came with V6 or V8 engines, including a high-performance SS model. The back seat is difficult to access, and

	1992	1993	1994	1995	1996
Size Class	Intermd.	Intermd.	Intermd.	Large	Large
Drive	Front	Front	Front	Front	Front
Crash Test	N/A	N/A	N/A	Vry. Gd.[1]	Vry. Gd.[1]
Airbags	None	None	None	Dual	Dual
ABS	4-Whl*	4-Whl*	4-Whl*	4-Whl*	4-Whl*
Parts Cost	Vry. Low	Low	Low	Average	Vry. Low
Complaints	Poor	Average	Good	Average	Vry. Gd.
Insurance	Discount	Discount	Discount	Discount	Discount
Fuel Econ.	19	17	19	19	20
Theft Rating	Low	Vry. Low	Low	Low	Vry. Low
Bumpers	Weak	Weak	Weak	Weak	Weak
Recalls	2	1	0	6	2
Trn. Cir. (ft.)	39	39	39	36.7	36
Weight (lbs.)	3115	3187	3333	3330	3330
Whlbase (in.)	107.5	107.5	107.5	107.5	107.5
Price	3-5,000	4-6,000	5-7,000	6-8,000	7-9,000
OVERALL				Vry. Gd.	BEST BET

[1]Data given for Lumina. Crash test for Monte Carlo is Good; [2]Data given for Lumina. Insurance rating for Monte Carlo in

1996 Chevrolet Monte Carlo

the trunk is smaller in exchange for styling.

Many 1990-93 Luminas, particularly those sold to rental fleets, have an underpowered 4-cylinder engine with a 3-speed automatic; a V6 was available and came with automatic or manual transmission. The hot Z-34 model, on Luminas and 1995 Monte Carlos, has a 4-cam V6 and 5-speed or automatic overdrive. Ride is okay. The handling is disappointing on the base models. Room inside is adequate for four. In 2001, the Lumina is only available for fleet sales.

	1997	1998	1999	2000	2001
Size Class	Large	Large	Large	Large	Large
Drive	Front	Front	Front	Front	Front
Crash Test	Vry. Gd.[1]	Vry. Gd.[1]	Vry. Gd.[1]	Vry. Gd.[1]	Vry. Gd.[1]
Airbags	Dual	Dual	Dual	Dual	Dual
ABS	4-Whl*	4-Whl	4-Whl	4-Whl	4-Whl
Parts Cost	Average	Low	Low	Low	Low
Complaints	Good	Average	Vry. Gd.	Vry. Gd.	Vry. Gd.
Insurance	Discount[2]	Discount	Discount	Discount	Discount
Fuel Econ.	20	20	20	20	20
Theft Rating	Vry. Low	Vry. Low	Vry. Low**	Vry. Low**	Vry. Low**
Bumpers	Weak	Weak			
Recalls	0	0	0	4	2
Trn. Cir. (ft.)	36.7	36.7	36.7	36.7	36.7
Weight (lbs.)	3243	3330	3330	3330	3330
Whlbase (in.)	107.5	107.5	107.5	107.5	107.5
Price	8-10,000	10-12,000	12-14,000	13-15,000	14-16,000
OVERALL	BEST BET	BEST BET	BEST BET	BEST BET	BEST BET

1997 is Regular; *Optional; **Estimate

Chev. Lumina '92-96, Venture '97-2001, Olds Silh. '92-2001, Pont. Tr. Sport '92-98, Montana '99-2001

GM's belated response to the front-wheel drive minivans made by Chrysler, these vehicles received significant changes for 1994, mainly new front-end styling that made them look more earthbound

1992 Chevrolet Lumina Minivan

than the previous models. A redesign for 1997 updated the exterior styling and improved the interior, and the Lumina was replaced with Venture. GM's minivans have conventional lap-shoulder belts for the front seats; 1994 models add a driver's airbag to the standard equipment list. Four-wheel ABS is standard from 1992-on.

The standard 3.1-liter V6 and 3-speed automatic, available through

	1992	1993	1994	1995	1996
Size Class	Minivan	Minivan	Minivan	Minivan	Minivan
Drive	Front	Front	Front	Front	Front
Crash Test	Vry. Gd.	Vry. Gd.	Good	Good	Good
Airbags	None	None	Driver	Driver	Driver
ABS	4-Whl	4-Whl	4-Whl	4-Whl	4-Whl
Parts Cost	Vry. Low	Vry. Low	Vry. Low	Vry. Low	Vry. Low
Complaints	Poor	Good	Average	Average	Vry. Gd.
Insurance	Discount	Discount	Discount	Discount	Discount
Fuel Econ.	18	18	19	19	19
Theft Rating	Average	Average	Average	Average	Average
Bumpers			Weak	Weak	Weak
Recalls	3	4	5	4	0
Trn. Cir. (ft.)	43.1	43.1	43.1	43.1	43.1
Weight (lbs.)	3370	3370	3554	3516	3593
Whlbase (in.)	109.8	109.8	109.8	109.8	109.8
Price	3-5,000	3-5,000	4-6,000	5-7,000	7-9,000
OVERALL	Good	Vry. Gd.	Good	Good	BEST BET

**Estimate

102

2001 Chevrolet Venture

1995, deliver substandard acceleration and gas mileage. The 3.8-liter V6 and automatic overdrive, optional from 1992-95, are far better suited to these vehicles. A new, more powerful 3.4-liter V6 from 1996-97 is standard. Like the Chrysler, the Venture offers sliding doors on both sides. Rear child seats are an excellent optional feature, worth seeking on 1994 and later models. Center and rear seats are easy to remove or install, but cargo room is small.

	1997	1998	1999	2000	2001
Size Class	Minivan	Minivan	Minivan	Minivan	Minivan
Drive	Front	Front	Front	Front	Front
Crash Test	Good	Good	Good	Good	Good
Airbags	Dual	Dual/Side	Dual/Side	Dual/Side	Dual/Side
ABS	4-Whl	4-Whl	4-Whl	4-Whl	4-Whl
Parts Cost	Low	Low	Average	Average	Average
Complaints	Average	Vry. Pr.	Vry. Pr.	Poor	Vry. Pr.
Insurance	Regular	Regular	Regular	Discount	Discount
Fuel Econ.	18	18	18	18	18
Theft Rating	Average	Average	Average**	Average**	Average**
Bumpers	Weak	Weak			
Recalls	2	3	0	1	1
Trn. Cir. (ft.)	37.4	37.4	37.4	37.4	37.4
Weight (lbs.)	3702	3699	3699	3699	3699
Whlbase (in.)	112	112	112	112	112
Price	9-11,000	14-16,000	16-18,000	18-20,000	22-24,000
OVERALL	Average	Average	Vry. Gd.	Vry. Gd.	Vry. Gd.

Chevrolet Malibu 1997-2001

Introduced in 1997, the Malibu is available in a base and LS. The base has a 2.4-liter engine, which delivers 150 hp. Optional on the base and standard on the LS is a 3.1-liter V6 engine. For 1999,

1997 Chevrolet Malibu

leather seats and a power seat for the driver were added to the LS model. A revised grill, which it borrowed from the Impala, was new for 2000.

The 2001 Chevrolet Malibu comes with a standard 3.1-liter V6 engine but few other changes. You'll find good interior room and fine handling. The Malibu is Chevy's challenge to the best-selling Taurus, Cam-

	1992	1993	1994	1995	1996
Size Class					
Drive					
Crash Test					
Airbags					
ABS					
Parts Cost					
Complaints					
Insurance		No Model Produced			
Fuel Econ.					
Theft Rating					
Bumpers					
Recalls					
Trn. Cir. (ft.)					
Weight (lbs.)					
Whlbase (in.)					
Price					
OVERALL					

2001 Chevrolet Malibu

ry, and Accord trio. The LS version comes with cruise control and a rear defogger.

	1997	1998	1999	2000	2001
Size Class	Intermediate	Intermediate	Intermediate	Intermediate	Intermediate
Drive	Front	Front	Front	Front	Front
Crash Test	Good	Good	Good	Good	Good
Airbags	Dual	Dual	Dual	Dual	Dual
ABS	4-Wheel	4-Wheel	4-Wheel	4-Wheel	4-Wheel
Parts Cost	High	High	Very High	High	High
Complaints	Average	Vry. Pr.	Poor	Average	Poor
Insurance	Regular	Regular	Regular	Regular	Regular
Fuel Econ.	20	23	22	20	20
Theft Rating	Average	Average	Average	Very Low	Very Low
Bumpers			Strong	Strong	Strong
Recalls	1	0	0	1	0
Trn. Cir. (ft.)	36.1	36.4	36.3	36.3	36.3
Weight (lbs.)	3051	3051	3051	3051	3051
Whlbase (in.)	107	107	107	107	107
Price	9-11,000	10-12,000	11-13,000	14-16,000	17-19,000
OVERALL	Average	Average	Average	Good	Average

Chevrolet S10 Blazer 1992-94, Blazer 1995-2001, Jimmy/Oldsmobile Bravada 1992-2001

GM's line of mid-size sport utilities has gone through many transitions in the past few years. What used to be the S10 Blazer is now simply the Blazer. This new Blazer is not to be confused with

1992 Chevrolet S10 Blazer

what used to be the larger Blazer, which is now the Tahoe. And finally, the fully-equipped Bravada, introduced in 1991 to compete against deluxe utility vehicles like the Ford Explorer and Nissan Pathfinder, was discontinued after 1994 but revived for 1996. The 1995 Blazer and Jimmy, with their updated styling and option choices, should be better competitors against their up-level sport utility competitors. All

	1992	1993	1994	1995	1996
Size Class	Sp. Util.	Sp. Util.	Sp. Util.	Sp. Util.	Sp. Util.
Drive	Rear/4	Rear/4	Rear/4	Rear/4	Rear/4
Crash Test	Vry. Pr.	Poor	Poor	Average	Average
Airbags	None	None	None	None	Driver
ABS	4-Whl	4-Whl	4-Whl	4-Whl	4-Whl
Parts Cost	Low	Low	Vry. Low	Vry. Low	Low
Complaints	Average[1]	Average[1]	Average	Vry. Pr.	Vry. Pr.
Insurance	Surchg.	Surchg.[2]	Surchg.	Surchg.	Surchg.[2]
Fuel Econ.	16	17	17	17	18
Theft Rating	High	Vry. High	Vry. High	Average	Vry. High
Bumpers					Weak
Recalls	1	1	2	6	5
Trn. Cir. (ft.)	34.6	34.6	34.6	35.2	39.5
Weight (lbs.)	3369	3365	3205	3306	4023
Whlbase (in.)	100.5	100.5	100.5	100.5	100.5
Price	4-6,000	5-7,000	6-8,000	9-11,000	10,12,000
OVERALL	Vry. Pr.	Vry. Pr.	Vry. Pr.	Vry. Pr.	Vry. Pr.

[1]Data given for S10 Blazer. Complaints rating for Jimmy in 2000 is Vry. Gd. Complaints rating for Bravada for 1992-93 is

2001 Oldsmobile Bravada

Bravadas before 1996 have conventional lap-shoulder belts but no airbags. Bravadas and 4-door Blazers and Jimmys have 4-wheel ABS from 1990 on; 2-door Blazers and Jimmys have rear-wheel ABS for 1990-92 and 4-wheel after 1992.

The S10 Blazer and Jimmy come with a V6 standard engine offering strength for hauling or trailer towing. You can choose from 5-speed or optional automatic overdrive and 2 or 4-wheel drive. Suspension packages help improve the ride and handling. Shop carefully to avoid paying for extra options you don't want.

	1997	1998	1999	2000	2001
Size Class	Sp. Util.	Sp. Util.	Sp. Util.	Sp. Util.	Sp. Util.
Drive	Rear/4	Rear/4	Rear/4	Rear/4	Rear/4
Crash Test	Average	Average	Average	Poor	Poor
Airbags	Driver	Dual	Dual	Dual	Dual
ABS	4-Whl	4-Whl	4-Whl	4-Whl	4-Whl
Parts Cost	Low	Low	Average	Average	Average
Complaints	Poor[1]	Average[1]	Average[1]	Average[1]	Poor
Insurance	Regular	Regular	Discount	Discount	Discount
Fuel Econ.	18	17	16	16	15
Theft Rating	Average	Average	Average	Average**	High**
Bumpers	Weak	Weak			
Recalls	3	3	0	1	1
Trn. Cir. (ft.)	35.2	35.2	35.2	34.8	34.8
Weight (lbs.)	3874	4046	3848	3518	3518
Whlbase (in.)	100.5	100.5	100.5	100.5	100.5
Price	12-14,000	13-15,000	15-17,000	17-19,000	22-24,000
OVERALL	Poor	Average	Vry. Gd.	Good	Poor

Vry. Pr.; 1997 is Good; 1998 is Poor; 1999-2000 is Vry. Pr.; [2]Data given for S10 Blazer. Insurance rating for Bravada is Regular; **Estimate

Chevrolet/GMC Suburban 1992-99, Chevrolet Suburban 2000-01

The Suburban is a 4-door station wagon version of a Chevrolet C/K pick-up. Neither Dodge nor Ford offered anything quite like it until 1997, when Ford introduced the Expedition. The Sub-urban is extremely large, over 5,000 pounds, and about as long as a Cadillac Fleetwood. The Suburban stayed the same for nearly 20 years, with GM waiting until 1992 before it changed the Suburban over, using the newer C/K chassis and sheet metal. For 2000, the Suburban was only a Chevy model, no GMC. four-wheel ABS has been standard since 1992, but a driver's side airbag was only added in 1995.

1996 GMC Suburban

	1992	1993	1994	1995	1996
Size Class	Sp. Util.	Sp. Util.	Sp. Util.	Sp. Util.	Sp. Util.
Drive	Rear/4	Rear/4	Rear/4	Rear/4	Rear/4
Crash Test	Vry. Gd.	Vry. Gd.	Vry. Gd.	Vry. Gd.	Vry. Gd.
Airbags	None	None	None	Driver	Driver
ABS	4-Whl	4-Whl	4-Whl	4-Whl	4-Whl
Parts Cost	Vry. Low	Vry. Low	Low	Vry. Low	Vry. Low
Complaints	Vry. Pr.	Vry. Pr.	Vry. Pr.	Vry. Pr.	Vry. Pr.
Insurance	Regular	Regular	Regular	Discount	Discount
Fuel Econ.	12	12	13	13	13
Theft Rating	High	High	High	Vry. High	Vry. High
Bumpers					
Recalls	2		2	7	3
Trn. Cir. (ft.)	46.1	47.8	47.8	47.5	43.7
Weight (lbs.)	4657	4657	4672	4691	4634
Whlbase (in.)	131.5	131.5	131.5	131.5	131.5
Price	11-13,000	12-14,000	13-15,000	15-17,000	18-20,000
OVERALL	Poor	Average	Poor	Average	Average

**Estimate

2001 Chevrolet Suburban

Given the Suburban's weight, even without any load, the standard 5.3-liter V8 has a lot of work to do. However, you can get a 6.0 liter V8 or 7.4-liter V8 option. Both engines come with automatic overdrive. The gas mileage is dreadful with the 5.3-liter, even worse with the 6.0 or 7.4. You can also find a 6.2-liter diesel that improves gas mileage somewhat, but its reliability on early models is questionable. Four-wheel drive is available. The cargo space is large and functional in shape, but the dash lacks the contemporary and functional look of better trucks or cars.

	1997	1998	1999	2000	2001
Size Class	Sp. Util.	Sp. Util.	Sp. Util.	Sp. Util.	Sp. Util.
Drive	Rear/4	Rear/4	Rear/4	Rear/4	Rear/4
Crash Test	Good	Good	Good	Good	Good
Airbags	Dual	Dual	Dual	Dual	Dual
ABS	4-Whl	4-Whl	4-Whl	4-Whl	4-Whl
Parts Cost	Low	Low	Low	Low	Low
Complaints	Vry. Pr.	Average	Vry. Pr.	Vry. Gd.	Average
Insurance	Discount	Discount	Discount	Discount	Discount
Fuel Econ.	13	13	14	14	14
Theft Rating	Vry. High	Vry. High	Vry. High	Vry. High**	Vry. High**
Bumpers					
Recalls	1	1	0	2	1
Trn. Cir. (ft.)	43.7	43.7	43.7	43.7	43.7
Weight (lbs.)	4802	4825	4820	4820	4820
Whlbase (in.)	131.5	131.5	131.5	131.5	131.5
Price	20-22,000	24-26,000	26-28,000	27-29,000	28-30,000
OVERALL	Average	Vry. Gd.	Good	BEST BET	BEST BET

Chrysler Cirrus 1995-2000, Dodge Stratus 1995-2001, Plymouth Breeze 1996-2000

In 1995, Chrysler replaced the LeBaron sedan and Dodge Spirit with the JA cars, the Chrysler Cirrus and Dodge Stratus. The JA cars looked similar to a Honda or Toyota in profile; however, the front fascias

1995 Chrysler Cirrus

were designed more aggressively. Plymouth rounded out the trio with the Breeze in 1996. Also new for '96 was the Sebring JT, a convertible based on the JA cars and not the Sebring coupe as the name suggests. Dual airbags and ABS were standard from their '95 introduction on. Like their LH cousins, their cab forward design increases the interior room.

	1992	1993	1994	1995	1996
Size Class				Intermd.	Intermd.
Drive				Front	Front
Crash Test				Vry. Gd.[1]	Vry. Gd.[1]
Airbags				Dual	Dual
ABS				4-Whl*	4-Whl*
Parts Cost				High	High
Complaints				Vry. Pr.	Vry. Pr.
Insurance		No Model Produced		Discount	Discount
Fuel Econ.				20	20
Theft Rating				Vry. Low	Vry. Low
Bumpers				Weak	Weak
Recalls				6	6
Trn. Cir. (ft.)				37	37
Weight (lbs.)				2931	2931
Whlbase (in.)				108	108
Price				7-9,000	8-10,000
OVERALL~					

**Estimate; *Optional; ~Cars without crash tests do not receive an overall rating. [1]Data given for 4 dr.; 2 dr. Good.

2001 Dodge Stratus

Three engine choices were available originally: 2.0-liter, 2.4-liter, and a powerful 2.5-liter. However, for '97, the 2.5-liter was replaced by a 2.4-liter V6. Consider the 2.4-liter, optional on the Stratus and standard on the upscale Cirrus. The Breeze is limited in options. The cars received an average rating in the government's crash tests. The Autostick, a combination stick and automatic, is an option on the Stratus. The Breeze and Cirrus were discontinued after 2000 but a new Stratus coupe was introduced for 2001 to take their place in the lineup.

	1997	1998	1999	2000	2001
Size Class	Intermd.	Intermd.	Intermd.	Intermd.	Intermd.
Drive	Front	Front	Front	Front	Front
Crash Test	Vry. Gd.[1]	Vry. Gd.[1]	Vry. Gd.[1]	Vry. Gd.[1]	Vry. Gd.[1]
Airbags	Dual	Dual	Dual	Dual	Dual
ABS	4-Whl*	4-Whl*	4-Whl*	4-Whl*	4-Whl*
Parts Cost	Low	Vry. Low	Low	Low	Very Low
Complaints	Good	Average	Good	Good	Average
Insurance	Regular	Regular	Regular	Regular	Surchg.
Fuel Econ.	20	19	19	19	20
Theft Rating	Vry. Low	Vry. Low	Vry. Low**	Vry. Low**	Average
Bumpers	Weak	Weak			Weak
Recalls	3	1	0	4	7
Trn. Cir. (ft.)	37	37	37	37	36.8
Weight (lbs.)	2920	3181	3146	3146	3226
Whlbase (in.)	108	108	108	108	108
Price	9-11,000	12-14,000	13-15,000	13-15,000	17-19,000
OVERALL~	Vry. Gd.	Vry. Gd.	BEST BET	Vry. Gd.	Good

Chrysler Concorde/Dodge Intrepid 1993-2001, Eagle Vision 1993-98

These three cars, dubbed "LH" cars, are Chrysler's successful first foray into cab-forward design. This design pushes the wheels farther toward the corners of the car, increasing interior room and improv-

1994 Dodge Intrepid

ing the ride and handling while not changing the overall size of the car. The Concorde and Intrepid have similar styling, though the Concorde is much more plush. Dual airbags have always been standard. ABS has been standard on the Concorde, optional on the Intrepid and Vision.

The base 2.7-liter V6 is both powerful and efficient enough; the 3.2-liter V6 or 3.5-liter V6 is slightly more powerful and just as efficient,

	1992	1993	1994	1995	1996
Size Class		Intermd.	Intermd.	Intermd.	Intermd.
Drive		Front	Front	Front	Front
Crash Test		Vry. Gd.	Vry. Gd.	Vry. Gd.	Vry. Gd.
Airbags		Dual	Dual	Dual	Dual
ABS		4-Whl*	4-Whl*	4-Whl*	4-Whl*
Parts Cost	No Model Produced	Vry. Low	Vry. Low	Vry. Low	Vry. Low
Complaints		Vry. Pr.	Vry. Pr.	Vry. Pr.	Average
Insurance		Discount	Discount	Discount	Discount
Fuel Econ.		20	20	20	19
Theft Rating		Low	Low	Low	Vry. Low
Bumpers					
Recalls		3	2	1	1
Trn. Cir. (ft.)		37.7	37.7	37.7	37.7
Weight (lbs.)		3320	3310	3310	3318
Whlbase (in.)		113	113	113	113
Price		4-6,000	5-7,000	7-9,000	9-11,000
OVERALL		Good	Vry. Gd.	Vry. Gd.	BEST BET

*Optional; **Estimate

2001 Dodge Intrepid

though you may have to use more expensive fuel. For a good balance between ride and handling, look for the "touring" suspension, optional in 1993 and standard thereafter; for a firmer ride, try to find an LH with the "performance" suspension. The cab-forward design yields a surprisingly large amount of interior space; the interior comfort is excellent, and the cars performed well on the crash tests.

	1997	1998	1999	2000	2001
Size Class	Intermd.	Intermd.	Intermd.	Intermd.	Intermd.
Drive	Front	Front	Front	Front	Front
Crash Test	Vry. Gd.	Good	Good	Good	Good
Airbags	Dual	Dual	Dual	Dual	Dual
ABS	4-Whl*	4-Whl*	4-Whl*	4-Whl*	4-Whl*
Parts Cost	Vry. Low	Low	Low	Low	Low
Complaints	Poor	Average	Average	Good	Poor
Insurance	Discount	Discount	Discount	Discount	Discount
Fuel Econ.	19	19	19	19	19
Theft Rating	Vry. Low	Vry. Low	Vry. Low**	Vry. Low**	Vry. Low**
Bumpers			Strong	Strong	Strong
Recalls	1	1	0	5	1
Trn. Cir. (ft.)	37.7	37.5	37.6	37.6	37.6
Weight (lbs.)	3411	3463	3556	3556	3556
Whlbase (in.)	113	113	113	113	113
Price	11-13,000	15-17,000	16-18,000	18-20,000	22-24,000
OVERALL	BEST BET	BEST BET	BEST BET	Vry. Gd.	Vry. Gd.

Chrysler New Yorker 1992-97, LHS 1994-2001, Dodge Dynasty 1992-93

The older New Yorker and Dynasty share almost nothing with the handsome LHS/New Yorker that was new for 1994. The early New Yorker shared its "square" styling with the new Dodge

1993 Chrysler New Yorker

Dynasty, catering to people who want the elegance of a Cadillac in a cheaper package. Landau and Salon models have different levels of equipment.

The Dynasty's base engine is a weak 2.5-liter 4-cylinder, while the New Yorker comes with a stronger V6 that's optional on the Dynasty and standard on the Dynasty LE. After 1994, a 3.5 V6 is plenty power-

	1992	1993	1994	1995	1996
Size Class	Intermd.	Intermd.	Large	Large	Large
Drive	Front	Front	Front	Front	Front
Crash Test	Good	Good	Good	Good	Good
Airbags	Driver	Driver	Dual	Dual	Dual
ABS	4-Whl*	4-Whl*	4-Whl	4-Whl	4-Whl
Parts Cost	Vry. Low	Vry. Low	Vry. Low	Low	Low
Complaints	Vry. Pr.	Average	Vry. Pr.	Average	Average
Insurance	Discount	Discount	Discount	Discount	Discount
Fuel Econ.	19	20	18	18	18
Theft Rating	Low	Vry. Low	Average	Average	Average
Bumpers	Weak	Weak			
Recalls	2	1	2	0	1
Trn. Cir. (ft.)	40	40	37.7	37.7	37.7
Weight (lbs.)	3346	3273	3483	3592	3596
Whlbase (in.)	104.3	104.3	113	113	113
Price	4-6,000	5-7,000	7-9,000	9-11,000	11-13,000
OVERALL	Good	Vry. Gd.	Good	BEST BET	BEST BET

*Optional; **Estimate

114

2001 Chrysler LHS

ful and delivers average mileage.

Handling can be sluggish, but ride is good on smooth roads. The interior is comfortable for four with generous trunk space. The gauges look misaligned; it's hard to tell which one is which. On later models, an array of luxury features comes standard with your only options being a sunroof and CD player, and the front controls improve greatly. The LHS is the only survivor for 2001 and it was completely redesigned in 1999. It's 5.3-liter V6 and numerous luxury and safety features herald it as Chrysler's flagship sedan.

	1997	1998	1999	2000	2001
Size Class	Large	Large	Large	Large	Large
Drive	Front	Front	Front	Front	Front
Crash Test	Good	Good	Average	Average	Average
Airbags	Dual	Dual	Dual	Dual	Dual
ABS	4-Whl	4-Whl	4-Whl	4-Whl	4-Whl
Parts Cost	Vry. Low	Low	Low	Low	Low
Complaints	Poor	Vry. Gd.	Vry. Pr.	Average	Vry. Pr.
Insurance	Discount	Discount	Discount	Discount	Discount
Fuel Econ.	17	17	18	18	18
Theft Rating	Average	Average	Average**	Average**	Average**
Bumpers					
Recalls	1	1	0	1	1
Trn. Cir. (ft.)	37.7	37.7	37.6	37.6	37.6
Weight (lbs.)	3619	3619	3579	3579	3579
Whlbase (in.)	113	113	113	113	113
Price	13-15,000	15-17,000	20-22,000	22-24,000	28-30,000
OVERALL	BEST BET	BEST BET	Good	BEST BET	Good

Chrysler Sebring 1995-2001, Dodge Avenger 1995-2000

Introduced in 1995, the Chrysler Sebring and Dodge Avenger quickly became attractive alternatives to Celica, Prelude, and Integra buyers. The Mitsubishi Galant is their less flashier Asian cousin. Sporty

1999 Dodge Avenger

yet practical is how Chrysler markets the Sebring/Avenger. The interior and exterior were redesigned in 1997, giving the Sebring/Avenger a minor facelift. Dual airbags have been standard since their introduction, and 4-wheel ABS was optional in 1995, standard since 1996. Excellent crash test performers, the Sebring and Avenger also come with 5-mph bumpers from '96 on.

	1992	1993	1994	1995	1996
Size Class				Compact	Compact
Drive				Front	Front
Crash Test				Vry. Gd.	Vry. Gd.
Airbags				Dual	Dual
ABS				4-Whl*	4-Whl*
Parts Cost				High	High
Complaints				Vry. Pr.	Vry. Pr.
Insurance				Surchg.	Surchg.
Fuel Econ.		No Model Produced		22	22
Theft Rating				Average	Average
Bumpers					
Recalls				1	4
Trn. Cir. (ft.)				39.4	39.4
Weight (lbs.)				2908	2908
Whlbase (in.)				103.7	103.7
Price				8-10,000	10-12,000
OVERALL~				Good	Vry. Pr.

*Optional; ~Cars without crash tests do not receive an overall rating.[1]Data given for 2 dr.

2001 Chrysler Sebring

The standard 2.0-liter 4-cylinder engine will probably not satisfy the sports car buyers Chrysler is hoping to reach. The peppier 2.5-liter V6 is a better choice. Fuel economy is merely average. You'll find ample head and leg room, even for rear passengers. Some negatives include a skimpy trunk, and repair bills tend to be high. Please note that the Chrysler Sebring JT convertible, introduced in '96, is not the same as the coupe hardtop Sebring; it is based on the Cirrus. For 2001, the Sebring is all-new and Chrysler added a sedan to the lineup.

	1997	1998	1999	2000	2001
Size Class	Compact	Compact	Compact	Compact	Compact
Drive	Front	Front	Front	Front	Front
Crash Test	Vry. Gd.	Vry. Gd.	Vry. Gd.	Vry. Gd.	Good[1]
Airbags	Dual	Dual	Dual	Dual	Dual
ABS	4-Whl*	4-Whl*	4-Whl*	4-Whl*	4-Whl*
Parts Cost	Vry. Low	Average	Average	Average	High
Complaints	Vry. Pr.	Vry. Pr.	Average	Average	Average
Insurance	Surchg.	Surchg.	Surchg.	Surchg.	Surchg.
Fuel Econ.	20	20	21	19	20
Theft Rating	Average	Average	Average	Very High	Very High
Bumpers			Strong	Strong	Strong
Recalls	4	3	0	0	6
Trn. Cir. (ft.)	39.4	39.4	39.4	39.4	36.1
Weight (lbs.)	2959	2595	2967	2967	3100
Whlbase (in.)	103.7	103.7	103.7	103.7	103.7
Price	12-14,000	14-16,000	15-17,0000	17-19,000	19-21,000
OVERALL~	Poor	Poor	Good	Good	Poor

Chrysler Town & Country 1992-2001

A luxury version of the wildly popular Dodge and Plymouth Grand Caravan/Grand Voyager, the Chrysler Town & Country, redesigned in 1996, has an extended wheelbase, giving it much more interior room. At a

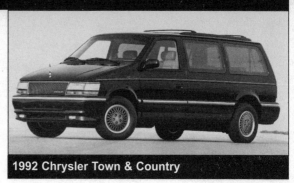

1992 Chrysler Town & Country

cost of about 20-40% more than its Dodge/Plymouth siblings, you'll get lots of power equipment and the option of leather upholstery, along with, on more recent models, a plethora of cup holders, captain's chairs, and other nice luxuries. In 1992, a driver airbag became standard, and in 1994, standard dual airbags were added. Optional ABS is available on 1993-95 models and became standard in 1996.

	1992	1993	1994	1995	1996
Size Class	Minivan	Minivan	Minivan	Minivan	Minivan
Drive	Front/All	Front/All	Front/All	Front/All	Front/All
Crash Test	Vry. Gd.	Vry. Gd.	Good	Good	Good
Airbags	Driver	Driver	Dual	Dual	Dual
ABS	None	4-Whl*	4-Whl*	4-Whl*	4-Whl*
Parts Cost	Vry. Low	Low	Low	Vry. Low	Low
Complaints	Vry. Pr.	Vry. Pr.	Vry. Pr.	Average	Vry. Pr.
Insurance	Discount	Discount	Discount	Discount	Discount
Fuel Econ.	18	19	18	20	20
Theft Rating	High	Vry. High	Vry. High	High	Vry. High
Bumpers			Weak	Weak	
Recalls	11	7	4	3	6
Trn. Cir. (ft.)	40.5	40.5	41	41	37.6
Weight (lbs.)	3187	3059	3135	3305	3528
Whlbase (in.)	119.3	119.3	119.3	119.3	119.3
Price	6-8,000	7-9,000	8-10,000	9-11,000	13-15,000
OVERALL	Good	Average	Average	Vry. Gd.	Average

*Optional;**Estimate

2001 Chrysler Town and Country

The Town & Country comes with a good 3.8-liter V6 with a standard automatic overdrive. Handling is decent, but you can't get the sport handling package found on the Dodge and Plymouth Grand models. Check out the trailer-towing package. The ride is comfortable on smooth roads. Inside there is plenty of room front and back. The earlier models seem trouble-prone. The controls and displays improve with time, and the optional child safety seats available after 1992 are worth looking for. The Town and Country, along with the rest of the Chrysler minivan line, was redesigned for 2001.

	1997	1998	1999	2000	2001
Size Class	Minivan	Minivan	Minivan	Minivan	Minivan
Drive	Front/All	Front/All	Front/All	Front/All	Front/All
Crash Test	Good	Good	Good	Good	Good
Airbags	Dual	Dual	Dual	Dual	Dual
ABS	4-Whl*	4-Whl*	4-Whl*	4-Whl	4-Whl
Parts Cost	Low	Vry. Low	Vry. Low	Vry. Low	Vry. Low
Complaints	Vry. Gd.	Vry. Gd.	Vry. Gd.	Good	Average
Insurance	Discount	Discount	Discount	Discount	Discount
Fuel Econ.	17	17	17	18	18
Theft Rating	Vry. High	Average	Average**	Average**	Average**
Bumpers	Weak	Weak		Strong	Strong
Recalls	3	1	0	0	1
Trn. Cir. (ft.)	37.6	39.5	39.5	39.4	39.4
Weight (lbs.)	3877	4082	4082	4045	4045
Whlbase (in.)	119.3	119.3	119.3	119.3	119.3
Price	15-17,000	17-19,000	22-24,000	27-29,000	28-30,000
OVERALL~	Vry. Gd.	BEST BET	BEST BET	BEST BET	Average

Dodge Caravan/Plymouth Voyager 1992-2000; Dodge Caravan/Chrysler Voyager 2001

These pioneering minivans, new for 1996, have become the standard against which all other minivans are judged. You have a choice between a short or extended wheelbase. The longer wheelbase

1992 Dodge Caravan

translates into more space behind the third seats. The longer versions are called "Grand" and are the most popular. In 1992, a driver's airbag became standard and rear child safety seats joined the option list. ABS is optional on 1993-95 models, standard for '96, and dual airbags became standard in 1994.

The base 4-cylinder engine is suitable only if you don't load the ve-

	1992	1993	1994	1995	1996
Size Class	Minivan	Minivan	Minivan	Minivan	Minivan
Drive	Front/All	Front/All	Front/All	Front/All	Front/All
Crash Test	Vry. Gd.	Vry. Gd.	Good	Good	Good
Airbags	Driver	Driver	Dual	Dual	Dual
ABS	None	4-Whl*	4-Whl*	4-Whl*	4-Whl*
Parts Cost	Vry. Low	Low	Low	Vry. Low	Low
Complaints	Vry. Pr.	Vry. Pr.	Vry. Pr.	Average	Vry. Pr.
Insurance	Discount	Discount	Discount	Discount	Discount
Fuel Econ.	18	19	18	20	20
Theft Rating	Average	Low	Average	Average	Vry. Low
Bumpers			Weak	Weak	
Recalls	12	7	3	3	8
Trn. Cir. (ft.)	40.5	40.5	41	41	37.6
Weight (lbs.)	3187	3059	3135	3305	3528
Whlbase (in.)	112.3	112.3	112.3	112.3	113.3
Price	3-5,000	4-6,000	5-7,000	7-9,000	11-13,000
OVERALL	Good	Average	Good	Vry. Gd.	Good

*Optional;**Estimate

2001 Dodge Caravan

hicle much; otherwise, look for the bigger 2.6-liter 4-cylinder or one of the V6 engines. All-wheel drive was a common option. Handling is okay on the base and Grand models; but, the heavy-duty suspension or the sport handling option improves it greatly. You'll find plenty of room inside. Buy the latest model you can afford and you can't go wrong. Controls and displays improved as time went on and the optional built-in child restraints (1992) are definitely worth looking for. The Plymouth line was dropped in 2001 and Plymouth's shorter wheelbase version became the Chrysler Voyager.

	1997	1998	1999	2000	2001
Size Class	Minivan	Minivan	Minivan	Minivan	Minivan
Drive	Front/All	Front/All	Front/All	Front/All	Front/All
Crash Test	Good	Good	Good	Good	Good
Airbags	Dual	Dual	Dual	Dual	Dual
ABS	4-Whl*	4-Whl*	4-Whl*	4-Whl*	4-Whl*
Parts Cost	Low	Low	Low	Vry. Low	Low
Complaints	Poor	Poor	Good	Good	Average
Insurance	Discount	Discount	Discount	Discount	Discount
Fuel Econ.	20	20	20	19	19
Theft Rating	Average	Vry. Low	Vry. Low**	Vry. Low**	Vry. Low**
Bumpers	Weak	Weak	Strong	Strong	Strong
Recalls	5	1	0	0	1
Trn. Cir. (ft.)	37.6	37.6	37.6	37.6	37.6
Weight (lbs.)	3533	3517	3517	3517	3517
Whlbase (in.)	113.3	113.3	113.3	113.3	113
Price	12-14,000	14-16,000	15-17,000	16-18,000	20-22,000
OVERALL	Good	Vry. Gd.	BEST BET	BEST BET	BEST BET

Dodge Shadow/Plymouth Sundance 1992-94

The Shadow and Sundance are the smallest sedans based on the K-car chassis. Most common are the 2- and 4-door hatchback form. For 1991 a convertible joined the Shadow lineup. The Shadow and

1993 Dodge Shadow

Sundance were discontinued early in 1994 to make room for the sporty Neon. The 1990-93 models have a driver airbag and conventional belts. The 1994 Shadows have a driver airbag, but the motorized shoulder belt and separate lap belt reappear for the front passenger. ABS first became optional in 1993.

Shadow/Sundance engines include a regular or turbocharged 2.2-

	1992	1993	1994	1995	1996
Size Class	Compact	Compact	Compact		
Drive	Front	Front	Front		
Crash Test	Good	Good	Good		
Airbags	Driver	Driver	Driver		
ABS	None	4-Whl*	4-Whl*		
Parts Cost	Vry. Low	Vry. Low	Low		
Complaints	Average	Good	Poor		
Insurance	Surchg.	Surchg.	Surchg.		
Fuel Econ.	23	23	22		
Theft Rating	Average	Average	Average		
Bumpers	Weak	Weak	Weak		
Recalls	3	0	0		
Trn. Cir. (ft.)	34	35	35		
Weight (lbs.)	2652	2613	2620		
Whlbase (in.)	97	97.2	97.2		
Price	<3,000	2-4,000	3-5,000		
OVERALL	Average	Good	Average		

No Model Produced

*Optional

122

1994 Dodge Shadow

liter 4-cylinder, a regular or turbocharged 2.5-liter 4-cylinder, or, starting in 1992, a 3-liter V6. The regular 2.5 offers a trade-off between economy and acceleration. The 5-speed is rougher to shift than Japanese cars. Automatic overdrive is available only on V6 models. Handling is good, but the ride isn't. Though big for subcompacts, the back seat is cramped for adults. The dashboard and controls are OK.

	1997	1998	1999	2000	2001
Size Class					
Drive					
Crash Test					
Airbags					
ABS					
Parts Cost					
Complaints					
Insurance					
Fuel Econ.					
Theft Rating		No Model Produced			
Bumpers					
Recalls					
Trn. Cir. (ft.)					
Weight (lbs.)					
Whlbase (in.)					
Price					
OVERALL					

Dodge Spirit/Plymouth Acclaim 1992-95

Chrysler removed standard items and trim levels from the Spirit and Acclaim, supposedly to keep their prices competitive, and the abandoned luxury models became the LeBarons. The Spirit and Acclaim received

1992 Dodge Spirit

driver airbags for 1990; in 1994, Chrysler added a motorized shoulder belt for the front passenger. ABS has been optional since 1991.

The standard 2.5-liter 4-cylinder accelerates adequately with the standard 3-speed automatic; the 5-speed stick improves highway mileage, but it was dropped for 1994. Many models have a turbocharged 4-cylinder or a V6; the Spirit R/T has a 225 hp turbo-charged

	1992	1993	1994	1995	1996
Size Class	Intermd.	Intermd.	Intermd.	Intermd.	
Drive	Front	Front	Front	Front	
Crash Test	Good	Good	Good	Good	
Airbags	Driver	Driver	Driver	Driver	
ABS	4-Whl*	4-Whl*	4-Whl*	4-Whl*	
Parts Cost	Vry. Low	Low	Low	Low	
Complaints	Average	Good	Average	Average	
Insurance	Discount	Discount	Discount	Regular	
Fuel Econ.	20	23	22	22	
Theft Rating	Average	Average	Average	Low	
Bumpers	Strong	Weak	Weak	Weak	
Recalls	1	0	1	0	
Trn. Cir. (ft.)	39	37	37	39	
Weight (lbs.)	2784	2784	2831	2862	
Whlbase (in.)	103.5	103.5	103.5	103.5	
Price	3-5,000	3-5,000	4-6,000	4-6,000	
OVERALL	BEST BET	Vry. Gd.	Good	Average	

No Model Produced

*Optional

124

4-cylinder. The V6 comes with a 3- or 4-speed automatic. Base Spirits prior to 1993 had a firmer suspension than the base Acclaims, giving them better handling. Suspension on ES and R/T models im-

1995 Plymouth Acclaim

proves handling. The rear seat is roomy. Controls and displays are complete and well designed on early models (except Acclaim base models).

	1997	1998	1999	2000	2001
Size Class					
Drive					
Crash Test					
Airbags					
ABS					
Parts Cost					
Complaints					
Insurance			No Model Produced		
Fuel Econ.					
Theft Rating					
Bumpers					
Recalls					
Trn. Cir. (ft.)					
Weight (lbs.)					
Whlbase (in.)					
Price					
OVERALL					

Dodge/Plymouth Colt 1992-94, Eagle Summit 1992-96

Based on the Mitsubishi Mirage the Dodge/Plymouth Colt and Eagle Summit were very popular cars. The 4-doors and wagons disappeared after 1990, and the Colt and Summit coupes were com-

1992 Dodge Colt

pletely restyled for 1993. In 1994, the Colt and Summit got a driver's side airbag and regular seat belt, but the right front seat kept a motorized belt and separate lap belt. In 1995, motorized belts were replaced when a second airbag and manual belts were added to the Summit, and the Colt was discontinued to make room for the new Neon. ABS became available in 1993, but only on top-line models.

	1992	1993	1994	1995	1996
Size Class	Intermediate	Intermediate	Intermediate	Intermediate	Compact
Drive	Front	Front	Front	Front	Front
Crash Test	Good	Good	Good	Average	Average
Airbags	None	None	Driver	Dual	Dual
ABS	None	4-Whl*	4-Whl*	4-Whl*	4-Whl*
Parts Cost	Very Low	Average	Average	Low	Vry. High
Complaints	Good[1]	Vry. Pr.	Good	Vry. Pr.	Vry. Gd.
Insurance	Surchg.	Regular	Surchg.	Surchg.	Surchg.
Fuel Econ.	20	27	28	33	26
Theft Rating	Average	Vry. Low	Average	Low	Very Low
Bumpers					
Recalls	1	5	1	0	1
Trn. Cir. (ft.)	30.2	30.2	30.2	33.4	32.8
Weight (lbs.)	2205	2195	2085	2085	2085
Whlbase (in.)	93.9[2]	96.1	96.1	96.1	96.1
Price	<3,000	2-4,000	3-5,000	4-6,000	5-7,000
OVERALL	Vry. Gd.	Poor	Average	Good	Average

[1]Data given for Dodge/Plymouth Colt. Complaints rating for Eagle Summit in 1992 is Vry. Pr.;[2]Data given for Colt. Wheel-

1996 Eagle Summit

Performance with the standard 4-cylinder (1.5- or 1.6-liter) is OK, but the heavier 1993-96 models do better with the 1.8-liter 4. Some models, such as the Premier and GT/GTS, have a turbo 4. The 5-speed is a better match than the 3-speed automatic for these engines. The ride is tolerable and the interior is fairly comfortable for four with ample trunk space on the newest models.

	1997	1998	1999	2000	2001
Size Class					
Drive					
Crash Test					
Airbags					
ABS					
Parts Cost					
Complaints					
Insurance					
Fuel Econ.					
Theft Rating					
Bumpers					
Recalls					
Trn. Cir. (ft.)					
Weight (lbs.)					
Whlbase (in.)					
Price					
OVERALL					

No Model Produced

base for Summit is 97.7.

Dodge/Plymouth Colt Vista 1992-94, Eagle Summit Wagon 1992-96

These vehicles first appeared on the U.S. market in 1984 and received minimal changes through 1991. In 1992, the Dodge edition was dropped, and the Eagle and Plymouth versions were restyled. These ve-

1993 Plymouth Colt Vista

hicles got motorized front shoulder belts with separate lap belts from 1990 to 1993. In 1994, the driver got an airbag with regular 3-point seat belt, but the front passenger seat kept the motorized shoulder belt and separate lap belt; in 1995, the Summit Wagon completed its journey into the modern era by adding a second airbag and losing all motorized belts. Also in 1995, the Plymouth models disappeared, leaving the

	1992	1993	1994	1995	1996
Size Class	Compact	Compact	Compact	Compact	Compact
Drive	Front	Front	Front	Front	Front
Crash Test	Good	Good	Good	Good	Good
Airbags	None	None	Driver	Dual	Dual
ABS	None	None	4-Whl*	4-Whl*	4-Whl*
Parts Cost	High	High	High	High	Vry. High
Complaints	Vry. Gd.	Vry. Gd.	Vry. Gd.	Average	Poor
Insurance	Regular	Regular	Regular	Regular	Surchg.
Fuel Econ.	19	20	20	24	24
Theft Rating	Low	Average	Average	Vry. Low	Vry. Low
Bumpers					
Recalls	5	5	1	1	1
Trn. Cir. (ft.)	33.5	33.5	33.5	33.5	33.5
Weight (lbs.)	2701	2976	2734	2734	2734
Whlbase (in.)	99.2	99.2	99.2	99.2	99.2
Price	2-4,000	3-5,000	4-6,000	5-7,000	6-8,000
OVERALL	Poor	Poor	Average	Good	Poor

*Optional

1996 Eagle Summit Wagon

Summit Wagon as the lone version. ABS was introduced in 1994, but only on deluxe trim levels.

The 1.8- and 2-liter engines are hard pressed to keep up with traffic, especially if you're loaded up with passengers and luggage. The 1992-94 deluxe models have a 2.4-liter 4 that's more powerful. Look for ABS on 1992-94 models; it does help. Handling is sluggish with a lot of lean in corners. The interior is fairly comfortable and easily converted to cargo carrying. Nearly all seating positions have lap-shoulder belts. Instruments and controls are generally well designed.

	1997	1998	1999	2000	2001
Size Class					
Drive					
Crash Test					
Airbags					
ABS					
Parts Cost					
Complaints					
Insurance					
Fuel Econ.					
Theft Rating					
Bumpers					
Recalls					
Trn. Cir. (ft.)					
Weight (lbs.)					
Whlbase (in.)					
Price					
OVERALL					

No Model Produced

Dodge/Plymouth Neon 1995-2001

The Neon is Chrysler's first small car to take advantage of the cab-forward design that has attracted so many customers to Chrysler's larger cars. Because of its design, the Neon has surprising

1995 Dodge Neon

room for such a small car. Sales have been quite high, though increasing complaints have taken their toll. You can find the Neon in either a two or four door version with three trim levels. Dual airbags have been standard since its inception; ABS is optional. Also, 1995 and 1996 models meet the 1997 government standards for side impact protection. For 2000, the Neon was redesigned.

	1992	1993	1994	1995	1996
Size Class				Subcomp.	Subcomp.
Drive				Front	Front
Crash Test				Poor	Average
Airbags				Dual	Dual
ABS				4-Whl*	4-Whl*
Parts Cost				Low	Low
Complaints				Vry. Pr.	Vry. Pr.
Insurance				Surchg.	Surchg.
Fuel Econ.				28	28
Theft Rating				Vry. Low	Vry. Low
Bumpers				Weak	Weak
Recalls		No Model Produced		7	2
Trn. Cir. (ft.)				35.4	35.4
Weight (lbs.)				2385	2385
Whlbase (in.)				104	104
Price				4-6,000	5-7,000
OVERALL				Poor	Poor

*Optional

130

2001 Dodge Neon

The single-cam version of the 2-liter engine that is found in the base sedan provides adequate power. For more zing, look for the dual-cam version of this same engine, it will give you more power without diminishing fuel economy very much. The cab-forward design leads to a wider and longer car that produces more interior room, and Chrysler has also raised the roof on the Neon to increase head room. Your best bet may be to find a coupe or sedan with the dual-cam engine. Also, look for the built in child restraints, as they are an excellent feature.

	1997	1998	1999	2000	2001
Size Class	Subcomp.	Subcomp.	Subcomp.	Subcomp.	Subcomp.
Drive	Front	Front	Front	Front	Front
Crash Test	Average	Good	Good	Good	Average
Airbags	Dual	Dual	Dual	Dual	Dual
ABS	4-Whl*	4-Whl*	4-Whl*	4-Whl*	4-Whl*
Parts Cost	Vry. Low	Vry. Low	Vry. Low	Vry. Low	Vry. Low
Complaints	Poor	Poor	Vry. Pr.	Vry. Pr.	Average
Insurance	Surchg.	Surchg.	Surchg.	Surchg.	Surchg.
Fuel Econ.	29	29	27	27	27
Theft Rating	Vry. Low	Vry. Low	Vry. Low	Vry. Low	Average
Bumpers	Weak	Weak			Strong
Recalls	1	0	1	2	0
Trn. Cir. (ft.)	35.4	35.4	35.4	35.5	35.5
Weight (lbs.)	2385	2470	2470	2564	2564
Whlbase (in.)	104	104	104	105	105
Price	6-8,000	7-9,000	9-11,000	10-12,000	12-14,000
OVERALL	Good	Good	Good	Good	Vry. Gd.

Eagle Talon 1992-98, Mitsubishi Eclipse 1992-2001, Plymouth Laser 1992-94

The Talon came out in the fall of 1989 as a 1990 model, and several months after the Talon, the identical Mitsubishi Eclipse and Plymouth Laser made their debuts. They received a modest restyling

1992 Eagle Talon

for 1992, eliminating the pop-up headlights of previous models. The Talon and Eclipse were redesigned for 1995, while the Laser was dropped after 1994. The Eclipse was completely redesigned for 2000. Like the Eclipse, the Talon is available in a 4-wheel drive model called the TSi AWD. These sports coupes had motorized shoulder belts and separate lap belts for front occupants until 1995, when dual airbags and

	1992	1993	1994	1995	1996
Size Class	Compact	Compact	Compact	Compact	Compact
Drive	Front/All	Front/All	Front/All	Front/All	Front/All
Crash Test	Vry. Gd.	Vry. Gd.	Vry. Gd.	Good	Good
Airbags	None	None	None	Dual	Dual
ABS	4-Whl*	4-Whl*	4-Whl*	4-Whl*	4-Whl*
Parts Cost	Vry. High	Vry. High	Vry. High	High[1]	Average
Complaints	Poor	Average	Average	Vry. Pr.	Poor
Insurance	Surchg.	Surchg.	Surchg.	Surchg.	Surchg.
Fuel Econ.	21	21	20	22	23
Theft Rating	Average	Vry. Low	Low	Average	Low
Bumpers	Strong	Strong	Strong		
Recalls	2	2	2	6	4
Trn. Cir. (ft.)	34.1	35.4	35.4	38.1	38.1
Weight (lbs.)	2531	2542	2542	2822	2767
Whlbase (in.)	97.2	97.2	97.2	98.8	98.8
Price	3-5,000	4-6,000	5-7,000	7-9,000	9-11,000
OVERALL	Vry. Pr.	Poor	Poor	Vry. Pr.	Poor

[1]Data given for Talon. Parts cost for Eclipse in 1995 is Average. *Optional;**Estimate

2001 Mitsubishi Eclipse

manual belts became standard. ABS was optional starting in 1991.

The base models of these coupes are well equipped, though some options such as a rear wiper and power locks are only available on the upper-level Laser RS, Talon ES and TSI, and Eclipse GS. The upper-level models' 2-liter twin-cam engine outperforms the base models' 1.8-liter, yet its gas mileage isn't much worse. Handling on the upper-level models is superior to the DL's. Ride is firm in all versions, exactly what you'd expect from a high-caliber sports car.

	1997	1998	1999	2000	2001
Size Class	Compact	Compact	Compact	Compact	Compact
Drive	Front/All	Front	Front	Front	Front
Crash Test	Good	Good	N/A	N/A	N/A
Airbags	Dual	Dual	Dual	Dual	Dual
ABS	4-Whl*	4-Whl*	4-Whl*	4-Whl*	4-Whl*
Parts Cost	Low	Average[1]	Low	Low	Low
Complaints	Average	Poor	Average	Vry. Pr.	Average
Insurance	Surchg.	Surchg.	Surchg.	Surchg.	Surchg.
Fuel Econ.	23	23	23	23	23
Theft Rating	Average	High**	High**	High**	High**
Bumpers			Strong	Strong	Strong
Recalls	4	5	0	3	4
Trn. Cir. (ft.)	38.1	38.1	38.1	36.5	36.5
Weight (lbs.)	2729	2729	2729	2822	2822
Whlbase (in.)	98.8	98.8	98.8	100.8	100.8
Price	10-12,000	11-13,000	15-17,000	18-20,000	22-24,000
OVERALL	Average	Poor			

Ford Aerostar 1992-97

A lackluster competitor through the years while up against Chrysler's minivans, Ford had hoped to change its luck in the minivan market with the new Windstar, which was added to the lineup in 1995. The Wind-

1993 Ford Aerostar

star was originally supposed to replace the Aerostar, but the Aerostar sold surprisingly well, despite all its deficiencies, prompting Ford to keep it around until 1997. The Aerostar has pressed on without major exterior changes since its debut in the early 80s.

Look for models with the 3-liter V6 and, if you often carry heavy loads, the 4-liter V6. The handling on the base models is mediocre but

	1992	1993	1994	1995	1996
Size Class	Minivan	Minivan	Minivan	Minivan	Minivan
Drive	Rear/4	Rear/4	Rear/4	Rear/4	Rear/4
Crash Test	Average	Average	Average	Average	Average
Airbags	Driver	Driver	Driver	Driver	Driver
ABS	2-Whl	2-Whl	2-Whl	2-Whl	2-Whl
Parts Cost	Low	Low	Average	Average	Low
Complaints	Poor	Poor	Average	Average	Good
Insurance	Discount	Discount	Discount	Discount	Discount
Fuel Econ.	17	18	16	17	18
Theft Rating	Low	Low	Average	Vry. Low	Vry. Low
Bumpers					
Recalls	2	2	2	4	4
Trn. Cir. (ft.)	42.4	42.4	42.4	42.4	42.4
Weight (lbs.)	3374	3296	3296	3400	3646
Whlbase (in.)	118.9	118.9	118.9	118.9	118.9
Price	3-5,000	4-6,000	5-7,000	6-8,000	7-9,000
OVERALL	Average	Average	Average	Average	Good

1997 Ford Aerostar

improves with 4-wheel drive. The ride is fairly good. Pass on the electronic dashboard, which is standard on the Eddie Bauer model.

Fold-out child restraints are an excellent option from 1993 on. The brakes are poor, especially on wet roads; the Aerostar really needs 4-wheel ABS to compete in this tough market. Early models had lots of mechanical problems, so get the latest model you can afford.

	1997	1998	1999	2000	2001
Size Class	Minivan				
Drive	Rear/4				
Crash Test	Average				
Airbags	Driver				
ABS	2-Whl				
Parts Cost	Average				
Complaints	Good				
Insurance	Discount				
Fuel Econ.	17				
Theft Rating	Vry. Low				
Bumpers	Weak				
Recalls	2				
Trn. Cir. (ft.)	42.4				
Weight (lbs.)	3646				
Whlbase (in.)	118.9				
Price	8-10,000				
OVERALL	Good				

No Model Produced

135

Ford Bronco 1992-96, Expedition 1997-2001

A descendant of the Bronco that was introduced in 1966 as a Astablemate of the Mustang, this vehicle represents Ford's first foray into what was to become modern-day sport utilities. New

1996 Ford Bronco

in 1997 was the Expedition, the replacement for the Bronco. The Expedition is designed to compete with the very successful Chevy Suburban. For the Bronco, styling changes were modest for the first 15 years or so. It received extensive facelifts in 1992. A driver's side airbag was finally added in 1994; dual airbags are standard for the Expedition. Rear-wheel ABS was available in 1990; 4-wheel ABS has been stan-

	1992	1993	1994	1995	1996
Size Class	Sp. Util.	Sp. Util.	Sp. Util.	Sp. Util.	Sp. Util.
Drive	Rear/4	Rear/4	Rear/4	Rear/4	Rear/4
Crash Test	Vry. Gd.	Vry. Gd.	Vry. Gd.	Vry. Gd.	Vry. Gd.
Airbags	None	None	Driver	Driver	Driver
ABS	2-Whl	4-Whl	4-Whl	4-Whl	4-Whl
Parts Cost	Average	Low	Low	Low	High
Complaints	Poor	Poor	Poor	Poor	Vry. Gd.
Insurance	Discount	Discount	Discount	Discount	Regular
Fuel Econ.	13	13	13	14	14
Theft Rating	High	Vry. High	Vry. High	Vry. High	Vry. High
Bumpers					
Recalls	4	5	4	0	0
Trn. Cir. (ft.)	36.6	36.6	36.6	36.6	36.6
Weight (lbs.)	4430	4587	4587	4587	4500
Whlbase (in.)	104.7	104.7	104.7	104.7	104.7
Price	8-10,000	9-11,000	10-12,000	12-14,000	14-16,000
OVERALL	Poor	Average	Average	Good	Good

**Estimate

2001 Ford Expedition

dard since 1993.

Both the 5-liter and 5.8-liter V8s available throughout the Bronco's recent history are adequate, though the 5.8 accelerates significantly better. The gas mileage with either engine is dreadful on this heavy vehicle. The Expedition comes with either a 4.6-liter V8 or a larger 5.4-liter engine. While driving, you'll find the handling is cumbersome because of the size of the Bronco and Expedition. The Bronco's rear seat won't be comfortable for adults on long trips, but it does improve on the Expedition.

	1997	1998	1999	2000	2001
Size Class	Sp. Util.	Sp. Util.	Sp. Util.	Sp. Util.	Sp. Util.
Drive	Rear/4	Rear/4	Rear/4	Rear/4	Rear/4
Crash Test	Vry. Gd.	Vry. Gd.	Vry. Gd.	Good	Good
Airbags	Dual	Dual	Dual	Dual	Dual
ABS	4-Whl	4-Whl	4-Whl	4-Whl	4-Whl
Parts Cost	Average	Average	High	High	High
Complaints	Poor	Poor	Poor	Average	Poor
Insurance	Regular	Regular	Regular	Discount	Discount
Fuel Econ.	14	15	15	15	15
Theft Rating	Vry. High	Vry. High	Vry. High**	Vry. High**	Vry. High**
Bumpers					
Recalls	3	3	1	1	1
Trn. Cir. (ft.)	36.6	40.4	40.4	40.4	40.4
Weight (lbs.)	4500	4500	4500	4500	4500
Whlbase (in.)	119	119.1	119.1	119.1	119.1
Price	196-21,000	22-24,000	25-27,000	27-29,000	>30,000
OVERALL	Poor	Average	Average	Vry. Gd.	Vry. Gd.

137

Ford Contour/Mercury Mystique 1995-2000

The Ford Contour and Mercury Mystique are the American versions of Ford's "world car." These cars represent Ford's efforts to enter the lucrative global auto market. Replacing the Tempo

1995 Ford Contour

and Topaz, the Contour/Mystique are marketed to a broader audience. Ford increased the length by six inches, increasing the interior room. Dual airbags have been standard since their 1995 introduction; ABS is still optional. The Mystique is the more upscale version and has a softer ride, while the Contour tends to be more utilitarian and aimed towards a broader audience.

	1992	1993	1994	1995	1996
Size Class				Compact	Compact
Drive				Front	Front
Crash Test				Good	Good
Airbags				Dual	Dual
ABS				4-Whl*	4-Whl*
Parts Cost				Average	Average
Complaints				Vry. Pr.	Poor
Insurance				Regular	Regular
Fuel Econ.				23	23
Theft Rating				Vry. Low	Vry. Low
Bumpers		No Model Produced		Weak	Weak
Recalls				8	4
Trn. Cir. (ft.)				36.5	36.5
Weight (lbs.)				2831	2831
Whlbase (in.)				106.5	106.5
Price				5-7,000	6-8,000
OVERALL				Average	Average

*Optional; **Estimate

2000 Mercury Mystique

The base GL on the Contour is basic, the LX is plusher. Both come with a 2-liter engine, barely adequate-the Mystique's base GS and mid-level LS also come with this engine. The Contour's sporty SE has a 2.5-liter V6 which is powerful and quiet. The 2.5-liter engine is optional for the Mystique. Ford guarantees these engines won't need a tune-up for the first 100,000 miles. The SE's sport suspension's handling is outstanding. The Contour will save you about $1,000 over the Mystique. Your best bet may be to look for an SE with the larger engine and other optional features.

	1997	1998	1999	2000	2001
Size Class	Compact	Compact	Compact	Compact	
Drive	Front	Front	Front	Front	
Crash Test	Good	Vry. Gd.	Vry. Gd.	Good	
Airbags	Dual	Dual	Dual/Side	Dual/Side	
ABS	4-Whl*	4-Whl*	4-Whl*	4-Whl*	
Parts Cost	Low	Low	Low	Low	
Complaints	Good	Vry. Pr.	Poor	Vry. Gd.	
Insurance	Regular	Regular	Regular	Regular	
Fuel Econ.	24	24	24	24	
Theft Rating	Vry. Low	Vry. Low	Vry. Low**	Vry. Low**	
Bumpers	Weak	Weak			
Recalls	3	5	2	1	
Trn. Cir. (ft.)	36.5	36.5	36.5	36.5	
Weight (lbs.)	2831	2811	2769	2769	
Whlbase (in.)	106.5	106.5	106.5	106.5	
Price	7-9,000	8-10,000	10-12,000	12-14,000	
OVERALL	Vry. Gd.	Good	Vry. Gd.	BEST BET	

No Model Produced

Ford Crown Victoria 1992-2001, Mercury Gr. Marquis 1992-2001

The Crown Victoria and Grand Marquis are almost identical and basically cheap versions of the Lincoln Town Car. In 1992, a major restyling occurred when Ford put an aerodynamic body on the

1993 Ford Crown Victoria

old chassis. The newest styling is a copy of Ford's successful Taurus and Sable. For 1992, both dropped the wagon line. These big Fords got standard driver airbags for 1990; dual front airbags became optional in 1992, standard on 1994 and later models. ABS is optional starting in 1991 for Ford, 1992 for Mercury. Also, crash-sverity sensors, seat-position sensors, and seat belt pretensioners are all standard for 2001.

	1992	1993	1994	1995	1996
Size Class	Large	Large	Large	Large	Large
Drive	Rear	Rear	Rear	Rear	Rear
Crash Test	Good	Good	Vry. Gd.	Vry. Gd.	Vry. Gd.
Airbags	Driver[#]	Driver[#]	Dual	Dual	Dual
ABS	4-Whl*	4-Whl*	4-Whl*	4-Whl*	4-Whl*
Parts Cost	Low	Low	Low	Low	Low
Complaints	Vry. Pr.	Poor	Average	Poor	Average
Insurance	Discount	Discount	Discount	Regular	Discount
Fuel Econ.	18	18	18	17	17
Theft Rating	Low	Vry. Low	Vry. Low	Vry. Low	Vry. Low
Bumpers					
Recalls	4	4	3	8	4
Trn. Cir. (ft.)	39.1	39.1	39.1	39.1	40.3
Weight (lbs.)	3748	3776	3786	3762	3780
Whlbase (in.)	114.4	114.4	114.4	114.4	114.4
Price	3-5,000	4-6,000	5-7,000	7-9,000	9-11,000
OVERALL	Average	Average	Vry. Gd.	Good	Vry. Gd.

*Optional; #Passenger Side Optional; **Estimate

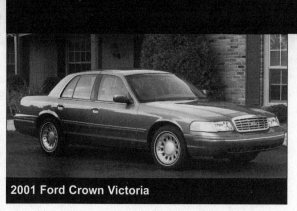
2001 Ford Crown Victoria

The modular 4.6-liter V8 engine is responsive with decent gas mileage. For 1996, you have the choice of an upgrade on the 4.6 V8 which will deliver 20 more horses with only a slight decrease in gas mileage. 1992 models and on got a tighter base suspension, which handles better. If you want good handling, look for a 1992 Touring Sedan, or a 1993-94 with the performance and handling package - firm suspension, improved steering and ABS. There's ample room for six plus luggage. Instruments and controls improved in 1992.

	1997	1998	1999	2000	2001
Size Class	Large	Large	Large	Large	Large
Drive	Rear	Rear	Rear	Rear	Rear
Crash Test	Vry. Gd.	Vry. Gd.	Vry. Gd.	Vry. Gd.	Vry. Gd.
Airbags	Dual	Dual	Dual	Dual	Dual
ABS	4-Whl*	4-Whl*	4-Whl*	4-Whl*	4-Whl*
Parts Cost	Average	Average	Average	Average	Average
Complaints	Good	Good	Average	Vry. Gd.	Good
Insurance	Discount	Discount	Discount	Discount	Discount
Fuel Econ.	17	17	17	17	18
Theft Rating	Vry. Low	Vry. Low	Vry. Low**	Vry. Low**	Vry. Low**
Bumpers			Strong	Strong	Strong
Recalls	2	1	1	3	2
Trn. Cir. (ft.)	40.3	40.3	40.3	40.3	40.3
Weight (lbs.)	3797	3917	3917	3917	3917
Whlbase (in.)	114.4	114.7	114.7	114.7	114.7
Price	11-13,000	13-15,000	15-17,000	18-20,000	22-24,000
OVERALL	Good	BEST BET	BEST BET	BEST BET	BEST BET

Ford Escort 1992-2001

The Ford Escort has had many upgrades and style changes since its introduction to the car market in 1981 as the Pinto replacement. In mid-1990 Ford introduced an all-new Escort and its twin,

1993 Ford Escort

the Mercury Tracer, both based on the Mazda Protégé. Finally, in 1997, the Escort went through its greatest change of all, as the vehicle was completely redesigned. The 1997 model has much rounder and smoother lines than previous models. Watch out for 1990-96 Escorts with motorized shoulder belts and separate lap belts; its very easy to forget the lap belt. 1997 models have conventional belts. The 1994

	1992	1993	1994	1995	1996
Size Class	Subcomp.	Subcomp.	Subcomp.	Subcomp.	Subcomp.
Drive	Front	Front	Front	Front	Front
Crash Test	Vry. Gd.	Vry. Gd.	Good	Average	Average
Airbags	None	None	Driver	Dual	Dual
ABS	None	None	None	4-Whl*	4-Whl*
Parts Cost	Low	Low	Low	Low	Low
Complaints	Good	Poor	Good	Average	Vry. Gd.
Insurance	Surchg.	Surchg.	Surchg.	Surchg.	Surchg.
Fuel Econ.	25	25	25	30	25
Theft Rating	Low	Vry. Low	Low	Average	Vry. Low
Bumpers	Weak	Weak	Weak	Weak	Weak
Recalls	3	2	1	4	0
Trn. Cir. (ft.)	31.5	31.5	31.5	31.5	31.5
Weight (lbs.)	2364	2419	2325	2355	2378
Whlbase (in.)	98.4	98.4	98.4	98.4	98.4
Price	<3,000	2-4,000	3-5,000	3-5,000	4-6,000
OVERALL	Average	Poor	Good	Average	Vry. Gd.

*Optional; **Estimate

2001 Ford Escort

models have a standard driver's airbag, and 1995 models added a passenger airbag. ABS was finally available beginning in 1995.

The Escort has offered several 4-cylinder engines; base engines are adequate. New engines for 1997 provide more power. The 5-speed is good but not delightful. The 1991-94 automatics have overdrive to help gas mileage. Comfort is good in front, only adequate in back; but both improved with the 1991 changeover. While not that flashy, Escorts are a good, solid buy. For 2001, they are only available for fleet sales.

	1997	1998	1999	2000	2001
Size Class	Subcomp.	Subcomp.	Subcomp.	Subcomp.	Subcomp.
Drive	Front	Front	Front	Front	Front
Crash Test	Average	Average	Average	Average	Average
Airbags	Dual	Dual	Dual	Dual	Dual
ABS	4-Whl*	4-Whl*	4-Whl*	4-Whl*	4-Whl*
Parts Cost	Average	Vry. Low	Vry. Low	Vry. Low	Vry. Low
Complaints	Good	Average	Average	Vry. Gd.	Average
Insurance	Surchg.	Surchg.	Surchg.	Surchg.	Surchg.
Fuel Econ.	26	28	28	28	28
Theft Rating	Vry. Low	Vry. Low**	Vry. Low**	Vry. Low**	Vry. Low**
Bumpers	Weak	Weak			
Recalls	0	0	0	0	0
Trn. Cir. (ft.)	31.5	31.5	31.5	31.5	31.5
Weight (lbs.)	2457	2468	2468	2468	2468
Whlbase (in.)	98.4	98.4	98.4	98.4	98.4
Price	6-8,000	7-9,000	8-10,000	10-12,000	11-13,000
OVERALL	Good	Good	Vry. Gd.	BEST BET	Vry. Gd.

Ford Explorer 1992-2001

The Ford Explorer has been the segment-leader for years, and its re-design in 1995 strengthened that position. The Explorer comes in two body styles, 2- or 4-door; the longer 4-door has

1993 Ford Explorer

more room for adults in the back. The Explorer had no airbags or other passive restraints until the 1995 re-design which, thankfully, brought dual airbags and side airbags are optional for 2001. 1991-93 Explorers have rear-wheel ABS; later models come with 4-wheel ABS.

The Explorer's engine is a 4-liter V6 with 5-speed manual or automatic overdrive, and 2- or part-time 4-wheel drive. A 5.0-liter V8 is

	1992	1993	1994	1995	1996
Size Class	Sp. Util.	Sp. Util.	Sp. Util.	Sp. Util.	Sp. Util.
Drive	Rear/4	Rear/4	Rear/4	Rear/4	Rear/4
Crash Test	Average	Average	Average	Good	Good
Airbags	None	None	None	Dual	Dual
ABS	2-Whl	2-Whl	4-Whl	4-Whl	4-Whl
Parts Cost	Low	Vry. Low	Vry. Low	Vry. Low	Vry. Low
Complaints	Poor	Vry. Pr.	Vry. Pr.	Good	Average
Insurance	Regular	Discount	Discount	Regular	Discount
Fuel Econ.	17	17	17	15	18
Theft Rating	Average	Vry. Low	Average	Vry. Low	Low
Bumpers					Weak
Recalls	8	11	6	6	5
Trn. Cir. (ft.)			35.6	37.3	37.3
Weight (lbs.)	3675	3890	3844	4189	4150
Whlbase (in.)	102.1	102.1	102.1	111.5	111.5
Price	5-7,000	6-8,000	7-9,000	10-12,000	12-14,000
OVERALL	Vry. Pr.	Poor	Poor	Vry. Gd.	Vry. Gd.

**Estimate

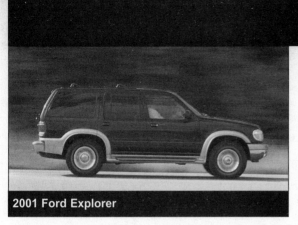
2001 Ford Explorer

also available. On both vehicles, power is adequate, and the gas mileage is better than most larger utility vehicles, but still worse than many full-size cars. In general, the handling is unresponsive and the ride is rough. Some dashboard controls aren't optimally placed. Up to four adults will be comfortable inside. The Explorer's front end was restyled for 1999.

	1997	1998	1999	2000	2001
Size Class	Sp. Util.	Sp. Util.	Sp. Util.	Sp. Util.	Sp. Util.
Drive	Rear/4	Rear/4	Rear/4	Rear/4	Rear/4
Crash Test	Good	Average	Average	Average	Average
Airbags	Dual	Dual	Dual	Dual/Side*	Dual/Side
ABS	4-Whl	4-Whl	4-Whl	4-Whl	4-Whl
Parts Cost	Average	Average	Low	Low	Low
Complaints	Poor	Vry. Pr.	Vry. Pr.	Good	Poor
Insurance	Discount	Discount	Regular	Regular	Discount
Fuel Econ.	16	16	16	16	15
Theft Rating	Low	Low	Low**	Average	Average
Bumpers	Weak	Weak			
Recalls	3	2	0	2	2
Trn. Cir. (ft.)	34.6	37.3	37.3	37.3	37.3
Weight (lbs.)	3707	3707	3707	3707	4250
Whlbase (in.)	111.5	111.5	111.5	111.5	111.6
Price	13-15,000	15-17,000	17-19,000	19-21,000	22-24,000
OVERALL	Good	Average	Average	Good	Vry. Gd.

Ford Festiva 1992-93, Aspire 1994-97

The Festiva is a Mazda-designed car which was built by Kia, which began exporting its own cars to America in 1994. The tiny Festiva is about seven inches shorter than the Geo Metro. The

1993 Ford Festiva

Festiva first appeared in early 1987 as a 1988 model and scarcely changed since then until it was replaced in mid-1994 by the more rounded Aspire. The 1990-93 Festivas have annoying motorized belts - you must remember to fasten the lap belts separately. The mid-1994 changeover to the Aspire brought standard dual airbags and optional ABS.

	1992	1993	1994	1995	1996
Size Class	Subcomp.	Subcomp.	Subcomp.	Subcomp.	Subcomp.
Drive	Front	Front	Front	Front	Front
Crash Test	N/A	N/A	Average	Average	Average
Airbags	None	None	Dual	Dual	Dual
ABS	None	None	4-Whl*	4-Whl*	4-Whl*
Parts Cost	Average	High	High	Low	Vry. High
Complaints	Vry. Gd.	Good	Average	Good	Good
Insurance	Surchg.	Surchg.	Regular	Regular	Surchg.
Fuel Econ.	35	35	36	36	34
Theft Rating	Low	Vry. Low	Vry. Low	Vry. Low	Vry. Low
Bumpers	Weak	Weak			
Recalls	1	1	2	0	0
Trn. Cir. (ft.)	28.9	28.9	29.5	29.5	30.8
Weight (lbs.)	1797	1797	2004	2004	2004
Whlbase (in.)	90.2	90.2	90.7	90.7	90.7
Price	<3000	<3000	<3000	2-4,000	3-5,000
OVERALL~			Average	BEST BET	Average

*Optional; ~Cars without crash tests do not receive an overall rating.

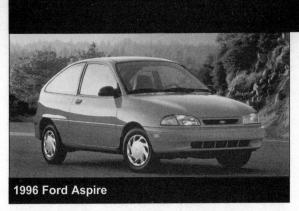

1996 Ford Aspire

The Festiva/Aspire's 1.3-liter 4-cylinder engine provides adequate power, though more so for the lighter Festiva than for the Aspire. You are better off with the 5-speed transmission—it allows better acceleration and fuel economy, and lets the engine run slower on the highway, reducing noise and improving engine life. The body leans during hard cornering, but handling is generally good. The Festiva comes in several trim levels; you have to get a GL in order to get items like air conditioning and a rear wiper. Front seat comfort is reasonably good. Cargo room for two people is easily expandable.

	1997	1998	1999	2000	2001
Size Class	Subcomp.				
Drive	Front				
Crash Test	Average				
Airbags	Dual				
ABS	4-Whl*				
Parts Cost	Vry. High				
Complaints	Good				
Insurance	Surchg.				
Fuel Econ.	34				
Theft Rating	Vry. Low				
Bumpers					
Recalls	0				
Trn. Cir. (ft.)	29.5				
Weight (lbs.)	2056				
Whlbase (in.)	90.7				
Price	4-6,000				
OVERALL~	Average				

No Model Produced

Ford Mustang 1992-2001

Up until the 1994 restyling, the Mustang remained virtually the same for over twenty years. It has competed with other pony cars, now only the Chevrolet Camaro and Pontiac Firebird, and

1993 Ford Mustang

done quite well for itself. The Mustang received a complete restyling for 1994, on an improved version of the old chassis. Beginning in 1990, Mustangs have a standard driver's airbag; dual airbags arrived for 1994. ABS was not available until 1994.

Engine choices on later models are extreme: a 2.3-liter 4 and a 5-liter V8, both with 5-speed manual or automatic. The 1994-95 Mustang of-

	1992	1993	1994	1995	1996
Size Class	Intermd.	Intermd.	Intermd.	Intermd.	Intermd.
Drive	Rear	Rear	Rear	Rear	Rear
Crash Test	Vry. Gd.[1]	Vry. Gd.[1]	Good	Good	Good[1]
Airbags	Driver	Driver	Dual	Dual	Dual
ABS	None	None	4-Whl*	4-Whl*	4-Whl*
Parts Cost	Vry. Low	Low	Low	Vry. Low	Average
Complaints	Good	Average	Average	Poor	Good
Insurance	Surchg.	Surchg.	Regular	Surchg.	Surchg.
Fuel Econ.	18	22	20	20	20
Theft Rating	High	Vry. High	Vry. High	Vry. High	Vry. High
Bumpers					
Recalls	1	2	4	5	2
Trn. Cir. (ft.)	37.4	37.4	38.3	38.3	38.3
Weight (lbs.)	2775	2775	3065	3077	3065
Whlbase (in.)	100.5	100.5	101.3	101.3	101.3
Price	5-7,000	6-8,000	7-9,000	8-10,000	10-12,000
OVERALL	Good	Average	Average	Poor	Poor

[1]Data given for coupe. Crash test for convertible 1992-93 is Good; 1996-97 is Vry. Good; *Optional; **Estimate

148

2001 Ford Mustang

fers a 3.8-liter V6 or the 5.0 V8, and the 1996 comes standard with the 3.8-liter V6 found the year before, but its optional engine is now a smaller and smoother 4.6-liter V8. The 4-cylinder Mustang is almost an economy car; the 3.8 V6 is much peppier. The 3.8-liter V6 actually meets Low Emission Vehicle requirements. The V8 transforms the Mustang into a muscle car; it's almost too much engine for the pre-1994 chassis. Handling is responsive, but with the V8 it's easy to get the car's rear end to swing out. The standard gauges are clear, and Ford has updated and improved the controls for 1994.

	1997	1998	1999	2000	2001
Size Class	Intermd.	Intermd.	Intermd.	Intermd.	Intermd.
Drive	Rear	Rear	Rear	Rear	Rear
Crash Test	Good[1]	Vry. Gd.	Vry. Gd.	Good	Good
Airbags	Dual	Dual	Dual	Dual	Vry. Gd.
ABS	4-Whl*	4-Whl*	4-Whl*	4-Whl*	4-Whl*
Parts Cost	High	Average	Average	Average	Average
Complaints	Poor	Average	Average	Poor	Good
Insurance	Surcharge	Surcharge	Surcharge	Surcharge	Surcharge
Fuel Econ.	20	20	20	20	20
Theft Rating	Vry. High	Vry. High	Vry. High**	Vry. High**	Vry. High**
Bumpers			Strong	Strong	Strong
Recalls	1	4	1	3	1
Trn. Cir. (ft.)	38.3	40.8	37.9	37.9	37.9
Weight (lbs.)	3084	3065	3069	3069	3069
Whlbase (in.)	101.3	101.3	101.3	101.3	101.3
Price	11-13,000	13-15,000	15-17,000	17-19,000	19-21,000
OVERALL	Poor	Poor	Average	Poor	Vry. Gd.

Ford Probe 1992-97

These Ford sport coupes share a chassis with the Mazda 626. The Probe was originally supposed to replace the Ford Mustang, but the Mustang's popularity and fresh new look changed Ford's mind. The Probe and its close relative, the Mazda MX-6, were all-new in 1993, when they were given a more modern, rounded styling. All Probes through 1992 have motorized shoulder belts with separate lap belts. The 1993 Probes have regular front belts and a driver's airbag; the 1994 models got a passenger airbag. ABS is optional throughout the model's history.

1993 Ford Probe

	1992	1993	1994	1995	1996
Size Class	Compact	Compact	Compact	Compact	Compact
Drive	Front	Front	Front	Front	Front
Crash Test	Vry. Gd.	Average	Vry. Gd.	Vry. Gd.	Vry. Gd.
Airbags	None	Driver	Dual	Dual	Dual
ABS	4-Whl*	4-Whl*	4-Whl*	4-Whl*	4-Whl*
Parts Cost	Vry. High	Vry. High	Vry. High	Vry. High	Vry. High
Complaints	Average	Vry. Pr.	Poor	Average	Good
Insurance	Surchg.	Regular	Surchg.	Surchg.	Surchg.
Fuel Econ.	19	24	22	21	26
Theft Rating	Average	Average	Average	Average	Average
Bumpers	Weak				
Recalls	4	1	1	1	1
Trn. Cir. (ft.)	34.8	34.8	35.8	35.8	35.8
Weight (lbs.)	3000	2619	2690	2921	2690
Whlbase (in.)	99	102.9	102.8	102.8	102.8
Price	3-5,000	4-6,000	5-7,000	6-8,000	7-9,000
OVERALL	Vry. Pr.	Vry. Pr.	Poor	Poor	Average

*Optional

1996 Ford Probe

The 1990-92 Probes have a 2.2-liter 4-cylinder, turbo-charged on GT models; a 3-liter V6 came standard on the 1990-92 LX. The engines for 1993-96 are a bit smaller, a 2-liter 4-cylinder or a 2.5-liter V6, though both are as powerful as the two they replace. The 5-speed is the better transmission choice; it's more enjoyable in daily use than the automatic. One benefit of the GT is a firmer suspension that gives excellent handling. Like other sporty cars, the Probe is really a 2-seater with a back seat for occasional use. The interior controls, especially the horn buttons, need some improvement.

	1997	1998	1999	2000	2001
Size Class	Compact				
Drive	Front				
Crash Test	Vry. Gd.				
Airbags	Dual				
ABS	4-Whl*				
Parts Cost	Vry. High				
Complaints	Good				
Insurance	Surchg.				
Fuel Econ.	26				
Theft Rating	Average				
Bumpers					
Recalls	1				
Trn. Cir. (ft.)	35.8				
Weight (lbs.)	2690				
Whlbase (in.)	102.8				
Price	8-10,000				
OVERALL	Average				

No Model Produced

Ford Taurus 1992-2001

The Taurus, introduced in 1986 with its twin, the Mercury Sable, popularized aerodynamic car design. Though widely imitated, the Taurus still holds its own; its redesign in 1996

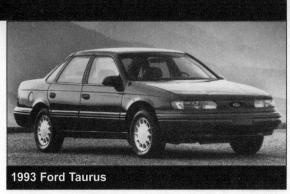

1993 Ford Taurus

only strengthened its industry-leading position. The Taurus originally came in L, GL, MT-5, and LX models and as a 4-door sedan or 4-door station wagon. For 1996, the Taurus received a total make-over as a new oval look was adopted. In 1990, a driver's airbag was added; a passenger airbag became optional in 1992, and standard in 1994. ABS is optional on sedans from 1990 on, and on wagons from 1991. It has typi-

	1992	1993	1994	1995	1996
Size Class	Intermd.	Intermd.	Intermd.	Intermd.	Intermd.
Drive	Front	Front	Front	Front	Front
Crash Test	Good[1]	Good[1]	Good	Good	Vry. Gd.
Airbags	Driver#	Driver#	Dual	Dual	Dual
ABS	4-Whl*	4-Whl*	4-Whl*	4-Whl*	4-Whl*
Parts Cost	Low	Low	Low	Low	Low
Complaints	Poor	Vry. Pr.	Poor	Poor	Average
Insurance	Discount	Discount	Discount	Discount	Discount
Fuel Econ.	20	21	19	20	20
Theft Rating	Low	Vry. Low	Vry. Low	Low	Vry. Low
Bumpers	Weak	Weak	Weak	Weak	Strong
Recalls	6	8	4	3	6
Trn. Cir. (ft.)	38.6	38.6	38.6	38.6	38
Weight (lbs.)	3111	3253	3104	3118	3326
Whlbase (in.)	106	106	106	106	108.5
Price	2-4,000	3-5,000	4-6,000	5-7,000	7-9,000
OVERALL	Average	Average	Good	Good	BEST BET

[1]Data given for sedan. Crash test for wagon is Vry. Good; *Optional; #Passenger Side Optional; **Estimate

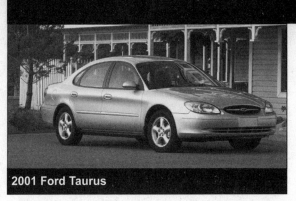
2001 Ford Taurus

cally done well on government crash tests and continues to do so.

Look for the 140 hp 3-liter V6 engine; it's more powerful and economical than the 2.5-liter 4-cylinder engine. The SHO comes only with a 5-speed through 1992 models. A 3.8-liter is optional on 1990-95 SHO models. The SHO's handling is precise; on other models, look for speed-sensitive steering. The dashboard is well laid-out, and the seating is excellent for four. The 1996 model features a longer wheelbase which added more room and made seating more comfortable than on past models.

	1997	1998	1999	2000	2001
Size Class	Intermd.	Intermd.	Intermd.	Intermd.	Intermd.
Drive	Front	Front	Front	Front	Front
Crash Test	Vry. Gd.	Vry. Gd.	Vry. Gd.	Vry. Gd.	Vry. Gd.
Airbags	Dual	Dual	Dual	Dual	Dual
ABS	4-Whl*	4-Whl*	4-Whl*	4-Whl*	4-Whl*
Parts Cost	Low	Average	Low	Low	Low
Complaints	Average	Good	Average	Vry. Gd.	Good
Insurance	Discount	Discount	Discount	Discount	Discount
Fuel Econ.	20	20	20	20	20
Theft Rating	Vry. Low	Vry. Low	Vry. Low	Vry. Low**	Vry. Low**
Bumpers	Strong	Strong			
Recalls	3	2	3	1	1
Trn. Cir. (ft.)	38	38	38	39.8	39.8
Weight (lbs.)	3326	3294	3329	3368	3368
Whlbase (in.)	108.5	108.5	108.5	108.5	108.5
Price	8-10,000	10-12,000	13-15,000	15-17,000	18-20,000
OVERALL	BEST BET	BEST BET	Vry. Gd.	BEST BET	BEST BET

Ford Tempo/Mercury Topaz 1992-94

The Ford Tempo and the Mercury Topaz have not change much since their 1984 debut. Ford remedied this in the fall of 1994, by replacing the average selling Tempo with the European-designed Contour.

1993 Mercury Topaz

For 1987, the Tempo was one of the first production cars to offer an optional driver's airbag, which Tempos kept until they were discontinued after the 1994 model year. The 1990-93 models without an airbag have motorized shoulder belts and separate lap belts. Unfortunately, ABS was never offered.

The standard 4-cylinder is a cut-down version of Ford's old in-line

	1992	1993	1994	1995	1996
Size Class	Compact	Compact	Compact		
Drive	Front	Front	Front		
Crash Test	Good[1]	Good	Good		
Airbags	Driver*	Driver*	Driver*		
ABS	None	None	None		
Parts Cost	Low	Low	Low		
Complaints	Average	Good	Average		
Insurance	Regular	Regular	Regular		
Fuel Econ.	21	22	22		
Theft Rating	Low	Vry. Low	Vry. Low		
Bumpers	Weak	Weak	Weak		
Recalls	2	2	1		
Trn. Cir. (ft.)	36.5	36.5	36.5		
Weight (lbs.)	2600	2600	2569		
Whlbase (in.)	99.9	99.9	99.9		
Price	<3000	2-4,000	3-5,000		
OVERALL	Good[2]	Vry. Gd.	Good		

No Model Produced

[1]Data given for model without airbags. Crash test for model with driver airbag is Average; [2]Data given for model without

154

1994 Ford Tempo

6-cylinder, which dates back to 1960; it's noisy, not very quick, and not that economical. Some of the 1990-92 models have 4-wheel drive. The optional 3-liter V6 is quicker, but it's handicapped by the 3-speed automatic, the only choice on any Tempo. The ride, comfort, and trunk space are average, and the handling is sloppy. This is a solid car; however, make sure you check out the engine and don=t buy one without an airbag.

	1997	1998	1999	2000	2001
Size Class					
Drive					
Crash Test					
Airbags					
ABS					
Parts Cost					
Complaints					
Insurance					
Fuel Econ.					
Theft Rating			No Model Produced		
Bumpers					
Recalls					
Trn. Cir. (ft.)					
Weight (lbs.)					
Whlbase (in.)					
Price					
OVERALL					

airbags. Overall rating for model with airbags may vary based on footnote; *Optional

Ford Thunderbird 1992-97

The Ford Thunderbird shares a body and chassis with the Mercury Cougar and the Lincoln Mark VII and VIII. The 1983 Thunderbird was the first Ford with the aerodynamic look that distinguished most of the company's cars by 1990. For 1996, Ford gave the Thunderbird a fresh, new look with redone front and back ends. The 1990-93 T-birds have motorized front shoulder belts and manual lap belts; the 1994 models have dual airbags and conventional belts. ABS has been optional since 1987 and standard on Turbo Coupes and Super Coupes.

1994 Ford Thunderbird

	1992	1993	1994	1995	1996
Size Class	Large	Large	Large	Large	Large
Drive	Rear	Rear	Rear	Rear	Rear
Crash Test	Vry. Gd.	Vry. Gd.	Vry. Gd.	Vry. Gd.	Vry. Gd.
Airbags	None	None	Dual	Dual	Dual
ABS	4-Whl*	4-Whl*	4-Whl*	4-Whl*	4-Whl*
Parts Cost	Low	Low	Low	Low	Average
Complaints	Poor	Vry. Pr.	Poor	Poor	Poor
Insurance	Discount	Discount	Regular	Discount	Discount
Fuel Econ.	17	17	18	19	19
Theft Rating	Average	Average	Average	Average	Average
Bumpers					
Recalls	2	2	0	0	2
Trn. Cir. (ft.)	37.5	36.6	36.6	36.6	36.6
Weight (lbs.)	3514	3575	3570	3536	3536
Whlbase (in.)	113	113	113	113	113
Price	4-6,000	5-7,000	6-8,000	7-9,000	8-10,000
OVERALL	Good	Average	Good	Vry. Gd.	Good

*Optional

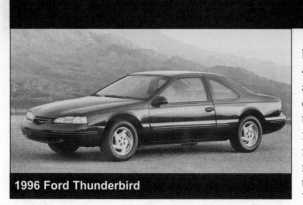
1996 Ford Thunderbird

Earlier Thunderbirds offer a turbo 4-cylinder, a V6, and a V8. The 4-cylinder may be the most enjoyable for 5-speed shifting. The newer models have a regular or supercharged V6 or, since 1991, a V8. This standard 6-cylinder is adequate; the other engines are roughly equal in power. The ride is comfortable, but base models' handling isn't as crisp as it should be; look for an SC or V8, which have a special handling package. The 1990-97 T-bird has enough room for four (five in a pinch) plus luggage. The gauges are nicely-designed; the electronic panel should be avoided.

	1997	1998	1999	2000	2001
Size Class	Large				
Drive	Rear				
Crash Test	Vry. Gd.				
Airbags	Dual				
ABS	4-Whl*				
Parts Cost	High				
Complaints	Average				
Insurance	Regular				
Fuel Econ.	18				
Theft Rating	Average				
Bumpers					
Recalls	0				
Trn. Cir. (ft.)	36.5				
Weight (lbs.)	3561				
Whlbase (in.)	113				
Price	10-12,000				
OVERALL~	Good				

No Model Produced

157

Ford Windstar 1995-2001

Ford unveiled the Windstar in 1995, in an attempt to stop the Chrysler minivan juggernauts—otherwise known as the Caravan/Voyager. The Windstar did received outstanding crash test ratings

1996 Ford Windstar

and offered standard dual airbags and 4-wheel ABS with optional built-in child seats. Plus, at over 200 inches, the Windstar came with more interior space than the Grand Caravan/Voyager. In the competitive minivan market, the Windstar was unable to lure many Chrysler buyers away, and problems appeared in 1997 as consumer complaints began to grow. The Windstar's redesign was not revolutionary; however,

	1992	1993	1994	1995	1996
Size Class				Minivan	Minivan
Drive				Front	Front
Crash Test				Vry. Gd.	Vry. Gd.
Airbags				Dual	Dual
ABS				4-Whl	4-Whl
Parts Cost			No Model Produced	Average	Average
Complaints				Vry. Pr.	Vry. Pr.
Insurance				Discount	Discount
Fuel Econ.				17	17
Theft Rating				Vry. Low	Vry. Low
Bumpers				Fair	Fair
Recalls				4	4
Trn. Cir. (ft.)				40.3	40.3
Weight (lbs.)				3733	3733
Whlbase (in.)				120.7	120.7
Price				8-10,000	9-11,000
OVERALL				Good	Good

**Estimate

158

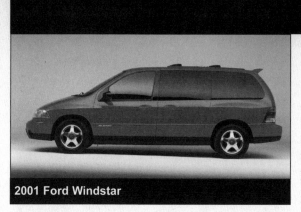
2001 Ford Windstar

a slight change in 1998 helped.

The base GL comes standard with the same 3-liter V6 available on the Aerostar and Ranger. A more powerful 3.8-liter V6 engine is optional, standard on the LX models. The 3.0-liter meets Low Emission Vehicle standards and the 3.8-liter meets Ultra Low Emission standards. With contemporary styling and decent handling, the Windstar provided a good challenge to the Chrysler minivans, but a high number of complaints lowers its overall ratings somewhat. Ride is good, and the cargo area is large and well designed. It added dual sliding doors for 1999.

	1997	1998	1999	2000	2001
Size Class	Minivan	Minivan	Minivan	Minivan	Minivan
Drive	Front	Front	Front	Front	Front
Crash Test	Vry. Gd.	Vry. Gd.	Vry. Gd.	Vry. Gd.	Vry. Gd.
Airbags	Dual	Dual	Dual	Dual	Dual
ABS	4-Whl	4-Whl	4-Whl	4-Whl	4-Whl
Parts Cost	High	High	High	High	High
Complaints	Vry. Gd.	Vry. Pr.	Vry. Pr.	Average	Vry. Pr.
Insurance	Discount	Discount	Discount	Discount	Discount
Fuel Econ.	17	18	17	17	17
Theft Rating	Vry. Low	Vry. Low	Vry. Low**	Vry. Low**	Vry. Low**
Bumpers	Fair	Fair	Strong	Strong	Strong
Recalls	1	5	0	1	2
Trn. Cir. (ft.)	40.3	40.3	40.3	40.3	40.3
Weight (lbs.)	3733	3733	3733	3733	3733
Whlbase (in.)	120.7	120.7	120.7	120.7	120.7
Price	10-12,000	13-15,000	16-18,000	19-21,000	21-23,000
OVERALL	BEST BET	Average	Good	BEST BET	Good

Geo Metro 1992-97, Chevrolet Metro 1998-2001, Suzuki Swift 1992-2001

A Geo Metro convertible arrived during 1990 and lasted until 1993. Convertibles have a driver's airbag with regular lap-shoulder belts in front. Other Metros and Swifts through 1994 have

1996 Geo Metro

the less-than-desirable door-mounted seat belts, with no airbags or ABS. In 1995, a redesign brought more modern styling, more headroom, dual airbags, conventional seat belts, optional ABS, and daytime running lights.

Metros and Sprints have a 1-liter 3-cylinder engine; Swifts get a 1.3-liter 4-cylinder with up to 100 horsepower, which it also shares with the

	1992	1993	1994	1995	1996
Size Class	Subcomp.	Subcomp.	Subcomp.	Subcomp.	Subcomp.
Drive	Front	Front	Front	Front	Front
Crash Test	Average	Average	Average	Good	Good
Airbags	None[1]	None[1]	None[1]	Dual	Dual
ABS	None	None	None	4-Whl*	4-Whl*
Parts Cost	High	High	Vry. High	High	Vry. High
Complaints	Good	Good	Average	Average	Average
Insurance	Surchg.	Surchg.	Surchg.	Surchg.	Surchg.
Fuel Econ.	44	36	39	44	39
Theft Rating	Low	Low	Low	Low	Vry. Low
Bumpers	Weak	Weak	Weak		
Recalls	1	1	0	1	0
Trn. Cir. (ft.)	30.2	30.2	31.5	31.5	31.5
Weight (lbs.)	1621	1694	1699	1751	1808
Whlbase (in.)	89.2	89.2	89.2	93.1	93.1
Price	<3,000	<3,000	<3,000	2-4,000	3-5,000
OVERALL	Poor	Poor	Vry. Pr.	Average	Good

[1]Data given for sedan/coupe. Airbags for convertible is Driver; *Optional; **Estimate

160

1995 Metro 4-door. The Metro and Swift have been among the industry fuel economy leaders for years. Stick to the standard 5-speed for best performance and gas mileage. In the hatchback, room for two is tight; the rear seat is for kids. Handling is quick and precise, but crosswinds and large trucks can blow the car off course.

2001 Suzuki Swift

	1997	1998	1999	2000	2001
Size Class	Subcomp.	Subcomp.	Subcomp.	Subcomp.	Subcomp.
Drive	Front	Front	Front	Front	Front
Crash Test	Good	Good	Good	Good	Good
Airbags	Dual	Dual	Dual	Dual	Dual
ABS	4-Whl*	4-Whl*	4-Whl*	4-Whl*	4-Whl*
Parts Cost	Vry. High	Vry. High	Vry. High	Vry. High	Vry. High
Complaints	Poor	Poor	Poor	Average	Average
Insurance	Surchg.	Surchg.	Surchg.	Surchg.	Surchg.
Fuel Econ.	44	41	39	41	30
Theft Rating	Vry. Low	Vry. Low	Vry. Low**	Vry. Low**	Vry. Low**
Bumpers					
Recalls	2	0	0	0	0
Trn. Cir. (ft.)	31.5	31.5	31.5	31.5	31.5
Weight (lbs.)	1878	1895	1895	1895	1895
Whlbase (in.)	93.1	93.1	93.1	93.1	93.1
Price	4-6,000	5-7,000	6-8,000	7-9,000	8-10,000
OVERALL	Average	Average	Average	Average	Average

Geo Prizm 1992-97, Chevrolet Prizm 1998-2001

The Prizm is a clone of Toyota's popular Corolla, but it never sold as well due to Toyota's better reputation. The Prizm comes with two trim levels and only in a sedan. Prizms from late

1996 Geo Prizm

1990 through 1992 had door-mounted shoulder belts with manual lap belts, so it may be wise to stay away from the Prizm during these years. The 1993 Prizm received a driver airbag and manual lap-shoulder belts and added a standard passenger airbag for 1994. ABS first became optional in 1993.

The standard Prizm engine, a 1.6-liter 4-cylinder, is adequate. The

	1992	1993	1994	1995	1996
Size Class	Subcomp.	Subcomp.	Subcomp.	Subcomp.	Compact
Drive	Front	Front	Front	Front	Front
Crash Test	Average	Average	Average	Good	Good
Airbags	None	Driver	Dual	Dual	Dual
ABS	None	4-Whl*	4-Whl*	4-Whl*	4-Whl*
Parts Cost	High	High	High	Average	Average
Complaints	Good	Average	Average	Good	Vry. Gd.
Insurance	Surchg.	Regular	Regular	Surchg.	Surchg.
Fuel Econ.	23	26	26	27	31
Theft Rating	Low	Vry. Low	Vry. Low	Low	Vry. Low
Bumpers	Weak				
Recalls	0	1	3	3	0
Trn. Cir. (ft.)	31.5	31.5	31.5	31.5	31.5
Weight (lbs.)	2435	2348	2355	2359	2359
Whlbase (in.)	95.7	97	97	97	97.1
Price	2-4,000	3-5,000	4-6,000	5-7,000	6-8,000
OVERALL	Poor	Poor	Vry. Pr.	Average	Good

*Optional; **Estimate

2001 Chevrolet Prizm

larger engine on 1993-97 models, with either a five-speed or automatic overdrive, is quieter and peppier, and gas mileage is equivalent. The 1994 and later models are fine choices among cars that are a bit bigger than a subcompact and at a very reasonable price. With the demise of the Geo nameplate, the Prizm fell under the Cherolet name starting in 1998. Where in early years the Prizm may have cost less than the Corolla, this is not true any more. If you are looking for a Toyota Corolla and can live without the Toyota name, the Prizm is still a good choice.

	1997	1998	1999	2000	2001
Size Class	Compact	Compact	Compact	Compact	Compact
Drive	Front	Front	Front	Front	Front
Crash Test	Good	Good	Good	Good	Good
Airbags	Dual	Dual/Side*	Dual/Side*	Dual/Side*	Dual/Side*
ABS	4-Whl*	4-Whl*	4-Whl*	4-Whl*	4-Whl*
Parts Cost	Vry. High	Vry. High	High	High	High
Complaints	Average	Vry. Gd.	Good	Vry. Gd.	Poor
Insurance	Surchg.	Surchg.	Surchg.	Surchg.	Surchg.
Fuel Econ.	30	31	31	31	31
Theft Rating	Vry. Low	Vry. Low	Vry. Low**	Vry. Low**	Vry. Low**
Bumpers		Weak		Strong	Strong
Recalls	2	0	0	0	0
Trn. Cir. (ft.)	31.5	34	34	34	34
Weight (lbs.)	2359	2403	2403	2403	2403
Whlbase (in.)	97.1	97	97.1	97.1	97.1
Price	7-9,000	9-11,000	10-12,000	11-13,000	14-16,000
OVERALL	Average	Good	Good	Vry. Gd.	Good

Geo Tracker 1992-97, Chevrolet Tracker 1998-2001, Suzuki Sidekick 1992-98

The Tracker, almost identical to the Suzuki Sidekick, is one of the smaller sport utility vehicles. The Tracker is available as a hardtop or convertible and only has 2 doors but can carry up to

1996 Geo Tracker

four people. Trackers haven't changed much since their introduction. All Trackers have conventional lap-shoulder belts in front. Airbags are not available on early models but come standard on the 1996 Tracker. 2-wheel ABS, available beginning in 1993, operates only on the rear wheels, but you can choose 4-wheel ABS starting in 1996.

Trackers have a 1.6-liter single-cam 4-cylinder, with either a stan-

	1992	1993	1994	1995	1996
Size Class	Sp. Util.	Sp. Util.	Sp. Util.	Sp. Util.	Sp. Util.
Drive	Rear/4	Rear/4	Rear/4	Rear/4	Rear/4
Crash Test	Vry. Pr.	Vry. Pr.	Vry. Pr.	Poor	Poor
Airbags	None	None	None	None	Dual
ABS	None	2-Whl	2-Whl	2-Whl	2-Whl[1]
Parts Cost	High	Vry. High	High	High	High
Complaints	Vry. Gd.	Vry. Gd.	Average	Average	Vry. Gd.
Insurance	Surchg.	Surchg.	Surchg.	Surchg.	Surchg.
Fuel Econ.	25	24	23	24	23
Theft Rating	High	Vry. High	Vry. High	Vry. High	Vry. High
Bumpers					
Recalls	0	2	4	0	2
Trn. Cir. (ft.)	32.2	32.2	32.2	32.2	32.2
Weight (lbs.)	2189	2270	2238	2246	2339
Whlbase (in.)	86.6	86.6	86.6	86.6	86.6
Price	<3,000	2-4,000	3-5,000	4-6,000	5-7,000
OVERALL	Vry. Pr.	Vry. Pr.	Vry. Pr.	Vry. Pr.	Poor

[1]Optional 4-Wheel; **Estimate

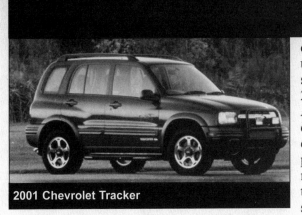

2001 Chevrolet Tracker

dard 5-speed manual or optional 3-speed automatic and 2- or 4-wheel drive. As with many subcompacts, the Tracker's fuel economy, performance, and noise improve with the 5-speed. Even so, the Tracker has poor acceleration. You'll find good handling and maneuverability, for a sport utility, with a stiff ride. Accommodations are OK in front for two, but tight for two in back. The instrument panel and controls are functional and simple. Along with the rest of the Geo lineup, the Tracker became a Chevrolet in 1998, when the Geo name was dropped.

	1997	1998	1999	2000	2001
Size Class	Sp. Util.	Sp. Util.	Sp. Util.	Sp. Util.	Sp. Util.
Drive	Rear/4	Rear/4	Rear/4	Rear/4	Rear/4
Crash Test	Poor	Poor	N/A	N/A	N/A
Airbags	Dual	Dual	Dual	Dual	Dual
ABS	2-Whl[1]	4-Whl*	4-Whl*	4-Whl*	4-Whl*
Parts Cost	Vry. High	Vry. High	Vry. High	Vry. High	Very Low
Complaints	Average	Vry. Pr.	Vry. Gd.	Average	Vry. Pr.
Insurance	Surchg.	Surchg.	Surchg.	Surchg.	Surchg.
Fuel Econ.	24	23	23	23	23
Theft Rating	Vry. High	Vry. High	Vry. High**	Vry. High**	Vry. High**
Bumpers					
Recalls	0	0	0	0	0
Trn. Cir. (ft.)	32.2	34.4	31.5	31.5	31.5
Weight (lbs.)	2339	2339	2596	2596	2596
Whlbase (in.)	86.6	86.6	86.6	86.6	86.6
Price	7-9,000	8-10,000	10-12,000	14-16,000	15-17,000
OVERALL	Vry. Pr.	Vry. Pr.			

Honda Accord 1992-2001

The Accord first showed up in American show-rooms almost 20 years ago. For the past decade, it has battled for the top sales spot with the Ford Taurus. The Accord has undergone a redesign for

1992 Honda Accord

the most part every four years since 1982. For 1996, Honda gave it a slightly redesigned front and rear, creating a more rounded appearance and the Accord received its most dramatic makeover in its 22-year history in 1998. At that time, changes were made to structure, engine, suspension, interior room and trunk space. Accord hatchbacks got door-mounted lap-shoulder belts in 1989; the 1990-92 coupes and sedans had

	1992	1993	1994	1995	1996
Size Class	Intermd.	Intermd.	Intermd.	Intermd.	Intermd.
Drive	Front	Front	Front	Front	Front
Crash Test	Vry. Gd.	Vry. Gd.[1]	Average	Average	Average
Airbags	Driver	Driver[#]	Dual	Dual	Dual
ABS	4-Whl*	4-Whl*	4-Whl*	4-Whl*	4-Whl*
Parts Cost	Low	Average	Average	Average	Average
Complaints	Good	Vry. Gd.	Good	Average	Vry. Gd.
Insurance	Regular	Regular	Regular	Regular	Regular
Fuel Econ.	22	22	23	25	25
Theft Rating	High	Vry. High	Vry. High	Vry. High	Average
Bumpers	Strong	Strong	Weak	Weak	Weak
Recalls	4	3	1	2	1
Trn. Cir. (ft.)	36.1	36.1	36.1	36.1	36.7
Weight (lbs.)	2733	2778	2800	2877	3219
Whlbase (in.)	107.1	107.1	106.9	106.9	106.9
Price	5-7,000	6-8,000	7-9,000	10-12,000	11-13,000
OVERALL	Good	Vry. Gd.[2]	Average	Average	Good

[1]Data given for model with driver airbag. Crash test for model with dual airbags is Good; [2]Data given for model with driver

2001 Honda Accord

motorized shoulder belts and manual lap belts. The 1991 wagons and all 1992-93 Accords have a driver's airbag and conventional belts; the 1993 SE sedan adds a passenger airbag. For 1994, all Accords have dual airbags. ABS became available in 1991.

The 4-cylinder engines are lively and, with the 5-speed, economical. Fuel-injected models (1989 LXi and all models from 1990 on) develop more power. The ride is comfortable and the Accord's instruments are superior. The Accord is competent and popular and a consistently good crash test performer.

	1997	1998	1999	2000	2001
Size Class	Intermd.	Intermd.	Intermd.	Intermd.	Intermd.
Drive	Front	Front	Front	Front	Front
Crash Test	Average	Good	Good	Good	Good
Airbags	Dual	Dual	Dual	Dual	Dual
ABS	4-Whl*	4-Whl*	4-Whl*	4-Whl*	4-Whl*
Parts Cost	High	Average	Average	Average	Average
Complaints	Vry. Gd.	Poor	Good	Average	Average
Insurance	Discount	Discount	Discount	Discount	Discount
Fuel Econ.	25	25	25	25	25
Theft Rating	Vry. High	Vry. High	Vry. High**	Vry. High**	Vry. High**
Bumpers	Weak				
Recalls	1	2	0	0	0
Trn. Cir. (ft.)	36.1	36.1	36.1	36.1	36.4
Weight (lbs.)	2855	2943	2943	3020	3031
Whlbase (in.)	106.9	106.9	105.1	106.9	106.9
Price	14-16,000	16-18,000	18-20,000	19-21,000	20-22,000
OVERALL	Vry. Gd.	Good	Vry. Gd.	Vry. Gd.	Vry. Gd.

airbag. Overall rating for model with dual airbags may vary based on footnote;*Optional; #Passenger Side Optional; **Estimate

Honda Civic 1992-2001

1992 Honda Civic

The Civic first appeared in the United States in 1973. There have been a lot of changes since then. Honda dropped the wagon and the sporty CRX from the redesigned 1992 lineup, but added a stylish coupe and the sporty targa-top del Sol for 1993. For 1996, the Civic was all-new, as Honda gave it a new look, a stronger body, and a firmer suspension. The 1990-91 hatchback coupes have door-mounted belts in front; other models have motorized shoulder belts and manual lap belts. In 1992, Civics got an optional driver airbag and regular front belts, which became standard for 1993. Dual airbags

	1992	1993	1994	1995	1996
Size Class	Subcomp.	Subcomp.	Subcomp.	Subcomp.	Subcomp.
Drive	Front	Front	Front	Front	Front
Crash Test	Average	Average	Average	Average	Vry. Gd.
Airbags	Driver*	Driver	Dual	Dual	Dual
ABS	4-Whl*	4-Whl*	4-Whl*	4-Whl*	4-Whl*
Parts Cost	Average	Average	Low	Average	Average
Complaints	Good	Vry. Gd.	Vry. Gd.	Good	Good
Insurance	Regular	Regular	Regular	Surchg.	Surchg.
Fuel Econ.	30	40	29	34	33
Theft Rating	Average	Vry. High	Average	High	High
Bumpers	Weak	Weak	Weak	Weak	Weak
Recalls	1	1	2	0	1
Trn. Cir. (ft.)	32.8	32.8	32.1	32.1	32.8
Weight (lbs.)	2094	2094	2108	2178	2262
Whlbase (in.)	101.3	101.3	101.3	101.3	103.2
Price	3-5,000	4-6,000	5-7,000	6-8,000	8-10,000
OVERALL	Good	Vry. Gd.	Vry. Gd.	Average	Vry. Gd.

*Optional; **Estimate

2001 Honda Civic

became standard on all models beginning in 1994. ABS is optional starting in 1992.

Honda claims the 1992-95 VX can deliver 55 mpg on the highway; other models aren't quite that economical, but in general, it is hard to do better than a Civic when it comes to fuel economy. The 5-speed shifts smoothly; the automatic isn't as pleasant. The rear seating is tight, especially in 2-doors. The ride is typical of subcompacts but, better from 1989 on. The Civic was all-new for 2001, gaining a new 1.7-liter engine and more interior space. The Civic ranks among the best subcompacts.

	1997	1998	1999	2000	2001
Size Class	Subcomp.	Subcomp.	Subcomp.	Subcomp.	Subcomp.
Drive	Front	Front	Front	Front	Front
Crash Test	Vry. Gd.	Vry. Gd.	Vry. Gd.	Vry. Gd.	Vry. Gd.
Airbags	Dual	Dual	Dual	Dual	Dual
ABS	4-Whl*	4-Whl*	4-Whl*	4-Whl*	4-Whl*
Parts Cost	Average	Vry. Low	Low	Low	Low
Complaints	Vry. Gd.	Good	Vry. Gd.	Vry. Gd.	Average
Insurance	Surchg.	Surchg.	Surchg.	Surchg.	Surchg.
Fuel Econ.	29	33	32	32	32
Theft Rating	Vry. High	Vry. High	Vry. High**	Vry. High**	Vry. High**
Bumpers	Weak	Weak			
Recalls	1	1	0	0	0
Trn. Cir. (ft.)	32.8	32.8	32.8	32.8	34.1
Weight (lbs.)	2238	2238	2339	2339	2421
Whlbase (in.)	103.2	103.2	103.2	103.2	103.1
Price	9-11,000	10-12,000	11-13,000	12-14,000	13-15,000
OVERALL	Vry. Gd.	Vry. Gd.	BEST BET	BEST BET	BEST BET

Honda Odyssey 2000-2001/Isuzu Oasis 1995-99

As is standard practice in the auto industry, automakers often sell each other's products as their own. In 1995, Honda introduced the Odyssey, an interesting as well as uniquely designed minivan, with high

1995 Honda Odyssey

hopes of cashing in on the hot-selling minivan market. Isuzu simply took the Odyssey and rebadged it into the Oasis. The Odyssey/Oasis is not a typical minivan. It is lower and narrower, making it easier to maneuver and handle. The low floor also makes it easier for kids to get in and out. Rather than sliding doors, the rear passengers used to have two sedan-type doors but now has two sliding doors as many of it competi-

	1992	1993	1994	1995	1996
Size Class				Minivan	Minivan
Drive				Front	Front
Crash Test				Good	Good
Airbags				Dual	Dual
ABS				4-Whl	4-Whl
Parts Cost		No Model Produced		Average	Vry. High
Complaints				Good	Good
Insurance				Discount	Discount
Fuel Econ.				20	21
Theft Rating				Average	Average
Bumpers					Weak
Recalls				0	0
Trn. Cir. (ft.)				37.6	37.6
Weight (lbs.)				3450	3473
Whlbase (in.)				111.4	111.4
Price				12-14,000	14-16,000
OVERALL				BEST BET	Vry. Gd.

**Estimate

2001 Honda Odyssey

tors. Dual airbags and ABS were standard from their introduction in 1995.

A standard 2.2-liter, 4-cylinder engine found on the Accord powers this minivan. Rumors of a V6 have been around for years, but it still isn't available. The Odyssey/Oasis performed well in government crash tests and comes with 5 mph bumpers. With a redesign in 1999, the Odyssey's new powerful 3.5-liter engine, full array of custom features, and interior size and space like other minivans has increased the popularity of this vehicle.

	1997	1998	1999	2000	2001
Size Class	Minivan	Minivan	Minivan	Minivan	Minivan
Drive	Front	Front	Front	Front	Front
Crash Test	Good	Good	Vry. Gd.	Vry. Gd.	Vry. Gd.
Airbags	Dual	Dual	Dual	Dual	Dual
ABS	4-Whl	4-Whl	4-Whl	4-Whl	4-Whl
Parts Cost	Vry. High	High	High	High	High
Complaints	Vry. Gd.	Average	Vry. Pr.	Vry. Pr.	Vry. Pr.
Insurance	Discount	Discount	Discount	Discount	Discount
Fuel Econ.	21	20	21	21	21
Theft Rating	Average	Average	Average**	Average**	Average**
Bumpers	Weak	Weak			
Recalls	0	0	1	4	0
Trn. Cir. (ft.)	37.6	37.6	37.7	37.7	37.7
Weight (lbs.)	3473	3450	4233	4233	4233
Whlbase (in.)	111.4	111.4	118.1	118.1	118.1
Price	16-18,000	18-20,000	23-25,000	24-26,000	25-27,000
OVERALL	Vry. Gd.	Good	Good	Good	Vry. Gd.

Honda Prelude 1992-2001

The Prelude is a combination sport/luxury coupe introduced to U.S. car buyers in 1979. The first Preludes were not much bigger than a Civic. In 1983, the Prelude grew in length, weight, wheelbase,

1992 Honda Prelude

and sales. In 1989, 4-wheel steering (4WS) was optional, but was dropped for 1995. For 1992, the Prelude received new, controversial styling with a strong GM influence on the dashboard and back end. In 1997, the Prelude was restyled and once again, its style was controversial. The 1992-93 models have a standard driver's airbag and optional passenger airbag (except S models). From 1994 on, models have stan-

	1992	1993	1994	1995	1996
Size Class	Compact	Compact	Compact	Compact	Compact
Drive	Front	Front	Front	Front	Front
Crash Test	Vry. Gd.	Vry. Gd.	Vry. Gd.	Vry. Gd.	Vry. Gd.
Airbags	Driver#	Driver#	Dual	Dual	Dual
ABS	4-Whl*	4-Whl*	4-Whl*	4-Whl*	4-Whl*
Parts Cost	Low	High	High	Vry. High	High
Complaints	Vry. Gd.	Vry. Gd.	Vry. Gd.	Vry. Gd.	Vry. Gd.
Insurance	Surchg.	Surchg.	Surchg.	Surchg.	Surchg.
Fuel Econ.	22	22	22	22	22
Theft Rating	High	Vry. High	Vry. High	Vry. High	Vry. High
Bumpers					
Recalls	0	0	0	0	0
Trn. Cir. (ft.)	34.8	34.8	35.9	35.9	35.9
Weight (lbs.)	2765	2765	2900	2866	2809
Whlbase (in.)	100.4	100.4	100.4	100.4	100.4
Price	6-8,000	7-9,000	8-10,000	11-13,000	13-15,000
OVERALL~	Good	Average	Good	Good	Good

*Optional; #Passenger Side Optional; **Estimate; ~Cars without crash tests do not receive an overall rating.

2001 Honda Prelude

dard dual airbags. ABS is optional from 1990 on.

The standard 4-cylinder is powerful enough, but if you want more horses, the Si and VTEC offer them. The Prelude's 5-speed is smooth, and automatic overdrive is excellent. While the handling is capable enough without 4-wheel steering, the ride is acceptably firm for a sporty coupe. The Prelude has just enough room for two; the rear seating is tiny. Pre-1992 Preludes have an easy to read instrument panel and well placed controls; however, the panel on 1992-96 Preludes is quite busy; the 1997 panel is better.

	1997	1998	1999	2000	2001
Size Class	Compact	Compact	Compact	Compact	Compact
Drive	Front	Front	Front	Front	Front
Crash Test	N/A	N/A	N/A	N/A	N/A
Airbags	Dual	Dual	Dual	Dual	Dual
ABS	4-Whl*	4-Whl*	4-Whl	4-Whl	4-Whl
Parts Cost	Vry. High	High	High	High	High
Complaints	Average	Poor	Good	Average	Average
Insurance	Surchg.	Surchg.	Surchg.	Surchg.	Surchg.
Fuel Econ.	22	22	22	22	22
Theft Rating	Vry. High	Vry. High	Vry. High**	Vry. High**	Vry. High**
Bumpers			Strong	Strong	Strong
Recalls	0	0	0	0	0
Trn. Cir. (ft.)	35.6	36.1	36.1	36.1	36.1
Weight (lbs.)	2954	2954	2954	2954	2954
Whlbase (in.)	101.8	101.8	101.8	101.8	101.8
Price	16-18,000	17-19,000	19-21,000	23-25,000	24-26,000
OVERALL~					

Hyundai Accent 1995-2001

1995 Hyundai Accent

If you are interested in an almost new subcompact and don't want to spend much, the Accent is the car for you. New Accents start around $9-10,000, so you should have little trouble finding an Accent to fit your budget. In 1995, Hyundai replaced the Excel with the Accent, a front wheel drive car with many improvements over the Excel. The Accent has more contemporary Civic-like styling with more interior room and horsepower than the aging Excel. Dual airbags are standard and ABS is optional.

A tiny 1.5-liter 4-cylinder engine is adequate to move this small car.

	1992	1993	1994	1995	1996
Size Class		No Model Produced		Subcomp.	Subcomp.
Drive				Front	Front
Crash Test				Average	Average
Airbags				Dual	Dual
ABS				4-Whl*	4-Whl*
Parts Cost				Low	Low
Complaints				Poor	Average
Insurance				Surchg.	Surchg.
Fuel Econ.				27	28
Theft Rating				Average	Average
Bumpers					
Recalls				4	3
Trn. Cir. (ft.)				31.8	31.8
Weight (lbs.)				2101	2101
Whlbase (in.)				94.5	94.5
Price				2-4,000	3-5,000
OVERALL~				Average	Average

*Optional; **Estimate; ~Cars without crash tests do not receive an overall rating.

2001 Hyundai Accent

Fuel economy is good, though not on par with misers like the Geo Metro. Compared to the Tercel, the Accent is just as powerful and roomy, but the Metro and Swift offer more interior room. Front seat passengers will be comfy in the Accent, but the back seat will be cramped for adults. The dashboard is rather bare, but this is a typical characteristic of inexpensive subcompacts. A redesign in 2000 improved the vehicle. It has an unbeatable 10-year/100,000 mile powertrain warranty along with second generation de-powered airbags and belt pretensioners to keep you safe.

	1997	1998	1999	2000	2001
Size Class	Subcomp.	Subcomp.	Subcomp.	Subcomp.	Subcomp.
Drive	Front	Front	Front	Front	Front
Crash Test	Average	Average	Average	N/A	N/A
Airbags	Dual	Dual	Dual	Dual	Dual
ABS	4-Whl*	4-Whl*	4-Whl*	4-Whl*	4-Whl*
Parts Cost	Low	Vry. Low	Vry. Low	Low	Low
Complaints	Average	Good	Good	Poor	Average
Insurance	Surchg.	Surchg.	Surchg.	Surchg.	Surchg.
Fuel Econ.	28	28	28	28	18
Theft Rating	Average	Vry. Low	Vry. Low	Vry. Low**	Average**
Bumpers			Strong	Strong	Strong
Recalls	2	0	0	2	0
Trn. Cir. (ft.)	31.8	31.8	31.8	31.8	31.8
Weight (lbs.)	2101	2101	2101	2240	2240
Whlbase (in.)	94.5	94.5	94.5	96.1	96.1
Price	4-6,000	5-7,000	7-9,000	8-10,000	9-11,000
OVERALL~	Average	Vry. Gd.	Vry. Gd.		

Hyundai Elantra 1992-2001

Around since 1992, the Elantra made its first real impact on the automotive world in 1996 with its first redesign since its inception. The 1996 redesign introduced a more rounded look and an improved

1992 Hyundai Elantra

interior. Pre-1996 models tend to feel outdated. Hyundai has positioned the Elantra between the cheaper Accent, the more expensive Sonata, and, new for 1997, the sporty Tiburon. Watch out for door-mounted lab/shoulder belts which appear in pre-1996 models. A drivers airbag first appears in 1994; dual airbags become standard in 1996 and side airbags are standard with the 2001 redesign. 4-wheel ABS is optional

	1992	1993	1994	1995	1996
Size Class	Compact	Compact	Compact	Compact	Compact
Drive	Front	Front	Front	Front	Front
Crash Test	Vry. Pr.	Vry. Pr.	Vry. Pr.	Vry. Pr.	Average
Airbags	None	None	Driver	Driver	Dual
ABS	None	None	4-Whl*	4-Whl*	4-Whl*
Parts Cost	Low	Low	Vry. Low	Vry. Low	Vry. Low
Complaints	Average	Good	Poor	Vry. Pr.	Poor
Insurance	Surchg.	Surchg.	Surchg.	Surchg.	Surchg.
Fuel Econ.	22	22	23	22	22
Theft Rating	Low	Low	Vry. Low	Low	Vry. Low
Bumpers					Weak
Recalls	0	0	2	1	1
Trn. Cir. (ft.)	33.8	33.8	33.8	34	34
Weight (lbs.)	2452	2452	2540	2500	2458
Whlbase (in.)	98.4	98.4	98.4	98.4	100.4
Price	<3,000	2-4,000	2-4,000	3-5,000	4-6,000
OVERALL	Vry. Pr.	Vry. Pr.	Vry. Pr.	Vry. Pr.	Average

*Optional

2001 Hyundai Elantra

starting in 1994.

1992-95 models come standard with a 1.6-liter 4-cylinder engine, which delivers adequate power with average fuel economy. The optional 1.8-liter engine on these models is slightly more powerful. Starting in 1996, only the 1.8-liter engine is available which has been refined and does a better job. You will be able to find the Elantra in either a sedan or wagon version and there are plenty of optional features. All-new for 2001, a longer wheelbase should make for a smother ride and space for more comfort inside.

	1997	1998	1999	2000	2001
Size Class	Compact	Compact	Compact	Compact	Compact
Drive	Front	Front	Front	Front	Front
Crash Test	Average	Average	Average	Good	Vry. Gd.
Airbags	Dual	Dual	Dual	Dual	Dual/Side
ABS	4-Whl*	4-Whl*	4-Whl*	4-Whl*	4-Whl*
Parts Cost	Low	Vry. Low	Vry. Low	Low	Low
Complaints	Poor	Poor	Average	Average	Average
Insurance	Surchg.	Surchg.	Surchg.	Surchg.	Surchg.
Fuel Econ.	24	24	24	24	25
Theft Rating	Vry. Low	Vry. Low	Vry. Low	Average	Average
Bumpers	Weak	Weak	Strong	Strong	Strong
Recalls	1	0	1	2	1
Trn. Cir. (ft.)	32.5	32.5	32.5	32.5	37.5
Weight (lbs.)	2458	2458	2458	2458	2635
Whlbase (in.)	100.4	100.4	100.4	100.4	102.7
Price	5-7,000	7-9,000	9-11,000	10-12,000	11-13,000
OVERALL	Average	Good	Good	Vry. Gd.	

Hyundai Excel 1992-94

The Excel was the first Korean-made automobile sold in the U.S. market. It initially sold well and so didn't change that much since its debut; however, it was replaced early in the 1995 model

1992 Hyundai Excel

year by the sleeker, roomier, and more powerful Accent. The Excel got new exterior sheet metal for 1990, but retained the look of the earlier models. Airbags and ABS aren't available.

The Excel is powered by a 1.5-liter 4, carbureted in pre-1990 cars, fuel injected after that. Power is merely adequate. The Excel suffers badly in quality and reliability when compared to its rivals. Ride is

	1992	1993	1994	1995	1996
Size Class	Subcomp.	Subcomp.	Subcomp.		
Drive	Front	Front	Front		
Crash Test	Good[1]	Good[1]	Good[1]		
Airbags	None	None	None		
ABS	None	None	None		
Parts Cost	Vry. Low	Low	Vry. Low		
Complaints	Average	Good	Good		
Insurance	Surchg.	Surchg.	Surchg.		
Fuel Econ.	28	29	27	No Model Produced	
Theft Rating	Low	Vry. Low	Vry. Low		
Bumpers	Weak	Weak	Weak		
Recalls	1	1	2		
Trn. Cir. (ft.)	31.7	31.7	31.7		
Weight (lbs.)	2202	2147	2147		
Whlbase (in.)	93.8	93.8	93.8		
Price	<3,000	<3,000	<3,000		
OVERALL	Average[2]	Average[2]	Average[2]		

[1]Data given for sedan. Crash test for coupe for 1992-94 is Vry. Good; [2]Data given for sedan. Overall rating for coupe may

1993 Hyundai Excel

worse than other small cars. Handling is sloppy, not what you'd expect from a subcompact. Rear seating is tight for adults and very uncomfortable for more than short trips. Because of rapid depreciation, the price of an Excel will undoubtedly be attractive, but it makes sense to consider something else.

	1997	1998	1999	2000	2001
Size Class					
Drive					
Crash Test					
Airbags					
ABS					
Parts Cost					
Complaints			No Model Produced		
Insurance					
Fuel Econ.					
Theft Rating					
Bumpers					
Recalls					
Trn. Cir. (ft.)					
Weight (lbs.)					
Whlbase (in.)					
Price					
OVERALL					

vary based on footnote.

Hyundai Scoupe 1992-95

The Scoupe is Hyundai's sportiest model, though that's a relative term. In reality, the Scoupe is a coupe body on an Excel chassis; it's an economy car with sporty styling, and it competes more

1992 Hyundai Scoupe

with the Toyota Paseo and Mazda MX-3 than with higher-priced sport coupes like the Nissan 240SX and Toyota Celica. Like other Hyundais, the Scoupe emphasizes a long list of standard features in a low-priced package, rather than state-of-the-art performance or safety features. The Scoupe's passive restraints are door-mounted shoulder belts with separate lap belts.

	1992	1993	1994	1995	1996
Size Class	Subcomp.	Subcomp.	Subcomp.	Subcomp.	
Drive	Front	Front	Front	Front	
Crash Test	Good	Good	Good	Good	
Airbags	None	None	None	None	
ABS	None	None	None	None	
Parts Cost	Low	Low	Vry. Low	Vry. Low	
Complaints	Average	Good	Average	Vry. Gd.	
Insurance	Surchg.	Surchg.	Surchg.	Surchg.	
Fuel Econ.	25	26	27	27	
Theft Rating	Average	Vry. Low	Average	Average	
Bumpers	Weak	Weak	Weak	Weak	
Recalls	0	0	0	0	
Trn. Cir. (ft.)	31.7	31.7	31.7	31.7	
Weight (lbs.)	2119	2217	2176	2176	
Whlbase (in.)	93.8	93.8	93.8	93.8	
Price	<3,000	<3,000	<3,000	2-4,000	
OVERALL	Poor	Average	Average	Good	

No Model Produced

1995 Hyundai Scoupe

Acceleration can be slow with the Scoupe's base engine, but fuel economy is good. The turbo option trades off better acceleration for worse gas mileage. The 5-speed is a more pleasant choice for this car than the automatic. Handling is OK, not as crisp as a true sports coupe's, and the ride tends to be jittery and unpleasant. The accommodations in the front are comfortable for two, and adults won't like the Scoupe's rear seat. The dashboard is fine, and the trunk space is good. Because of the lack of safety features and the presence of door mounted seat belts, the Scoupe doesn't stand out as a good choice.

	1997	1998	1999	2000	2001
Size Class					
Drive					
Crash Test					
Airbags					
ABS					
Parts Cost					
Complaints					
Insurance					
Fuel Econ.					
Theft Rating		No Model Produced			
Bumpers					
Recalls					
Trn. Cir. (ft.)					
Weight (lbs.)					
Whlbase (in.)					
Price					
OVERALL					

Hyundai Sonata 1992-2001

The Sonata, Hyundai's mid-size car, went six years without a major change—an unusually long time in this competitive market. The 1995 Sonata, new from the ground up, re-

1992 Hyundai Sonata

placed the old model in the spring of 1994 and brought with it more contemporary styling and a longer wheelbase that translates into more legroom. The Sonata, unfortunately, has motorized front shoulder belts and separate lap belts as passive restraints in lieu of airbags through 1994; the 1995 model finally gets dual airbags, but you're still stuck with motorized belts. And to get ABS, available beginning in 1992,

	1992	1993	1994	1995	1996
Size Class	Compact	Compact	Compact	Intermd.	Intermd.
Drive	Front	Front	Front	Front	Front
Crash Test	Poor	Poor	Poor	Average	Average
Airbags	None	None	None	Dual	Dual
ABS	4-Whl*	4-Whl*	4-Whl*	4-Whl*	4-Whl*
Parts Cost	Average	Vry. Low	Vry. Low	Vry. Low	Low
Complaints	Poor	Vry. Pr.	Vry. Gd.	Vry. Pr.	Average
Insurance	Surchg.	Surchg.	Surchg.	Surchg.	Surchg.
Fuel Econ.	20	20	20	21	22
Theft Rating	Average	High	Low	Low	Vry. High
Bumpers	Weak	Weak	Weak	Weak	Weak
Recalls	1	1	1	2	1
Trn. Cir. (ft.)	35.7	35.7	35.7	34.6	34.6
Weight (lbs.)	2723	2723	2850	2864	2964
Whlbase (in.)	104.3	104.3	104.3	106.3	106.3
Price	<3,000	2-4,000	3-5,000	4-6,000	5-7,000
OVERALL	Vry. Pr.	Vry. Pr.	Average	Poor	Average

*Optional; **Estimate

2001 Hyundai Sonata

you'll have to look for the more expensive GL or GLS models. For 2001, side airbags become standard as well.

The Sonata is Hyundai's most competent model but still falls several notches below the really good mid-size cars. Ride isn't as smooth or quiet as on other mid-size cars; handling, though, is pretty good. Interior room and comfort are good—comparable to other mid-size cars. Thicker glass and a redesigned cabin contribute to a quieter ride for the 2001 model year. Trunk space is adequate; the dashboard is easy to use.

	1997	1998	1999	2000	2001
Size Class	Intermd.	Intermd.	Intermd.	Intermd.	Intermd.
Drive	Front	Front	Front	Front	Front
Crash Test	Average	Average	Average	Average	N/A
Airbags	Dual	Dual	Dual	Dual	Dual
ABS	4-Whl*	4-Whl*	4-Whl*	4-Whl*	4-Whl*
Parts Cost	Low	Low	Low	Low	Low
Complaints	Good	Poor	Average	Good	Average
Insurance	Surchg.	Surchg.	Surchg.	Surchg.	Surchg.
Fuel Econ.	21	21	21	21	21
Theft Rating	Low	Average**	Average**	Average**	Average**
Bumpers	Weak		Strong	Strong	Strong
Recalls	1	0	2	1	0
Trn. Cir. (ft.)	34.6	34.6	34.6	34.6	34.6
Weight (lbs.)	2935	2935	2935	3072	3072
Whlbase (in.)	106.3	106.3	106.3	106.3	106.3
Price	7-9,000	8-10,000	11-13,000	13-15,000	16-18,000
OVERALL	Average	Average	Average	Good	

Infiniti G20 1992-96, 1999-2001

Styling is pretty bland on the G20 compared to the other Infiniti models, but it's certainly on par with its American competitors. A bargain-basement Infiniti at about the price of other companies'

1992 Infiniti G20

mid-range offerings, the G20 is clearly less of a status symbol, and, if you can live without the nameplate, you might want to consider a Nissan Sentra with all the options for less money. If you buy an early G20, you'll be stuck with motorized belts and no airbags; conventional belts and dual airbags became standard mid-way through the 1993 model year. ABS has been standard throughout the G20's history. Side airbags

	1992	1993	1994	1995	1996
Size Class	Compact	Compact	Compact	Compact	Compact
Drive	Front	Front	Front	Front	Front
Crash Test	N/A	N/A	N/A	N/A	N/A
Airbags	Dual	Dual	Dual	Dual	Dual
ABS	4-Whl	4-Whl	4-Whl	4-Whl	4-Whl
Parts Cost	Low	Low	Low	High	Average
Complaints	Vry. Gd.	Good	Vry. Gd.	Good	Good
Insurance	Regular	Regular	Regular	Regular	Discount
Fuel Econ.	22	22	22	24	24
Theft Rating	Average	Average	Average	Average	Average
Bumpers					
Recalls	2	3	2	1	1
Trn. Cir. (ft.)	35.4	35.4	35.4	35.4	35.4
Weight (lbs.)	2745	2745	2877	2877	2877
Whlbase (in.)	100.4	100.4	100.4	100.4	100.4
Price	5-7,000	6-8,000	7-9,000	8-10,000	10-12,000
OVERALL~					

**Estimate; ~Cars without crash tests do not receive an overall rating.

184

2001 Infiniti G20

became standard in 1999.

The G20 shares its 4-cylinder 140 hp engine with the Sentra SE; you'll probably be happier with the 5-speed manual transmission than with the 4-speed automatic, and you'll get better mileage. Ride is firm and handling can be a bit challenging in sudden high-speed maneuvers, but otherwise it's predictable and responsive. The instrument panel is a pleasure to use, but the car is small for four adults. The added features, such as an excellent warranty, make this car fairly attractive. If you do choose a G20, stick with the 1993 and later models that have airbags and conventional belts.

	1997	1998	1999	2000	2001
Size Class			Compact	Compact	Compact
Drive			Front	Front	Front
Crash Test			N/A	N/A	N/A
Airbags			Dual/Side	Dual/Side	Dual/Side
ABS			4-Whl	4-Whl	4-Whl
Parts Cost			High	Average	High
Complaints			Vry. Gd.	Vry. Gd.	Vry. Gd.
Insurance			Regular	Regular	Regular
Fuel Econ.			23	23	24
Theft Rating			Average**	Average**	Average**
Bumpers				Strong	Strong
Recalls			0	0	0
Trn. Cir. (ft.)			37.4	37.4	37.4
Weight (lbs.)			2913	2913	2913
Whlbase (in.)			102.4	102.4	102.4
Price			18-20,000	19-21,000	22-24,000
OVERALL~					

No Model Produced

Infiniti I30 1996-2001

In 2000, the all-new second generation I30 has a revised version of the 3.0 liter V6 that produces 227 horsepower. The exterior has new styling, including increased dimensions, and interior is all-new as well.

1996 Infiniti I30

In addition to standard ABS and driver and front passenger airbags and side airbags, there is now head protection. It also has rear child seat tethers, which ensure your child seat is secured properly. The optional navigation system is 3-D and rises from the dash for easy visibility. Essentially an upscale Nissan Maxima, the I30 received minor changes through 1998-99. If you can live without the name plate, con-

	1992	1993	1994	1995	1996
Size Class					Large
Drive					Front
Crash Test					Average
Airbags					Dual
ABS					4-Whl
Parts Cost					Vry. High
Complaints					Vry. Gd.
Insurance					Surchg.
Fuel Econ.		No Model Produced			21
Theft Rating					Vry. High
Bumpers					
Recalls					0
Trn. Cir. (ft.)					34.8
Weight (lbs.)					3090
Whlbase (in.)					106.3
Price					14-16,000
OVERALL~					Average

~Cars without crash tests do not receive an overall rating.

2001 Infiniti I30

sider a fully-loaded Maxima and save a couple thousand dollars.

	1997	1998	1999	2000	2001
Size Class	Large	Large	Large	Large	Large
Drive	Front	Front	Front	Front	Front
Crash Test	Average	Good	Good	Good	Good
Airbags	Dual	Dual/Side	Dual/Side	Dual/Side	Dual/Side
ABS	4-Whl	4-Whl	4-Whl	4-Whl	4-Whl
Parts Cost	Vry High	Vry High	Vry High	Vry High	Vry High
Complaints	Vry. Gd.	Average	Vry. Gd.	Average	Average
Insurance	Surchg	Surchg	Surchg	Surchg	Surchg
Fuel Econ.	21	21	21	20	18
Theft Rating	Vry High	Vry High	Vry High	Vry High	Vry High
Bumpers			Strong	Strong	Strong
Recalls	0	0	0	0	0
Trn. Cir. (ft.)	34.8	34.8	34.8	35.4	35.4
Weight (lbs.)	3090	3090	3150	3342	3342
Whlbase (in.)	106.3	106.3	106.3	108.3	108.3
Price	16-18,000	18-20,000	21-23,000	29-31,000	>30,000
OVERALL~	Average	Average	Good	Good	Good

Infiniti Q45 1992-2001

The Q45 is Infiniti's biggest and most impressive model. Along with the ill-fated M30 coupe, the Q45 was among Infiniti's first ventures in 1990 as the premium car division of Nissan, and the

1992 Infinit Q45

Q45 continues to be Infiniti's flagship, the model in which they've invested their future. The Q45 got a new front end treatment, including a small, chrome grille in 1995, and it was all-new for 1997. All Q45 models have a driver's airbag and ABS is standard. The 1994 models added a passenger airbag.

The Q45's 4.5-liter 272 hp V8 with automatic overdrive accelerates

	1992	1993	1994	1995	1996
Size Class	Large	Large	Large	Large	Large
Drive	Rear	Rear	Rear	Rear	Rear
Crash Test	N/A	N/A	N/A	N/A	N/A
Airbags	Driver	Driver	Dual	Dual	Dual
ABS	4-Whl	4-Whl	4-Whl	4-Whl	4-Whl
Parts Cost	High	Vry. High	High	High	High
Complaints	Poor	Vry. Gd.	Poor	Vry. Gd.	Good
Insurance	Discount	Discount	Discount	Discount	Discount
Fuel Econ.	16	17	17	17	17
Theft Rating	High	High	Vry. High	Vry. High	Vry. High
Bumpers					
Recalls	0	0	0	0	0
Trn. Cir. (ft.)	37.3	37.4	37.4	37.4	37.4
Weight (lbs.)	3950	3929	4039	4039	4039
Whlbase (in.)	113.2	113.2	113.2	113.4	113.4
Price	12-14,000	13-15,000	14-16,000	16-18,000	19-21,000
OVERALL~					

**Estimate; ~Cars without crash tests do not receive an overall rating.

2001 Infiniti Q45

rapidly, but gulps enough fuel to qualify for a hefty gas guzzler tax. New models have a slightly smaller and less powerful 4.1-liter engine. The Q45 comes with just about everything you could imagine; you can find cars with active suspension (Q45a), a touring package (Q45t), or traction control, which is worth looking for. Handling is excellent. The Q45 accommodates two sumptuously; people in back may not be quite as pleased. The ride is generally smooth, but more sensitive than most other luxury cars.

	1997	1998	1999	2000	2001
Size Class	Large	Large	Large	Large	Large
Drive	Rear	Rear	Rear	Rear	Rear
Crash Test	N/A	N/A	N/A	N/A	N/A
Airbags	Dual	Dual/Side	Dual/Side	Dual/Side	Dual/Side
ABS	4-Whl	4-Whl	4-Whl	4-Whl	4-Whl
Parts Cost	Vry. High	Vry. High	Vry. High	Vry. High	Vry. High
Complaints	Vry. Gd.	Vry. Gd.	Vry. Gd.	Vry. Gd.	Vry. Gd.
Insurance	Regular	Regular	Regular	Regular	Regular
Fuel Econ.	18	18	17	17	17
Theft Rating	Vry. High	Vry. High**	Vry. High**	Vry. High**	Vry. High**
Bumpers	Weak	Weak			
Recalls	1	0	0	0	0
Trn. Cir. (ft.)	36.1	36.1	36.1	36.1	36.1
Weight (lbs.)	3879	3879	4007	4007	4007
Whlbase (in.)	111.4	111.4	111.4	111.4	111.4
Price	23-25,000	29-31,000	>30,000	>30,000	>30,000
OVERALL~					

Isuzu Amigo 1992-95, 1998-99

Based on the Isuzu pickup chassis, this 2-door sport utility has changed little since its introduction in 1989. From the doors forward, it is identical to the pickup, but the rear is chopped off and

1995 Isuzu Amigo

the partial hardtop roof ends with a soft top portion above the rear seats/cargo area. The Amigo lagged behind its competition by never offering airbags. ABS was added in 1993, but only on the rear wheels.

The Amigo weighs a lot for such a small vehicle, so the 2.6-liter 4-cylinder engine has a lot of work to do. As a result, gas mileage suffers. Because of the Amigo's short wheelbase, the ride is rougher than oth-

	1992	1993	1994	1995	1996
Size Class	Sp. Util.	Sp. Util.	Sp. Util.	Sp. Util.	
Drive	Rear/4	Rear/4	Rear/4	Rear/4	
Crash Test	Poor	Poor	Poor	Poor	
Airbags	None	None	None	None	
ABS	None	2-Whl	2-Whl	2-Whl	
Parts Cost	Vry. Low	Vry. Low	Vry. Low	Vry. Low	
Complaints	Vry. Gd.	Vry. Gd.	Vry. Gd.	Good	
Insurance	Surchg.	Surchg.	Surchg.	Surchg.	
Fuel Econ.	16	18	16	16	
Theft Rating	High	Vry. High	Vry. High	Vry. High	
Bumpers					
Recalls	0	0	1	0	
Trn. Cir. (ft.)	33.5	33.5	33.5	33.5	
Weight (lbs.)	2905	2905	2905	2905	
Whlbase (in.)	91.7	91.7	91.7	91.7	
Price	4-6,000	5-7,000	6-8,000	7-9,000	
OVERALL~	Poor	Poor	Poor	Poor	

No Model Produced

~Cars without crash tests do not receive an overall rating.**Estimate

er Isuzu light trucks. Handling is pretty good, but take those corners slowly. The instrument panel is poorly-designed with too many buttons and knobs. Being a relatively tall vehicle with a narrow

1999 Isuzu Amigo

track width, the Amigo is quite unstable—so be careful. Overall, you can find a much better vehicle to spend your money on.

	1997	1998	1999	2000	2001
Size Class		Sp. Util.	Sp. Util.		
Drive		Rear/4	Rear/4		
Crash Test		N/A	N/A		
Airbags		Dual	Dual		
ABS		4-Whl	4-Whl		
Parts Cost		Average	Average		
Complaints		Vry Poor	Average		
Insurance		Surchg.	Surchg.		
Fuel Econ.		20	20		
Theft Rating		Vry. High	Vry. High**		
Bumpers					
Recalls		4	0		
Trn. Cir. (ft.)		34.1	34.1		
Weight (lbs.)		3329	3329		
Whlbase (in.)		96.9	96.9		
Price		12-14,000	14-16,000		
OVERALL~					

No Model Produced (1997)

No Model Produced (2000-2001)

Isuzu Rodeo 1992-2001, Honda Passport 1994-2001

The Passport, which represents Honda's first entry in the highly competitive U.S. sport utility market, is basically a Rodeo. These sport utilities are intended to compete with vehicles like the Jeep

1999 Honda Passport

Grand Cherokee, but they always seem to be a step behind. These twins had no airbags until 1996, and have performed poorly in government crash tests until recently. ABS is standard beginning in 1992, but only on the rear wheels. In 1996 and 1997, you have to pay extra for 4-wheel ABS.

Available in 2- or 4-wheel drive and with automatic or manual trans-

	1992	1993	1994	1995	1996
Size Class	Sp. Util.	Sp. Util.	Sp. Util.	Sp. Util.	Sp. Util.
Drive	Rear/4	Rear/4	Rear/4	Rear/4	Rear/4
Crash Test	Poor	Poor	Poor	Poor	Average
Airbags	None	None	None	None	Dual
ABS	2-Whl	2-Whl	2-Whl	2-Whl	2-Whl[1]
Parts Cost	Low	Low	Low	Low	Vry. Low
Complaints	Vry. Pr.	Good	Good	Poor	Average
Insurance	Regular	Regular	Regular	Surchrg.	Surchrg.
Fuel Econ.	14	18	16	16	16
Theft Rating	Average	Average	High	Average	Average
Bumpers					Weak
Recalls	0	1	4	2	0
Trn. Cir. (ft.)	37.7	37.7	37.7	37.7	37.7
Weight (lbs.)	3535	3470	3490	3545	3593
Whlbase (in.)	108.7	108.7	108.7	108.7	108.7
Price	5-7,000	6-8,000	7-9,000	9-11,000	10-12,000
OVERALL	Vry. Pr.	Poor	Vry. Pr.	Vry. Pr.	Average

[1]Optional 4-Wheel ABS; *Optional; **Estimate

2001 Isuzu Rodeo

mission, the ride and handling are adequate. 2-wheel drive models come with a standard in-line 4-cylinder that is not powerful enough, even with only two passengers aboard. The 4-wheel drive models are better equipped with a more powerful V6. The sloping roof cuts down on cargo space and there is a lot of interior noise. Neither the Rodeo or Passport is a strong competitor against Jeep Grand Cherokee or later Ford Expeditions and Explorers.

	1997	1998	1999	2000	2001
Size Class	Sp. Util.	Sp. Util.	Sp. Util.	Sp. Util.	Sp. Util.
Drive	Rear/4	Rear/4	Rear/4	Rear/4	Rear/4
Crash Test	Average	Average	Average	Average	Average
Airbags	Dual	Dual	Dual	Dual	Dual
ABS	2-Whl[1]	4-Whl*	4-Whl	4-Whl	4-Whl
Parts Cost	High	High	High	Very Low	Low
Complaints	Good	Vry. Pr.	Vry. Pr.	Vry. Gd.	Vry. Pr.
Insurance	Regular	Regular	Regular	Regular	Regular
Fuel Econ.	16	16	16	16	17
Theft Rating	Average	High**	High**	High**	Average
Bumpers	Weak				
Recalls	0	4	0	0	0
Trn. Cir. (ft.)	37.7	38.4	38.4	38.4	38.4
Weight (lbs.)	3705	3860	3860	3848	3848
Whlbase (in.)	108.7	106.4	106.4	106.4	106.4
Price	12-14,000	14-16,000	14-16,000	17-19,000	20-22,000
OVERALL	Average	Vry. Pr.	Poor	Vry. Gd.	Average

Isuzu Trooper 1992-2001, Trooper II 1992

The Trooper is the original and largest sport utility vehicle. In 1992, the Trooper was re-designed, but only came as a 4-door; though Isuzu did introduce the 2-door for 1993. Troopers didn't have

1993 Isuzu Trooper

airbags or passive belts through 1994, but 1995 and later models have dual airbags, a welcome addition. Rear brakes on 1991 and later models have ABS; 4-wheel ABS is available on certain Troopers beginning in 1994, standard in 1997.

The regular 4-cylinder or turbo-diesel engines struggle with any significant load. A V6, first offered in 1989, provides more power. With

	1992	1993	1994	1995	1996
Size Class	Sp. Util.	Sp. Util.	Sp. Util.	Sp. Util.	Sp. Util.
Drive	All	All	All	All	All
Crash Test	Poor	Poor	Poor	Average	Average
Airbags	None	None	None	Dual	Dual
ABS	2-Whl	2-Whl	4-Whl*	4-Whl*	4-Whl*
Parts Cost	Average	High	Low	Low	Average
Complaints	Average	Average	Average	Poor	Poor
Insurance	Regular	Regular	Discount	Regular	Discount
Fuel Econ.	16	15	15	15	16
Theft Rating	Average	Low	Average	Average	Average
Bumpers					
Recalls	1	1	1	0	4
Trn. Cir. (ft.)	34.1	32.8	32.8	32.8	38.1
Weight (lbs.)	4155	4210	4155	4060	4315
Whlbase (in.)	91.71	91.71	91.71	91.71	91.71
Price	7-9,000	8-10,000	9-11,000	11-13,000	14-16,000
OVERALL	Vry. Pr.	Vry. Pr.	Average	Average	Average

*Optional; **Estimate

2001 Isuzu Trooper

the 1992 weight increase to over two tons, the V6, even the twin-cam version, is barely enough. It is no surprise that gas mileage is poor with the V6. Engines come with 5-speed manual or automatic overdrive, and part-time 4-wheel drive. The handling is worse than average for sport utility vehicles. The ride is poor on all Troopers, but fairly quiet on newer models. Like many sport utilities, the high center of gravity may increase the likelihood of rollover in certain maneuvers. It has not been crash tested.

	1997	1998	1999	2000	2001
Size Class	Sp. Util.	Sp. Util.	Sp. Util.	Sp. Util.	Sp. Util.
Drive	Front/All	Front/All	Front/All	Front/All	Front/All
Crash Test	Average	Average	N/A	N/A	N/A
Airbags	Dual	Dual	Dual	Dual	Dual
ABS	4-Whl	4-Whl	4-Whl	4-Whl	4-Whl
Parts Cost	Vry. High	Vry. High	Vry. High	Vry. High	Vry. High
Complaints	Vry. Gd.	Good	Good	Vry. Gd.	Good
Insurance	Discount	Discount	Discount	Discount	Discount
Fuel Econ.	14	16	16	16	16
Theft Rating	Average	Average**	Average**	Average**	Average**
Bumpers					
Recalls	4	1	0	1	0
Trn. Cir. (ft.)	38.1	38.1	38.1	38.1	38.1
Weight (lbs.)	4315	4540	4540	4465	4465
Whlbase (in.)	91.71	108.7	108.7	108.7	108.7
Price	15-17,000	16-18,000	18-20,000	20-22,000	27-29,000
OVERALL	Average	Good			

Jeep Cherokee 1992-2001

These models, first introduced in 1984, pioneered and popularized 4-door sport-utility vehicles. Original-ly slated to be re-placed by the mod-ern Grand Chero-kee in 1993, Jeep decided to keep

1996 Jeep Cherokee

both models around, and the Cherokee has carried on. For 1997, the Cherokee is all-new with a freshened appearance. A driver airbag fi-nally became available on the 1995 Jeep Cherokee; dual airbags are standard for 1997. ABS became available after 1991, but it may be hard to find on cheaper trim lines.

The standard engine is a slow but economical 2.5-liter 4-cylinder. A

	1992	1993	1994	1995	1996
Size Class	Sp. Util.	Sp. Util.	Sp. Util.	Sp. Util.	Sp. Util.
Drive	Rear/4	Rear/4	Rear/4	Rear/4	Rear/4
Crash Test	Average	Average	Average	Good	Good
Airbags	None	None	None	Driver	Driver
ABS	4-Whl*	4-Whl*	4-Whl*	4-Whl*	4-Whl*
Parts Cost	Vry. Low	Vry. Low	Vry. Low	Vry. Low	Vry. Low
Complaints	Average	Vry. Pr.	Vry. Pr.	Vry. Pr.	Poor
Insurance	Discount	Regular	Regular	Regular	Discount
Fuel Econ.	17	17	15	17	19
Theft Rating	High	Vry. High	Vry. High	High	Vry.High
Bumpers					
Recalls	2	3	3	4	4
Trn. Cir. (ft.)	35.9	35.9	35.9	35.9	35.9
Weight (lbs.)	2808	2808	2932	2932	2905
Whlbase (in.)	101.4	101.4	101.4	101.4	101.4
Price	3-5,000	4-6,000	5-7,000	7-9,000	9-11,000
OVERALL	Average	Vry. Pr.	Vry. Pr.	Average	Good

*Optional; **Estimate

2001 Jeep Cherokee

2.8-liter V6 was optional for several years, but it was replaced in 1989 with a 4-liter 6. In 2001, you have the option of buying the Cherokee with the 4-liter inline-6 offered on the Grand Cherokee. With either engine, you can find a 5-speed manual or an automatic, and you can choose between a 2-wheel drive or two 4-wheel drive systems. Handling is pretty good for a sport utility vehicle, but the ride is stiff and bumpy except on the smoothest roads. The Cherokee has some virtues in basic form, particularly the low price. The Cherokee is being phased out and may be replaced for the 2002 model year.

	1997	1998	1999	2000	2001
Size Class	Sp. Util.	Sp. Util.	Sp. Util.	Sp. Util.	Sp. Util.
Drive	Rear/4	Rear/4	Rear/4	Rear/4	Rear/4
Crash Test	Poor	Poor	Poor	Poor	Poor
Airbags	Dual	Dual	Dual	Dual	Dual
ABS	4-Whl*	4-Whl*	4-Whl*	4-Whl*	4-Whl*
Parts Cost	Low	Vry. Low	Vry. Low	Vry. Low	Vry. Low
Complaints	Poor	Poor	Poor	Average	Average
Insurance	Discount	Discount	Discount	Discount	Discount
Fuel Econ.	19	19	19	19	19
Theft Rating	Vry. High	Vry. High	Vry. High**	Vry. High**	Vry. High**
Bumpers					
Recalls	3	2	0	0	1
Trn. Cir. (ft.)	35.9	35.1	35.1	35.1	35.1
Weight (lbs.)	2947	3150	3150	3150	3150
Whlbase (in.)	101.4	101.4	101.4	101.4	101.4
Price	10-12,000	12-14,000	14-16,000	15-17,000	20-22,000
OVERALL	Average	Good	Good	Vry. Gd.	Vry. Gd.

Jeep Grand Cherokee 1993-2001

The Jeep Grand Cherokee, one of the better sport utilities on the market, was originally scheduled to replace the Cherokee. With its redesign in 1993, it was given rounded corners, a better

1993 Jeep Grand Cherokee

suspension, and a more modern interior design than the boxy, rough-and-tumble Cherokee. It was introduced in the spring of 1992 as a 1993 model, but did not end up replacing the Cherokee. A driver's airbag and 4-wheel ABS became standard with the 1993 redesign. Starting in 1996, dual airbags are standard.

The 1989-91 models came standard with a powerful 5.9-liter V8. The

	1992	1993	1994	1995	1996
Size Class		Sp. Util.	Sp. Util.	Sp. Util.	Sp. Util.
Drive		Rear/4	Rear/4	Rear/4	Rear/4
Crash Test		Average	Average	Average	Average
Airbags		Driver	Driver	Driver	Dual
ABS		4-Whl	4-Whl	4-Whl	4-Whl
Parts Cost	No Model Produced	Low	Average	Vry. Low	Vry. Low
Complaints		Poor	Poor	Average	Average
Insurance		Regular	Regular	Regular	Discount
Fuel Econ.		16	15	15	15
Theft Rating		Vry. High	Vry. High	Vry. High	Vry. High
Bumpers					Weak
Recalls		7	1	2	3
Trn. Cir. (ft.)		36.6	36.6	36.6	36.6
Weight (lbs.)		3449	3530	3567	3614
Whlbase (in.)		105.9	105.9	105.9	105.9
Price		7-9,000	8-10,000	10-12,000	13-15,000
OVERALL		Vry. Pr.	Vry. Pr.	Average	Good

**Estimate

2001 Jeep Grand Cherokee

1993-97 Grand Cherokees have a powerful 4-liter 190 hp engine or an optional 5.2-liter 220 hp V8 with automatic overdrive. The larger engine is ideal for towing. Because its body is one single unit, rather than the body-on-frame approach other sport utilities are based on, the Grand Cherokee has a more solid feel to it. All Grand Cherokees/Grand Wagoneers are available in both rear- and 4-wheel drive, and Jeep gives you three different 4-wheel drive systems to meet your demands. Gas mileage is about what you'd expect from a sport utility vehicle, and cargo room is adequate.

	1997	1998	1999	2000	2001
Size Class	Sp. Util.	Sp. Util.	Sp. Util.	Sp. Util.	Sp. Util.
Drive	Rear/4	Rear/4	Rear/4	Rear/4	Rear/4
Crash Test	Average	Average	Average	Poor	Poor
Airbags	Dual	Dual	Dual	Dual	Dual
ABS	4-Whl	4-Whl	4-Whl	4-Whl	4-Whl
Parts Cost	Vry. Low	Vry. Low	Vry. Low	Vry. Low	Vry. Low
Complaints	Poor	Poor	Vry. Pr.	Average	Vry. Pr.
Insurance	Discount	Discount	Discount	Discount	Discount
Fuel Econ.	15	15	15	15	15
Theft Rating	Vry. High	Vry. High	Vry. High**	Vry. High**	Vry. High**
Bumpers	Weak	Weak			
Recalls	4	1	1		
Trn. Cir. (ft.)	37.5	36.7	36.7	36.7	36.7
Weight (lbs.)	3609	3800	3800	3800	3800
Whlbase (in.)	105.9	105.9	105.9	105.9	105.9
Price	17-19,000	17-19,000	22-24,000	23-25,000	29-31,000
OVERALL	Good	Good	Average	Good	Good

Jeep Wrangler 1992-2001

The Wrangler replaced the CJ-series Jeeps that were direct descendants of World War II–era Jeeps. The Wrangler is basic transportation in a 4-wheel drive vehicle; other than the addition of trim

1992 Jeep Wrangler

packages and options, it barely changed between 1989 and 1996. A new version debuted in 1997 and is a much better vehicle. Unfortunately, airbags aren't available until 1997. ABS became optional on 6-cylinder Wranglers in 1991 and optional on all models beginning in 1992.

The standard 2.5-liter 4-cylinder offers adequate power, or you can choose an optional 4-liter 6 that offers more than enough power. Wran-

	1992	1993	1994	1995	1996
Size Class	Sp. Util.	Sp. Util.	Sp. Util.	Sp. Util.	Sp. Util.
Drive	Rear/4	Rear/4	Rear/4	Rear/4	Rear/4
Crash Test	Average	Average	Poor	Poor	Poor
Airbags	None	None	None	None	None
ABS	4-Whl*	4-Whl*	4-Whl*	4-Whl*	4-Whl*
Parts Cost	Vry. Low	Low	Vry. Low	Vry. Low	Vry. Low
Complaints	Poor	Poor	Average	Average	Average
Insurance	Surchg.	Regular	Regular	Regular	Regular
Fuel Econ.	17	16	17	19	19
Theft Rating	High	Vry. High	Vry. High	Vry. High	Vry. High
Bumpers					
Recalls	3	2	1	0	0
Trn. Cir. (ft.)	32.9	32.9	32.9	32.9	32.9
Weight (lbs.)	3080	3080	2935	2934	2934
Whlbase (in.)	93.4	93.4	93.4	93.4	93.4
Price	6-8,000	7-9,000	8-10,000	8-10,000	13-15,000
OVERALL	Vry. Pr.	Vry. Pr.	Poor	Poor	Poor

*Optional; **Estimate

2001 Jeep Wrangler

glers come with part-time 4-wheel drive and a 5-speed manual or 3-speed automatic. You'll find handling is average for sport utility vehicles and notably worse than a typical passenger car's. Wrangler's element is really off the road, but the ride is awful on any surface. Ride improves in the 1997 version. The rear seat is definitely cramped and uncomfortable for adults. Interior comfort and weather sealing are minimal with the soft top, but the heater is powerful.

	1997	1998	1999	2000	2001
Size Class	Sp. Util.	Sp. Util.	Sp. Util.	Sp. Util.	Sp. Util.
Drive	Rear/4	Rear/4	Rear/4	Rear/4	Rear/4
Crash Test	Vry. Gd.	Vry. Gd.	Vry. Gd.	Good	Good
Airbags	Dual	Dual	Dual	Dual	Dual
ABS	4-Whl*	4-Whl*	4-Whl*	4-Whl*	4-Whl*
Parts Cost	Low	Average	Vry. Low	Vry. Low	Vry. Low
Complaints	Vry. Pr.	Vry. Pr.	Vry. Gd.	Vry. Pr.	Poor
Insurance	Surchg.	Surchg.	Surchg.	Surchg.	Surchg.
Fuel Econ.	17	17	16	16	16
Theft Rating	Vry. High	Vry. High**	Vry. High**	Vry. High**	Vry. High**
Bumpers					
Recalls	4	2	0	0	2
Trn. Cir. (ft.)	33.6	32.8	32.8	32.8	32.8
Weight (lbs.)	3092	3045	3045	3045	3045
Whlbase (in.)	93.4	93.4	93.4	93.4	93.4
Price	13-15,000	15-17,000	16-18,000	16-18,000	17-19,000
OVERALL	Poor	Vry. Pr.	Vry. Gd.	Average	Average

Kia Sephia 1994-2001

Kia was the first new manufacturer to enter the U.S. auto market in several years. However, they had experience—for years, Kia made Festivas and Aspires for Ford. The Sephia debuted into a very

1994 Kia Sephia

crowded and competitive subcompact market in 1994. During its first year, the Sephia did not offer airbags or ABS, but Kia quickly remedied this in 1995 when Sephias came standard with dual airbags; optional ABS was added in 1996.

In 1994, your only engine choice was a meek 88 horsepower 1.6-liter engine; however, with the changes in safety features in 1995, Kia also

	1992	1993	1994	1995	1996
Size Class			Subcomp.	Subcomp.	Subcomp.
Drive			Front	Front	Front
Crash Test			Average	Average	Average
Airbags			None	None	Dual
ABS			None	None	4-Whl*
Parts Cost			High	High	Average
Complaints			Average	Vry. Pr.	Vry. Pr.
Insurance			Surchg.	Surchg.	Surchg.
Fuel Econ.			25	25	29
Theft Rating			Average	Average	Average
Bumpers					Weak
Recalls			1	0	0
Trn. Cir. (ft.)			33.5	33.5	33.5
Weight (lbs.)			2405	2405	2476
Whlbase (in.)			98.4	98.4	98.4
Price			2-4,000	3-5,000	4-6,000
OVERALL			Vry. Pr.	Vry. Pr.	Poor

Across columns 1992–1993: No Model Produced

*Optional; **Estimate

2001 Kia Sephia

upgraded its engine. For 1995 and later models, the Sephia is equipped with an impressive 1.8-liter 4-cylinder engine which can produce 122 horsepower, enough to move this small car. Unlike many of Sephia's competitors, Kia only offers one body style, the sedan. You do, however, have several trim levels to choose from. The styling is similar to the old Mazda 323, which should not be too surprising, as Mazda is a part owner of Kia. Interior space is adequate, but trunk space is skimpy.

	1997	1998	1999	2000	2001
Size Class	Subcomp.	Subcomp.	Subcomp.	Subcomp.	Subcomp.
Drive	Front	Front	Front	Front	Front
Crash Test	Average	Good	Good	Good	Good
Airbags	Dual	Dual	Dual	Dual	Dual
ABS	4-Whl*	4-Whl*	4-Whl*	4-Whl*	4-Whl*
Parts Cost	High	High	Average	Average	Low
Complaints	Vry. Pr.	Vry. Pr.	Vry. Pr.	Vry. Pr.	Average
Insurance	Surchg.	Surchg.	Surchg.	Surchg.	Surchg.
Fuel Econ.	28	28	24	23	24
Theft Rating	Vry. Low	Vry. Low	Vry. Low**	Vry. Low**	Low
Bumpers	Weak		Strong	Weak	Weak
Recalls	0	0	0	0	0
Trn. Cir. (ft.)	33.5	33.5	33.5	32.16	32.16
Weight (lbs.)	2476	2476	2476	2478	2478
Whlbase (in.)	98.4	98.4	98.4	100.8	100.8
Price	5-7,000	6-8,000	7-9,000	8-10,000	11-13,000
OVERALL	Poor	Poor	Poor	Poor	Good

Kia Sportage 1995-2001

Kia's small sport utility has been increasing its safety package over the past few years. NO airbags were offered until the standard driver's in 1996. In 1998, Kia offered dual airbags as standard. A sim-

1995 Kia Sportage

ilar upgrade occurred with ABS; none available in 1995, 2-wheel in 1996, and optional 4-wheel ABS for 1998-2000.

The 2-liter 4-cylinder engine is adequate and fuel economy is average for this segment of vehicle. A more powerful engine would be nice; unfortunately, none is offered. The model lineup is fairly simple, with only a base model and an optional EX package that comes with some

	1992	1993	1994	1995	1996
Size Class				Sp. Util.	Sp. Util.
Drive				Rear/4	Rear/4
Crash Test				Poor	Poor
Airbags				Driver	Driver
ABS				2-Whl	2-Whl
Parts Cost		No Model Produced		High	High
Complaints				Vry. Pr.	Vry. Pr.
Insurance				Discount	Discount
Fuel Econ.				19	19
Theft Rating				Average	Average
Bumpers					
Recalls				1	2
Trn. Cir. (ft.)				34.8	34.8
Weight (lbs.)				3252	3252
Whlbase (in.)				104.4	104.4
Price				6-8,000	8-10,000
OVERALL				Vry. Pr.	Vry. Pr.

*Optional; **Estimate

2001 Kia Sportage

luxury amenities. Four wheel drive is optional. In 1999, Kia introduced 2-door models for the first time.

	1997	1998	1999	2000	2001
Size Class	Sp. Util.	Sp. Util.	Sp. Util	Sp. Util	Sp. Util
Drive	Rear/4	Rear/4	Rear/4	Rear/4	Rear/4
Crash Test	Poor	Poor	Poor	N/A	N/A
Airbags	Driver	Dual	Dual	Dual	Dual
ABS	2-Whl	4-Whl*	4-Whl*	4-Whl*	4-Whl*
Parts Cost	High	High	High	High	High
Complaints	Vry. Pr.	Vry. Pr.	Vry. Pr.	Poor	Vry. Pr.
Insurance	Discount	Discount	Discount	Discount	Discount
Fuel Econ.	19	19	19	19	19
Theft Rating	Average	Average	Average	Average**	Average**
Bumpers				Weak	Weak
Recalls	1	1	1	0	0
Trn. Cir. (ft.)	34.8	34.8	34.8	34.8	34.8
Weight (lbs.)	3303	3303	3303	3303	3303
Whlbase (in.)	104.4	104.3	104.3	104.3	104.3
Price	9-11,000	10-12,000	11-13,000	12-14,000	16-18,000
OVERALL	Vry. Pr.	Poor	Vry. Pr.		

Land Rover Discovery 1995-98, Discovery Series II 1999-2001

Land Rover has geared this rugged model to the wealthier sport utility buyer. Although it's slightly smaller than the Range Rover, you should have no problem doing any necessary suburban hauling in comfort.

1996 Land Rover Discovery

And if you're on of the few sport utility owners who actually take the vehicle off the pavement, you'll find the Discovery holds its own. In 1995, Land Rover was one of the first sport utility manufacturers to provide standard dual airbags.

The Discovery comes with a 3.9-liter V8 engine, standard four wheel drive, and ABS brakes. You'll want to note the high price of replace-

	1992	1993	1994	1995	1996
Size Class				Sp. Util.	Sp. Util.
Drive				All	All
Crash Test				Average	Average
Airbags				Dual	Dual
ABS				4-Whl	4-Whl
Parts Cost		No Model Produced		Vry. High	Vry. High
Complaints				Poor	Poor
Insurance				Regular	Regular
Fuel Econ.				13	13
Theft Rating				Average	Average
Bumpers					
Recalls				2	4
Trn. Cir. (ft.)				39.4	39.4
Weight (lbs.)				4465	4465
Whlbase (in.)				100	100
Price				15-17,000	17-19,000
OVERALL~				Vry. Pr.	Vry. Pr.

**Estimate; ~Cars without crash tests do not receive an overall rating.

2001 Land Rover Discovery Series II

ment parts, low fuel efficiency, and steady number of recalls in the early years. It also has not been crash tasted since it's re-design and name change in 1999. It has been known since then as the Discovery Series II.

	1997	1998	1999	2000	2001
Size Class	Sp. Util.	Sp. Util.	Sp. Util.	Sp. Util.	Sp. Util.
Drive	All	All	All	All	All
Crash Test	Average	Average	N/A	N/A	N/A
Airbags	Dual	Dual	Dual	Dual	Dual
ABS	4-Whl	4-Whl	4-Whl	4-Whl	4-Whl
Parts Cost	Vry. High	Vry. High	Vry. High	Vry. High	Vry. High
Complaints	Average	Average	Vry. Pr.	Average	Average
Insurance	Regular	Regular	Regular	Regular	Regular
Fuel Econ.	13	14	14	14	14
Theft Rating	Average	Average**	Average**	Average**	Average**
Bumpers					
Recalls	3	2	3	0	0
Trn. Cir. (ft.)	39.4	39.4	39.4	39.4	39.4
Weight (lbs.)	4465	4465	4465	4465	4465
Whlbase (in.)	100	100	100	100	100
Price	20-22,000	25-27,000	28-30,000	29-31,000	>30,000
OVERALL~	Poor	Poor			

Land Rover Range Rover 1992-2001

The Land Rover Range Rover has been around since 1970, before the sport utility fad, but still hasn't been crash tested. The original Range Rover lasted 14 years until a new model was intro-

1994 Land Rover Range Rover

duced for model year 1995. Like the Discovery, the Range Rover got dual airbags in 1995; 4-wheel ABS was an earlier feature.

The naming changed slightly after 1995. Prior to the remake, the Classic Range Rover was the only model available and came with a 3.5-liter V8 engine. The 4.0-liter SE and 4.6-liter HSE became available in 1995. The larger engines mean stronger engines; the 4.6 HSE can tow

	1992	1993	1994	1995	1996
Size Class	Sp. Util.	Sp. Util.	Sp. Util	Sp. Util.	Sp. Util.
Drive	All	All	All	All	All
Crash Test	N/A	N/A	N/A	N/A	N/A
Airbags	None	None	None	Dual	Dual
ABS	4-Whl	4-Whl	4-Whl	4-Whl	4-Whl
Parts Cost	Vry. High	Vry. High	Vry. High	Vry. High	Vry. High
Complaints	Poor	Good	Average	Poor	Vry. Pr.
Insurance	Average	Average	Average	Average	Average
Fuel Econ.	12	12	12	12	12
Theft Rating	Average	Average	Average	Average	Average
Bumpers					
Recalls	0	0	0	6	1
Trn. Cir. (ft.)	39	39.4	39.4	39	39
Weight (lbs.)	4400	4401	4401	4960	4960
Whlbase (in.)	108	108	108	108.1	108.1
Price	14-16,000	15-17,000	17-19,000	20-22,000	28-30,000
OVERALL~					

**Estimate; ~Cars without crash tests do not receive an overall rating.

2001 Land Rover Range Rover

almost 4 tons. Four wheel drive and an automatic transmission are standard. The Range Rover weighs about 4,500 lbs., so acceleration is fairly slow and fuel economy is dismal. Typical of this class of vehicles, the handling is sluggish, though the ride is comfortable. These trucks were made to go off-road which is why their drive is rougher.

	1997	1998	1999	2000	2001
Size Class	Sp. Util.	Sp. Util.	Sp. Util.	Sp. Util.	Sp. Util.
Drive	All	All	All	All	All
Crash Test	N/A	N/A	N/A	N/A	N/A
Airbags	Dual	Dual	Dual	Dual	Dual
ABS	4-Whl	4-Whl	4-Whl	4-Whl	4-Whl
Parts Cost	Vry. High	Vry. High	Vry. High	Vry. High	Vry. High
Complaints	Poor	Vry. Pr.	Vry. Pr.	Good	Average
Insurance	Average	Average	Average	Average	Average
Fuel Econ.	13	13	13	13	13
Theft Rating	Average	Average	Average**	Average**	Average**
Bumpers					
Recalls	1	1	2	3	1
Trn. Cir. (ft.)	39	39	39	39	39
Weight (lbs.)	4960	4960	4960	4960	4960
Whlbase (in.)	108.1	108.1	108.1	108.1	108.1
Price	>30,000	>30,000	>30,000	>30,000	>30,000
OVERALL~					

Lexus ES300 1992-2001

Billed as an entry-level luxury car, the ES is basically a dressed up version of the Toyota Camry. The ES has most of the Camry's options as standard equipment, including a V6 and stereo with

1993 Lexus ES300

CD player. Styling on the 1992 model was altered slightly, and the ES300 has gotten progressively sleeker over the past few years, while the Camry has remained somewhat more conservative. For 1992, the ES got a standard driver airbag, and dual airbags became standard the following year. ABS has always been standard on all 4 wheels.

Some models have a smaller engine, but the larger V6 is much more

	1992	1993	1994	1995	1996
Size Class	Large	Large	Large	Large	Large
Drive	Front	Front	Front	Front	Front
Crash Test	Good	Good	Good	Good	Good
Airbags	Driver	Dual	Dual	Dual	Dual
ABS	4-Whl	4-Whl	4-Whl	4-Whl	4-Whl
Parts Cost	High	High	High	Vry. High	High
Complaints	Vry. Gd.	Good	Vry. Gd.	Vry. Gd.	Vry. Gd.
Insurance	Discount	Discount	Discount	Discount	Discount
Fuel Econ.	17	18	20	20	20
Theft Rating	High	Average	Vry. High	High	Vry. High
Bumpers					
Recalls	1	0	0	0	0
Trn. Cir. (ft.)	36.7	36.7	36.7	36.7	36.7
Weight (lbs.)	3362	3362	3374	3374	3373
Whlbase (in.)	103.1	103.1	103.1	103.1	103.1
Price	11-13,000	12-14,000	14-16,000	16-18,000	18-20,000
OVERALL	Good	Vry. Gd.	Vry. Gd.	Vry. Gd.	Vry. Gd.

**Estimate

2001 Lexus ES300

satisfying and just as fuel efficient. Earlier ES models were available with either manual or automatic transmission. In 1994, Lexus, realizing that someone seeking a luxury car would want an automatic, dropped the manual. Handling is adequate, and the ride is pleasantly firm. In front, room and comfort are ample, less so in the rear. A good, solid car, but you can save almost $10,000 by buying a well-equipped Camry.

	1997	1998	1999	2000	2001
Size Class	Large	Large	Large	Large	Large
Drive	Front	Front	Front	Front	Front
Crash Test	Good	Vry. Gd.	Vry. Gd.	Vry. Gd.	Vry. Gd.
Airbags	Dual	Dual/Side	Dual/Side	Dual/Side	Dual/Side
ABS	4-Whl	4-Whl	4-Whl	4-Whl	4-Whl
Parts Cost	Vry. High	High	High	High	High
Complaints	Vry. Gd.	Vry. Gd.	Vry. Gd.	Vry. Gd.	Vry. Gd.
Insurance	Discount	Discount	Discount	Discount	Discount
Fuel Econ.	19	19	19	19	19
Theft Rating	Vry. High	Vry. High	Vry. High**	Vry. High**	Vry. High**
Bumpers			Strong	Weak	Weak
Recalls	1	0	0	0	0
Trn. Cir. (ft.)	36.7	36.7	36.7	36.7	36.7
Weight (lbs.)	3296	3378	3351	3373	3373
Whlbase (in.)	105.1	105.1	105.1	105.1	105.1
Price	22-24,000	24-26,000	28-30,000	>30,000	>30,000
OVERALL	Vry. Gd.	BEST BET	BEST BET	BEST BET	BEST BET

Lexus GS300 1994-2001

Lexus' newest entry into the luxury market was designed to bridge the nearly $20,000 gap between the entry-level ES300 and the luxurious LS400. Little has changed on the GS300 since its in-

1994 Lexus GS300

ception until its full revision in 1999. It got an increased wheelbase which allows for more interior room and a bigger trunk. As you would expect, dual airbags and ABS have been standard on the GS300 since its inception. Side airbags became standard in 1998 as well.

The GS300 is powered by a very strong but inefficient 3-liter 6-cylinder engine that provides poor gas mileage, but no worse than its

	1992	1993	1994	1995	1996
Size Class			Large	Large	Large
Drive			Rear	Rear	Rear
Crash Test			Average	Average	Average
Airbags			Dual	Dual	Dual
ABS			4-Whl	4-Whl	4-Whl
Parts Cost			Vry. High	Vry. High	High
Complaints			Vry. Gd.	Very Gd.	Average
Insurance			Regular	Regular	Regular
Fuel Econ.			18	18	18
Theft Rating	No Model Produced		Vry. Low	Vry. Low	Vry. High
Bumpers					
Recalls			1	0	0
Trn. Cir. (ft.)			36.1	36.1	36.1
Weight (lbs.)			3660	3660	3660
Whlbase (in.)			109.4	109.4	109.4
Price			18-20,000	20-22,000	24-26,000
OVERALL~			Average	Good	Average

**Estimate; ~Cars without crash tests do not receive an overall rating.

212

2001 Lexus GS300

corporate siblings, the ES300 and the LS400. A five speed automatic transmission makes driving enjoyable, and as the GS300 emphasizes a smooth, silent ride. Front seat occupants will ride in comfort, but the back seat will be cramped for adults and the cargo space is just average. The GS300 is a solid, if expensive, choice. Before settling on it, keep in mind that you can find less expensive cars with the GS300's same luxurious feel. For example, be sure to look at the BMW 3-Series.

	1997	1998	1999	2000	2001
Size Class	Large	Large	Large	Large	Large
Drive	Rear	Rear	Rear	Rear	Rear
Crash Test	Average	N/A	N/A	N/A	N/A
Airbags	Dual	Dual/Side	Dual/Side	Dual/Side	Dual/Side
ABS	4-Whl	4-Whl	4-Whl	4-Whl	4-Whl
Parts Cost	Vry. High	High	High	High	High
Complaints	Average	Poor	Vry. Gd.	Vry. Gd.	Vry. Gd.
Insurance	Discount	Discount	Discount	Discount	Discount
Fuel Econ.	18	20	20	20	20
Theft Rating	Vry. High	Vry. High	Vry. High**	Vry. High**	Vry. High**
Bumpers					
Recalls	0	1	0	0	0
Trn. Cir. (ft.)	36.1	36.1	37.1	37.1	37.1
Weight (lbs.)	3660	3635	3638	3638	3638
Whlbase (in.)	109.4	110.2	110.2	110.2	110.2
Price	27-29,000	>30,000	>30,000	>30,000	>30,000
OVERALL~	Good				

Lexus LS400/LS430 1992-2001

The LS400, the flagship sedan, is the biggest, most expensive Lexus you can buy. It received a host of detail improvements and price increases between its 1990 introduction and its redesign in 1995.

1992 Lexus LS400

The 1995 overhaul brought a sleeker, lighter and more powerful model. For 2001, another redesign brings more interior space and a smoother ride along with a new designation, the LS430. All LS400 models have standard driver's airbag and ABS. Dual airbags first became standard in 1993. Standard side airbags for both the driver and front passenger appear in 1997 models.

	1992	1993	1994	1995	1996
Size Class	Large	Large	Large	Large	Large
Drive	Rear	Rear	Rear	Rear	Rear
Crash Test	N/A	N/A	N/A	N/A	N/A
Airbags	Driver	Dual	Dual	Dual	Dual
ABS	4-Whl	4-Whl	4-Whl	4-Whl	4-Whl
Parts Cost	High	Vry. High	Vry. High	Vry. High	Vry. High
Complaints	Vry. Gd.	Vry. Gd.	Vry. Gd.	Vry. Gd.	Vry. Gd.
Insurance	Discount	Regular	Discount	Discount	Discount
Fuel Econ.	18	18	18	19	19
Theft Rating	High	High	Average	Average	Vry. High
Bumpers					
Recalls	0	0	0	1	1
Trn. Cir. (ft.)	36.1	36.1	36.1	34.8	34.8
Weight (lbs.)	3759	3858	3859	3650	3649
Whlbase (in.)	110.8	110.8	110.8	112.2	112.2
Price	17-19,000	18-20,000	20-22,000	24-26,000	27-29,000
OVERALL~					

**Estimate; ~Cars without crash tests do not receive an overall rating.

214

2001 Lexus LS430

The LS400 has a very smooth, powerful four-cam V8 with automatic overdrive, and the 1995 and later versions are even more powerful. The LS400 is thoroughly equipped in base form, but you should look for a car with optional traction control. While handling isn't quite up to the level of the best sedans, it's still pretty good and the ride is superlative. The front seats are outstanding, and the rear seat is nearly as roomy and comfortable. The instrument panel and controls are about the best you can get.

	1997	1998	1999	2000	2001
Size Class	Large	Large	Large	Large	Large
Drive	Rear	Rear	Rear	Rear	Rear
Crash Test	N/A	N/A	N/A	N/A	N/A
Airbags	Dual	Dual/Side	Dual/Side	Dual/Side	Dual/Side
ABS	4-Whl	4-Whl	4-Whl	4-Whl	4-Whl
Parts Cost	Vry. High	Vry. High	Vry. High	Vry. High	Vry. High
Complaints	Vry. Gd.	Vry. Gd.	Vry. Gd.	Vry. Gd.	Vry. Gd.
Insurance	Discount	Discount	Discount	Discount	Discount
Fuel Econ.	19	19	18	18	18
Theft Rating	Vry. High	Vry. High**	Vry. High**	Vry. High**	Vry. High**
Bumpers	Weak	Weak	Weak	Strong	Strong
Recalls	1	0	0	0	0
Trn. Cir. (ft.)	34.8	34.8	34.8	34.8	37.4
Weight (lbs.)	3726	3890	3890	3890	3955
Whlbase (in.)	112.2	112.2	112.2	112.2	115.2
Price	>30,000	>30,000	>30,000	>30,000	>30,000
OVERALL~					

Lexus SC300/SC400 1992-2001

The SC300 and 400 are nearly identical except for the engines and luxury appointments. Many of the standard features that you will find on the more expensive SC400 will be optional on the

1992 Lexus SC300

cheaper SC300. Both of these coupes have remained virtually unchanged same since their inception in 1992. 4-wheel ABS is standard on all models. A driver's airbag became standard in 1992; dual airbags became standard starting in 1993.

The SC300 shares a powerful 3-liter 6-cylinder engine with the GS300 and the Toyota Supra. For more power, look for the SC400,

	1992	1993	1994	1995	1996
Size Class	Large	Large	Large	Large	Large
Drive	Rear	Rear	Rear	Rear	Rear
Crash Test	N/A	N/A	N/A	N/A	N/A
Airbags	Dual	Dual	Dual	Dual	Dual
ABS	4-Whl	4-Whl	4-Whl	4-Whl	4-Whl
Parts Cost	Vry. High	Vry. High	Vry. High	Vry. High	Vry. High
Complaints	Average	Average	Average	Average	Average
Insurance	Discount	Discount	Discount	Discount	Regular
Fuel Econ.	18	18	18	18	18
Theft Rating	Vry. High	Vry. High	Vry. High	Vry. High	Vry. High
Bumpers					
Recalls	0	0	0	0	0
Trn. Cir. (ft.)	36.1	36.1	36.1	36.1	36.1
Weight (lbs.)	3506	3506	3506	3660	3610
Whlbase (in.)	105.9	105.9	105.9	105.9	105.9
Price	14-16,000	15-17,000	17-19,000	20-22,000	24-26,000
OVERALL~					

**Estimate; ~Cars without crash tests do not receive an overall rating.

2001 Lexus SC400

which comes with the 4-liter V8 that is found in the large LS400. The SC400 will cost you more in both sticker price and at the pump. Also, look for a model with traction control; this will help control the engine's power on slippery roads. As you would expect, handling is excellent, and the ride is comfortably firm. The front seats are very comfortable; however, the rear seats are cramped and uncomfortable for adults. Because it is a relatively small coupe, the trunk space is below average.

	1997	1998	1999	2000	2001
Size Class	Large	Large	Large	Large	Large
Drive	Rear	Rear	Rear	Rear	Rear
Crash Test	N/A	N/A	N/A	N/A	N/A
Airbags	Dual	Dual	Dual	Dual	Dual
ABS	4-Whl	4-Whl	4-Whl	4-Whl	4-Whl
Parts Cost	Vry. High	Vry. High	High	High	High
Complaints	Average	Average	Vry. Pr.	Vry. Pr.	Vry. Pr.
Insurance	Surchg.	Surchg.	Surchg.	Surchg.	Surchg.
Fuel Econ.	18	19	18	18	18
Theft Rating	Vry. High	Vry. High	Vry. High**	Vry. High**	Vry. High**
Bumpers			Strong	Strong	Strong
Recalls	1	1	0	0	0
Trn. Cir. (ft.)	36.1	36.1	36.1	36.1	36.1
Weight (lbs.)	3538	3560	3655	3655	3655
Whlbase (in.)	105.9	105.9	105.9	105.9	105.9
Price	28-30,000	>30,000	>30,000	>30,000	>30,000
OVERALL~					

Lincoln Continental 1992-2001

Lincoln has been applying the Continental name to a variety of cars for over fifty years. The 1982-87 models were based on the low-priced Ford Fairmont chassis. For 1988, the Continental

1993 Lincoln Continental

converted dramatically to a stretched version of the modern Taurus/Sable chassis. In 1995, another major redesign with much more modern styling came along, and another revision occurred in 1998. Continentals have come in several trim levels, including some designer series. Continentals have dual airbags for 1989 and 1992-97; for 1990-91, it's hit or miss because of supply problems during manufac-

	1992	1993	1994	1995	1996
Size Class	Large	Large	Large	Large	Large
Drive	Front	Front	Front	Front	Front
Crash Test	N/A	N/A	N/A	N/A	N/A
Airbags	Dual	Dual	Dual	Dual	Dual
ABS	4-Whl	4-Whl	4-Whl	4-Whl	4-Whl
Parts Cost	Vry. High	Vry. High	Vry. High	High	High
Complaints	Vry. Pr.	Vry. Pr.	Vry. Pr.	Good	Good
Insurance	Discount	Discount	Discount	Regular	Discount
Fuel Econ.	17	17	18	17	17
Theft Rating	Average	Average	Low	Low	Average
Bumpers					
Recalls	3	4	4	2	2
Trn. Cir. (ft.)	38.4	38.4	38.4	41.1	41.1
Weight (lbs.)	3628	3595	3576	3969	3911
Whlbase (in.)	109	109	109	109	109
Price	5-7,000	6-8,000	7-9,000	11-13,000	13-15,000
OVERALL~					

**Estimate; ~Cars without crash tests do not receive an overall rating.

218

2001 Lincoln Continental

turing. The 1985 Continentals were the first U.S. cars with optional 4-wheel ABS, standard from 1986 on.

The Continental's engines are strong and smooth but hardly economical; the 1995 4.6-liter V8 is particularly powerful. The Continental is very quiet and comfortable, though often unresponsive. The muffler was upgraded in 1999 to be quiet. The digital instrument panel shows only one gauge at a time, which can be frustrating. The Continental has plenty of room for six and a large trunk.

	1997	1998	1999	2000	2001
Size Class	Large	Large	Large	Large	Large
Drive	Front	Front	Front	Front	Front
Crash Test	N/A	N/A	N/A	N/A	N/A
Airbags	Dual	Dual	Dual/Side	Dual/Side	Dual/Side
ABS	4-Whl	4-Whl	4-Whl	4-Whl	4-Whl
Parts Cost	Vry. High	Vry. High	High	High	High
Complaints	Poor	Poor	Vry. Gd.	Poor	Average
Insurance	Discount	Discount	Discount	Discount	Discount
Fuel Econ.	17	17	17	17	17
Theft Rating	Average	Average	Average**	Average**	Average**
Bumpers			Strong	Strong	Strong
Recalls	1	2	1	1	0
Trn. Cir. (ft.)	41.1	41.1	41.1	41.1	41.1
Weight (lbs.)	3884	3868	3868	3868	3868
Whlbase (in.)	109	109	109	109	109
Price	16-18,000	20-22,000	24-26,000	27-29,000	>30,000
OVERALL~					

Lincoln Mark VII 1992, Mark VIII 1993-98

The Mark series is based on the same chassis as the Mercury Cougar and Ford Thunderbird, but it costs substantially more—about twice what you'd pay for a Mercury Cougar V8. However, the

1994 Lincoln Mark VIII

Mark series does have a distinctive style all its own and a slightly better ride. The Mark VII lasted without major styling changes through the 1992 model year. For 1993, Lincoln replaced it with an all-new Mark VIII, based on the newer 1989 Thunderbird/Cougar chassis. For 1997, the Mark VIII received a fresh new exterior and interior. A driver's airbag was standard on the 1990-92 Mark VII; the Mark VIII went far-

	1992	1993	1994	1995	1996
Size Class	Large	Large	Large	Large	Large
Drive	Rear	Rear	Rear	Rear	Rear
Crash Test	N/A	Vry. Gd.	Vry. Gd.	Vry. Gd.	Vry. Gd.
Airbags	Driver	Dual	Dual	Dual	Dual
ABS	4-Whl	4-Whl	4-Whl	4-Whl	4-Whl
Parts Cost	Low	Average	Average	Average	Average
Complaints	Vry. Gd.	Poor	Average	Average	Good
Insurance	Discount	Regular	Discount	Discount	Discount
Fuel Econ.	17	17	18	18	18
Theft Rating	High	Vry. High	High	High	Vry. High
Bumpers					
Recalls	0	2	1	0	0
Trn. Cir. (ft.)	40.1	40.1	37.2	37.2	37.2
Weight (lbs.)	3768	3752	3768	3768	3767
Whlbase (in.)	108.5	113	113	113	113
Price	7-9,000	8-10,000	9-11,000	12-14,000	13-15,000
OVERALL~		Average	Vry. Gd.	Vry. Gd.	Vry. Gd.

**Estimate; ~Cars without crash tests do not receive an overall rating.

1994 Lincoln Mark VIII

ther, featuring standard dual airbags for 1993. All Marks going back to 1986 had standard ABS; it was even available on many 1985 models.

From 1987-92, the models were available in an LSC version, which featured a firmer suspension, bigger tires, and analog gauges. Otherwise, handling is nothing special on the Mark series. Starting in 1993, Lincoln has offered only one version. The LSC deserves a look, but if you can live without the Lincoln name and distinctive style, the Ford Thunderbird and Mercury Cougar are similar cars at much lower prices.

	1997	1998	1999	2000	2001
Size Class	Large	Large			
Drive	Rear	Rear			
Crash Test	Vry. Gd.	Vry. Gd.			
Airbags	Dual	Dual			
ABS	4-Whl	4-Whl			
Parts Cost	High	Vry. High			
Complaints	Poor	Vry. Pr.			
Insurance	Discount	Discount			
Fuel Econ.	18	18			
Theft Rating	Vry. High	Average**			
Bumpers					
Recalls	0	0			
Trn. Cir. (ft.)	37.2	37.2			
Weight (lbs.)	3778	3765			
Whlbase (in.)	113	113			
Price	18-20,000	22-24,000			
OVERALL~	Good	Average			

No Model Produced

Lincoln Town Car 1992-2001

The Town Car is about as big as cars get—just five inches shorter than the Cadillac Fleetwood. And, Lincoln doesn't change the Town Car much; 1980 and 1990 were the last redesigns, although it did re-

1993 Lincoln Town Car

ceive minor cosmetic changes in 1995. Since 1970, the Town Car has shared the Ford Crown Victoria/Mercury Grand Marquis chassis, and it's one of the last rear-wheel drive vehicles being produced in the U.S. For 1990, the edges were smoothed off. The base-model Town Cars are fully equipped, but fancier models have an extra touch of decadence. Dual airbags were supposed to be standard on 1990-91 models, but

	1992	1993	1994	1995	1996
Size Class	Large	Large	Large	Large	Large
Drive	Rear	Rear	Rear	Rear	Rear
Crash Test	Vry. Gd.	Vry. Gd.	Vry. Gd.	Vry. Gd.	Vry. Gd.
Airbags	Dual	Dual	Dual	Dual	Dual
ABS	4-Whl	4-Whl	4-Whl	4-Whl	4-Whl
Parts Cost	Low	Low	Low	Vry. Low	Low
Complaints	Poor	Average	Good	Good	Good
Insurance	Discount	Discount	Discount	Discount	Discount
Fuel Econ.	19	18	18	17	17
Theft Rating	High	Vry. High	High	High	Vry. High
Bumpers					
Recalls	2	2	3	5	4
Trn. Cir. (ft.)	40	40	40	40	42
Weight (lbs.)	4024	4040	4039	4031	4040
Whlbase (in.)	117.4	117.4	117.4	117.4	117.4
Price	7-9,000	8-10,000	9-11,000	12-14,000	14-16,000
OVERALL	Vry. Gd.	Vry. Gd.	BEST BET	BEST BET	Vry. Gd.

**Estimate

2001 Lincoln Town Car

many cars only have a driver's airbag because of supply problems that were resolved in 1992. ABS became optional in 1990, standard in 1991.

The 1991-97 models got the modular 4.6-liter V8, a responsive and fairly fuel-efficient power plant. It is now up to 225 horsepower. Typical of American luxury cars, the Town Car rides smoothly, but it protests during corners or sudden maneuvers. The optional, and rare, handling package makes the Town Car far more satisfying to drive. Watch out for the digital dashboard, it can be hard to read. The Town Car is a very good choice.

	1997	1998	1999	2000	2001
Size Class	Large	Large	Large	Large	Large
Drive	Rear	Rear	Rear	Rear	Rear
Crash Test	Vry. Gd.	Good	Good	Good	Good
Airbags	Dual	Dual	Dual/Side	Dual/Side	Dual/Side
ABS	4-Whl	4-Whl	4-Whl	4-Whl	4-Whl
Parts Cost	Average	Average	Very High	Low	Very Low
Complaints	Average	Averge	Good	Good	Average
Insurance	Discount	Discount	Discount	Discount	Discount
Fuel Econ.	17	17	17	17	18
Theft Rating	Vry. High	Vry. High**	Vry. High**	Vry. High**	Vry. High**
Bumpers			Strong	Strong	Strong
Recalls	2	2	2	4	3
Trn. Cir. (ft.)	42	42.2	42	42	42
Weight (lbs.)	4040	3860	4015	4015	4015
Whlbase (in.)	117.4	117.7	117.7	117.7	117.7
Price	18-20,000	21-23,000	24-26,000	27-29,000	>30,000
OVERALL	Vry. Gd.	Good	Vry. Gd.	BEST BET	BEST BET

Mazda 323 1992-94, Protégé 1992-2001

For 1990, Mazda restyled its subcompact and split off the sedans (under the name Protégé) from the 323 hatchback coupe. In 1995, the 323 was discontinued, and the 4-door Protégé was slightly

1992 Mazda 323

redesigned. For the first time, Mazda no longer offered a coupe in the competitive subcompact market. The 1990-94 323 and Protégé have motorized front shoulder belts and separate lap belts. 1995 was the first year optional ABS was offered on upper-level models and dual airbags were standard on all models. Side airbags became on option in 2000.

Power on base models is adequate; for more kick, look for the turbo

	1992	1993	1994	1995	1996
Size Class	Subcomp.	Subcomp.	Subcomp.	Subcomp.	Subcomp.
Drive	Front	Front	Front	Front	Front
Crash Test	Average	Average	Average	N/A	N/A
Airbags	None	None	None	Dual	Dual
ABS	None	None	None	4-Whl*	4-Whl*
Parts Cost	Low	Low	Average[1]	Average	Average
Complaints	Average	Good	Good	Average	Good
Insurance	Surchg.	Surchg.	Surchg.	Surchg.	Surchg.
Fuel Econ.	29	28	26	31	32
Theft Rating	Low	Low	Low	Vry. Low	Vry. Low
Bumpers					
Recalls	1	1	1	2	0
Trn. Cir. (ft.)	31.5	31.5	31.5	34.8	33.4
Weight (lbs.)	2238	2238	2238	2445	2385
Whlbase (in.)	98.43	98.43	98.43	102.6	102.6
Price	<3,000	2-4,000	3-5,000	5-7,000	6-8,000
OVERALL~	Average	Average	Vry. Pr.		

[1]Data given for Protégé. Parts Cost for 323 is Low; *Optional; **Estimate; ~Cars without crash tests do not receive an

2001 Mazda Protege

or twin-cam models. The standard five-speed transmission is slick-shifting and the later automatic transmission has an overdrive gear for better gas mileage. The 323 and Protégé fall behind other subcompacts in high-speed handling, which can be erratic. The interior has enough room for four, though the 1995 and later models are somewhat more spacious. Trunk space is adequate, and front seat comfort is reasonably good. The ride and noise are typical of subcompacts.

	1997	1998	1999	2000	2001
Size Class	Subcomp.	Subcomp.	Subcomp.	Subcomp.	Subcomp.
Drive	Front	Front	Front	Front	Front
Crash Test	N/A	N/A	Good	Good	Good
Airbags	Dual	Dual	Dual	Dual	Dual
ABS	4-Whl*	4-Whl*	4-Whl*	4-Whl*	4-Whl*
Parts Cost	High	High	High	High	High
Complaints	Average	Average	Good	Average	Average
Insurance	Surchg.	Surchg.	Surchg.	Surchg.	Surchg.
Fuel Econ.	30	30	29	29	29
Theft Rating	Vry. Low	Vry. Low**	Vry. Low**	Vry. Low**	Vry. Low**
Bumpers					
Recalls	0	0	0	0	0
Trn. Cir. (ft.)	33.4	33.4	33.4	34.1	34.1
Weight (lbs.)	2385	2385	2385	2434	2434
Whlbase (in.)	102.6	102.6	102.6	102.6	102.6
Price	7-9,000	8-10,000	10-12,000	12-14,000	14-16,000
OVERALL~			Good	Good	Good

overall rating.

Mazda 626 1992-2001

Mazda restyled the 626 again for 1993 and dropped the hatchback model. Minor cosmetic changes were done to the 626 in 1996. 1989-92 models have motorized shoulder belts and man-

1993 Mazda 626

ual lap belts. The 1993 626 has a driver's airbag and conventional belts; 1994 models added a passenger airbag. ABS can be found on various models beginning in 1991.

The base 4-cylinder is lively enough and reasonably economical. For more power but higher fuel costs, consider the turbocharged 4-cylinder or the 2.5-liter V6. The 626's automatic, which shifts harshly and of-

	1992	1993	1994	1995	1996
Size Class	Compact	Compact	Compact	Compact	Compact
Drive	Front	Front	Front	Front	Front
Crash Test	N/A	Good	Good	Good	Good
Airbags	None	Driver	Dual	Dual	Dual
ABS	4-Whl*	4-Whl*	4-Whl*	4-Whl*	4-Whl*
Parts Cost	Low	High	High	High	High
Complaints	Vry. Gd.	Average	Poor	Poor	Poor
Insurance	Surchg.	Surchg.	Regular	Regular	Surchg.
Fuel Econ.	22	23	23	23	26
Theft Rating	Average	Vry. Low	Average	Vry. Low	Vry. Low
Bumpers	Weak	Weak	Weak	Weak	Weak
Recalls	2	0	0	2	1
Trn. Cir. (ft.)	36	35.4	35.4	34.8	34.8
Weight (lbs.)	2610	2606	2606	2743	2828
Whlbase (in.)	101.4	102.8	102.8	102.8	102.8
Price	3-5,000	4-6,000	5-7,000	6-8,000	8-10,000
OVERALL~		Poor	Average	Poor	Poor

*Optional; **Estimate; ~Cars without crash tests do not receive an overall rating.

2001 Mazda 626

ten, is the car's worst feature. While the handling is fairly precise, the body tends to lean. Like most Japanese mid-sized cars, the base 626 has plenty of standard equipment. The interior and trunk areas are spacious, functional, and comfortable for four. With a good crash test, later models are a solid choice.

	1997	1998	1999	2000	2001
Size Class	Compact	Compact	Compact	Compact	Compact
Drive	Front	Front	Front	Front	Front
Crash Test	Good	N/A	Vry. Good	Vry. Gd.	Vry. Gd.
Airbags	Dual	Dual	Dual	Dual/Side	Dual/Side
ABS	4-Whl*	4-Whl*	4-Whl*	4-Whl*	4-Whl*
Parts Cost	Average	Low	Average	Average	Average
Complaints	Average	Good	Good	Vry. Gd.	Poor
Insurance	Surchg.	Surchg.	Surchg.	Surchg.	Surchg.
Fuel Econ.	26	26	26	26	26
Theft Rating	Vry. Low	Average	Average**	Average**	Average**
Bumpers	Weak		Strong	Strong	Strong
Recalls	2	2	1	1	0
Trn. Cir. (ft.)	34.8	34.8	34.8	36.1	36.1
Weight (lbs.)	2749	2749	2749	2749	2749
Whlbase (in.)	102.8	102.8	102.8	105.1	105.1
Price	10-12,000	11-13,000	13-15,000	14-16,000	20-22,000
OVERALL~	Average		Vry. Gd.	BEST BET	Vry. Gd.

227

Mazda 929 1992-96

Designed to compete against the Infiniti J30 and other less expensive luxury models, the 929 was Mazda's priciest sedan. The 929 comes in one model, but you can choose expensive option packages to

1992 Mazda 929

dress it up even more. The 929 was discontinued after the 1996 model year. You'll find manual lap-shoulder belts through 1989, motorized shoulder belts with separate lap belts from 1990-91, and standard dual airbags from 1992 on. ABS was optional from 1990-91, standard after that.

The 929 emphasizes a plush ride with handling more like a Buick

	1992	1993	1994	1995	1996
Size Class	Large	Large	Large	Large	Large
Drive	Rear	Rear	Rear	Rear	Rear
Crash Test	N/A	N/A	N/A	N/A	N/A
Airbags	Dual	Dual	Dual	Dual	Dual
ABS	4-Whl	4-Whl	4-Whl	4-Whl	4-Whl
Parts Cost	High	High	High	Vry. High	Vry. High
Complaints	Poor	Poor	Average	Vry. Gd.	Vry. Gd.
Insurance	Discount	Discount	Discount	Regular	Regular
Fuel Econ.	19	19	19	19	19
Theft Rating	High	Vry. High	Vry. High	Vry. High	Vry. High
Bumpers					
Recalls	1	0	0	0	0
Trn. Cir. (ft.)	36.7	36.7	36.7	36.7	36.7
Weight (lbs.)	3596	3596	3627	3627	3627
Whlbase (in.)	112.2	112.2	112.2	112.2	112.2
Price	7-9,000	8-10,000	9-11,000	10-12,000	11-13,000
OVERALL~					

~Cars without crash tests do not receive an overall rating.

1995 Mazda 929

Roadmaster than a Mazda RX-7. The rare 1989-90 929S had sportier suspension tuning and standard ABS - it is worth seeking out. From 1989 on, all models have automatic overdrive. If you like real wood trim inside, look for 1992 and later models with the optional premium package. Another great option senses hot interior temperatures and activates a special ventilation system. The brakes and transmission are very good; however, the trunk is rather skimpy for a car this size.

	1997	1998	1999	2000	2001
Size Class					
Drive					
Crash Test					
Airbags					
ABS					
Parts Cost					
Complaints			No Model Produced		
Insurance					
Fuel Econ.					
Theft Rating					
Bumpers					
Recalls					
Trn. Cir. (ft.)					
Weight (lbs.)					
Whlbase (in.)					
Price					
OVERALL~					

Mazda Miata 1992-2001

1992 Mazda Miata

The Miata was an amazing phenomenon for Mazda when introduced early in the summer of 1989 and is still going strong in its twelfth year. The Miata is a modern, Japanese rendition of a traditional English sports car with all the fun, while adding improved comfort and a minimum of reliability problems. When the Miata first went on sale, you had to wait in line and pay well above sticker price in most cities in order to get one. The body was redesigned in 1999 to give it a more modern look. All Miatas have a driver's airbag. For 1994, the passenger gets an airbag, too. ABS is available beginning with 1991 mod-

	1992	1993	1994	1995	1996
Size Class	Subcomp.	Subcomp.	Subcomp.	Subcomp.	Subcomp.
Drive	Rear	Rear	Rear	Rear	Rear
Crash Test	Average	Average	Average	Average	Average
Airbags	Driver	Driver	Dual	Dual	Dual
ABS	4-Whl*	4-Whl*	4-Whl*	4-Whl*	4-Whl*
Parts Cost	Average	Average	Low	Average	High
Complaints	Good	Vry. Gd.	Vry. Gd.	Average	Good
Insurance	Surchg.	Regular	Regular	Regular	Regular
Fuel Econ.	24	24	23	23	23
Theft Rating	Average	Low	Average	Average	Low
Bumpers					
Recalls	1	1	0	0	0
Trn. Cir. (ft.)	30.8	30.8	30	30	30
Weight (lbs.)	2216	2222	2293	2293	2293
Whlbase (in.)	89.2	89.2	89.2	89.2	89.2
Price	6-8,000	7-9,000	8-10,000	9-11,000	10-12,000
OVERALL~	Poor	Good	Vry. Gd.	Average	Average

*Optional; ~Cars without a crash test do not receive an overall rating.

230

2001 Mazda Miata

els, but it comes only with one of the expensive options packages.

All 1990-93 Miatas have a twin-cam 1.6-liter 4-cylinder engine. For 1994, the Miata gets a more powerful 1.8-liter twin-cam 4, but the gas mileage drops with the larger engine. You get crisp, responsive handling, automatic overdrive or a precise-shifting 5-speed, and a modern climate control system. Don't expect a quiet ride, spacious interior, or oversize trunk in a Miata. If you fit inside, don't mind the noise, and don't need any extra space, the Miata is a good choice in a sports car. However, the current model has not been crash tested.

	1997	1998	1999	2000	2001
Size Class	Subcomp.	Subcomp.	Subcomp.	Subcomp.	Subcomp.
Drive	Rear	Rear	Rear	Rear	Rear
Crash Test	Average	Average	Vry. Gd.	Vry. Gd.	Vry. Gd.
Airbags	Dual	Dual	Dual	Dual	Dual
ABS	4-Whl*	4-Whl*	4-Whl*	4-Whl*	4-Whl*
Parts Cost	High	Average	High	High	High
Complaints	Good	Average	Vry. Pr.	Vry. Pr.	Vry. Pr.
Insurance	Regular	Regular	Regular	Regular	Regular
Fuel Econ.	23	23	25	25	25
Theft Rating	Average	Average	Average	High	High
Bumpers					
Recalls	0	0	1	1	1
Trn. Cir. (ft.)	30	30	30.2	30.2	30.2
Weight (lbs.)	2293	2293	2299	2299	2299
Whlbase (in.)	89.2	89.2	89.2	89.2	89.2
Price	12-14,000	15-17,000	17-19,000	21-23,000	22-24,000
OVERALL~	Average	Average	Average	Average	Average

Mazda Millenia 1995-2001

In 1995, the Millenia was introduced and billed as a performance luxury sedan with subtle styling. Dual airbags and ABS were standard from the start. When the 929 was discontinued in 1996, the

1995 Mazda Millenia

Millenia was moved to the forefront to pick up the lost 929 sales. For '97, slight interior and exterior changes were made. In 1999, the Millenia was restyled in hopes that it would be a winner in the competitive intermediate market.

The standard 2.5-liter V6 engine on the base model is more than adequate; however, the Millenia S model comes with a more powerful and

	1992	1993	1994	1995	1996
Size Class				Intermd.	Intermd.
Drive				Front	Front
Crash Test				Vry. Gd.	Vry. Gd.
Airbags				Dual	Dual
ABS				4-Whl	4-Whl
Parts Cost				Vry. High	Vry. High
Complaints		No Model Produced		Average	Good
Insurance				Regular	Regular
Fuel Econ.				20	20
Theft Rating				High	High
Bumpers				Weak	Weak
Recalls				0	0
Trn. Cir. (ft.)				37.4	37.4
Weight (lbs.)				3216	3216
Whlbase (in.)				108.3	108.3
Price				10-12,000	13-15,000
OVERALL				Average	Good

**Estimate

2001 Mazda Millenia

responsive "Miller cycle," a supercharged version of the same engine. Performance is the difference, as the S model is meant to appeal to younger drivers. The base can get by on regular fuel, but the S engine requires premium fuel, increasing operating costs. You'll find that this front-wheel drive sedan is slightly smaller than the old 929, but it should still be big enough for four passengers, five in a pinch. In government crash tests, the Millenia performed excellently. Overall, the Millenia is a good choice is a crowded luxury market.

	1997	1998	1999	2000	2001
Size Class	Intermd.	Intermd.	Intermd.	Intermd.	Intermd.
Drive	Front	Front	Front	Front	Front
Crash Test	Vry. Gd.	Vry. Gd.	Vry. Gd.	Vry. Gd.	Vry. Gd.
Airbags	Dual	Dual	Dual	Dual	Dual
ABS	4-Whl	4-Whl	4-Whl	4-Whl	4-Whl
Parts Cost	Vry. High	Vry. High	Vry. High	Vry. High	Vry. High
Complaints	Vry. Gd.	Vry. Gd.	Good	Good	Vry. Gd.
Insurance	Regular	Regular	Regular	Regular	Regular
Fuel Econ.	20	20	20	20	20
Theft Rating	High	Vry. High	Vry. High**	Vry. High**	Vry. High**
Bumpers	Weak	Weak	Weak	Weak	Weak
Recalls	0	0	0	0	0
Trn. Cir. (ft.)	37.4	37.4	37.4	34.1	34.1
Weight (lbs.)	3216	3216	3216	3241	3241
Whlbase (in.)	108.3	108.3	108.3	108.3	108.3
Price	15-17,000	17-19,000	19-21,000	25-27,000	28-30,000
OVERALL	Good	Good	Average	Average	Good

Mazda MPV 1992-98, 2000-2001

The Mazda MPV, multipurpose passenger vehicle, takes its name from a U.S. government regulatory classification originally created to exempt vans and light trucks from safety standards that applied

1993 Mazda MPV

to cars. The MPV didn't change at all from its introduction through 1995. However, it was all-new in '96. There wasn't an official 1999 model year and it was introduced as all new for 2000. A driver's airbag is standard beginning in 1993, and dual airbags become standard in 1996. ABS is standard on the rear wheels from 1990-95, but 4-wheel ABS is not available until 1996. Optional side airbags were available

	1992	1993	1994	1995	1996
Size Class	Minivan	Minivan	Minivan	Minivan	Minivan
Drive	Rear/4	Rear/4	Rear/4	Rear/4	Rear/4
Crash Test	Average	Average	Average	Average	Vry. Gd.
Airbags	None	Driver	Driver	Driver	Dual
ABS	2-Whl	2-Whl	2-Whl	2-Whl	4-Whl
Parts Cost	Low	Average	Average	Average	High
Complaints	Poor	Poor	Average	Good	Average
Insurance	Discount	Regular	Regular	Regular	Discount
Fuel Econ.	17	16	16	16	16
Theft Rating	Low	Average	Average	Average	Vry. High
Bumpers			Weak	Weak	Weak
Recalls	0	0	0	0	0
Trn. Cir. (ft.)	36.1	36.1	36.1	36.1	36.1
Weight (lbs.)	3295	3515	3595	3745	3730
Whlbase (in.)	110.4	110.4	110.4	110.4	110.4
Price	5-7,000	6-8,000	7-9,000	8-10,000	12-14,000
OVERALL	Average	Poor	Poor	Average	Good

**Estimate

2001 Mazda MPV

in 2000.

You can choose an adequate 2.6-liter 4 or an optional 3-liter V6; all-wheel drive is available with the V6. The new 2000 model has a 2.5-liter V6 and less space than some of it's competitors. The 4-cylinder engine was discontinued for 1995 along with the five-person seating configuration, leaving customers with the more-powerful V6 and seven-person seating. Brakes, handling, and ride are inferior to most minivans. The interior is typical of the class. Not an outstanding vehicle; you'll likely be happier and better off with one of Chrysler's minivans.

	1997	1998	1999	2000	2001
Size Class	Minivan	Minivan		Minivan	Minivan
Drive	Rear/4	Rear/4		Rear/4	Rear/4
Crash Test	Vry. Gd.	Vry. Gd.		Vry. Gd.	Good
Airbags	Dual	Dual		Dual	Dual
ABS	4-Whl	4-Whl		4-Whl	4-Whl
Parts Cost	High	Vry. High	No Model Produced	High	High
Complaints	Good	Good		Good	Average
Insurance	Regular	Regular		Regular	Regular
Fuel Econ.	16	16		16	16
Theft Rating	Average	Average		Average**	Average**
Bumpers	Weak	Weak			
Recalls	0	0		0	0
Trn. Cir. (ft.)	36.1	36.1		37.4	37.4
Weight (lbs.)	3790	3790		3657	3657
Whlbase (in.)	110.4	110.4		111.8	111.8
Price	14-16,000	16-18,000		18-20,000	23-25,000
OVERALL	Good	Good		Good	Good

Mazda MX-6 1992-97

Actually the coupe version of the 626 (with a shorter wheelbase), the MX-6 entered the market in 1988. The MX-6 chassis formed the basis of Ford's Probe, a completely different looking car that came out in

1992 Mazda MX-6

1989. A 4-wheel-steering system was optional from 1989-90, but it's hard to find today. Mazda completely restyled the MX-6 for 1993, using a longer-wheelbase chassis shared with the new 626. The 1988-92 MX-6 coupes have motorized shoulder belts and manual lap belts. For 1993, the MX-6 got conventional belts and a driver's airbag; a passenger airbag was added in 1994. ABS is optional on all models after 1991.

	1992	1993	1994	1995	1996
Size Class	Compact	Compact	Compact	Compact	Compact
Drive	Front	Front	Front	Front	Front
Crash Test	Good	Vry. Gd.	Vry. Gd.	Vry. Gd.	Vry. Gd.
Airbags	None	Driver	Dual	Dual	Dual
ABS	4-Whl*	4-Whl*	4-Whl*	4-Whl*	4-Whl*
Parts Cost	Low	Vry. High	Vry. High	High	High
Complaints	Good	Poor	Average	Poor	Average
Insurance	Surchg.	Regular	Surchg.	Surchg.	Surchg.
Fuel Econ.	22	23	23	26	26
Theft Rating	Average	Average	Average	Average	Low
Bumpers	Weak				
Recalls	1	1	0	1	1
Trn. Cir. (ft.)	35.3	35.4	35.4	35.4	35.4
Weight (lbs.)	2560	2604	2625	2625	2625
Whlbase (in.)	99	102.8	102.8	102.8	102.8
Price	3-5,000	4-6,000	5-7,000	7-9,000	10-12,000
OVERALL	Average	Poor	Average	Poor	Average

*Optional

1997 Mazda MX-6

The base MX-6 has a 2-liter 4-cylinder engine. For more power, look for the turbo or a 2.5-liter V6. The MX-6 uses the 626's rough-shifting automatic transmission, so avoid it. The handling is responsive due to different suspension tuning; you'll find it a notch below the Probe's. The ride tends to be harsh, and the controls could stand some improvement. The 1993 MX-6, though longer, has less room in back, adequate for just two. However, the driving position and front seat comfort are as good as the best sporty cars.

	1997	1998	1999	2000	2001
Size Class	Compact				
Drive	Front				
Crash Test	Vry. Gd.				
Airbags	Dual				
ABS	4-Whl*				
Parts Cost	Average				
Complaints	Average				
Insurance	Surchg.				
Fuel Econ.	26				
Theft Rating	Average		No Model Produced		
Bumpers					
Recalls	1				
Trn. Cir. (ft.)	35.4				
Weight (lbs.)	2625				
Whlbase (in.)	102.8				
Price	12-14,000				
OVERALL	Average				

Mazda RX-7 1992-96

1993 Mazda RX-7

The 1993 RX-7 model is a deliberately bare-bones sports car with unique styling. It's all business, without the gadgets and clutter of the 300ZX, Corvette, Stealth, and 3000GT. The 1990-92 models have an optional driver's airbag; the 1993 model has a standard driver's airbag; the 1994 RX-7 adds a passenger airbag. ABS became optional in 1990, standard in 1993.

The rotary engine provides ample smooth power but inferior gas mileage. The later models with the more conventional engines perform slightly better. The 5-speed on either engine choice is excellent. You'll

	1992	1993	1994	1995	1996
Size Class	Compact	Compact	Compact	Compact	Compact
Drive	Rear	Rear	Rear	Rear	Rear
Crash Test	N/A	N/A	N/A	N/A	N/A
Airbags	Driver*	Driver	Dual	Dual	Dual
ABS	4-Whl*	4-Whl	4-Whl	4-Whl	4-Whl
Parts Cost	Average	Average	Vry. High	Vry. High	Average
Complaints	Vry. Gd.	Average	Poor	Good	Vry. Gd.
Insurance	Regular	Regular	Regular	Surchg.	Surchg.
Fuel Econ.	16	18	17	17	17
Theft Rating	High	Vry. High	High	High	Vry. High
Bumpers					
Recalls	0	3	3	1	0
Trn. Cir. (ft.)	35.4	35.4	35.4	35.4	35.4
Weight (lbs.)	2789	2789	2826	2830	2830
Whlbase (in.)	95.5	95.5	95.5	95.5	95.5
Price	14-16,000	15-17,000	16-18,000	19-21,000	20-22,000
OVERALL~					

*Optional; ~Cars without crash tests do not receive an overall rating.

1995 Mazda RX-7

find the handling superb, extraordinary on the newest models, and so is braking. While the controls need some improvement, the displays are functional. The cockpit is a snug fit. This is a solid sports car.

	1997	1998	1999	2000	2001
Size Class					
Drive					
Crash Test					
Airbags					
ABS					
Parts Cost					
Complaints					
Insurance					
Fuel Econ.					
Theft Rating					
Bumpers					
Recalls					
Trn. Cir. (ft.)					
Weight (lbs.)					
Whlbase (in.)					
Price					
OVERALL~					

No Model Produced

Mercedes-Benz C-Class 1994-2001

As the smallest member of the Mercedes-Benz family, the C-Class has managed to make a name for itself as the least expensive member, though it still may not be considered affordable by some.

1994 Mercedes-Benz C-Class

The C-Class, which debuted in 1994 as the replacement for the 190E, competes mainly with the cheaper luxury offerings from Infiniti (J30) and Lexus (ES300). As with other luxury models from Mercedes, the C-Class comes with a large list of standard features, including dual airbags and 4-wheel ABS. The C-Class is all-new for 2001 and gains more interior space and head airbags to complement the side airbags.

	1992	1993	1994	1995	1996
Size Class			Intermd.	Intermd.	Intermd.
Drive			Rear	Rear	Rear
Crash Test			Good	Good	Good
Airbags			Dual	Dual	Dual
ABS			4-Whl	4-Whl	4-Whl
Parts Cost			Vry. High	Vry. High	Vry. High
Complaints			Average	Average	Average
Insurance			Regular	Discount	Discount
Fuel Econ.			23	23	23
Theft Rating			High	High	High
Bumpers		No Model Produced			
Recalls			1	0	1
Trn. Cir. (ft.)			35.2	35.2	35.2
Weight (lbs.)			3150	3150	3150
Whlbase (in.)			105.9	105.9	105.9
Price			15-17,000	18-20,000	20-22,000
OVERALL~			Vry. Gd.	Average	Good

**Estimate; ~Cars without crash tests do not receive an overall rating.

2001 Mercedes-Benz C-Class

Like the E-Class, the C stands for the car's platform, while the number following it tells you which engine the car has. The standard offering is a 2.2-liter 4-cylinder engine (C220) which will deliver average power and average gas mileage. The 2.2 was replaced in 1997 with a larger 2.3-liter engine. A larger 2.8-liter 6-cylinder (C280) and a 3.6-liter 6-cylinder (C360) are available, both of which will provide more power at the expense of fuel economy. A six-speed manual transmission is also available. The front seats are firm and comfortable, but the back is cramped with three adults.

	1997	1998	1999	2000	2001
Size Class	Intermd.	Intermd.	Intermd.	Intermd.	Intermd.
Drive	Rear	Rear	Rear	Rear	Rear
Crash Test	Good	Good	Good	Average	N/A
Airbags	Dual	Dual/Side	Dual/Side	Dual/Side	Dual/Side
ABS	4-Whl	4-Whl	4-Whl	4-Whl	4-Whl
Parts Cost	Vry. High	Vry. High	Vry. High	Vry. High	Vry. High
Complaints	Average	Average	Poor	Average	Average
Insurance	Discount	Discount	Discount	Discount	Discount
Fuel Econ.	23	23	21	21	21
Theft Rating	Vry. High	Vry. High	Vry. High**	Vry. High**	Vry. High**
Bumpers					
Recalls	0	0	0	0	0
Trn. Cir. (ft.)	35.2	35.2	35.2	35.2	35.3
Weight (lbs.)	3195	3250	3316	3316	3310
Whlbase (in.)	105.9	105.9	105.9	105.9	106.9
Price	23-25,000	26-28,000	29-31,000	>30,000	>30,000
OVERALL~	Good	Vry. Gd.	Good	Good	

Mercedes-Benz E 1992, E-Class 1993-2001

The E-Class, Mercedes' mid-level series, received new, aerodynamic styling for 1996 that was a sweeping departure from the traditional Mercedes look and feel. Filling the gap between the smaller 190-series (now

1993 Mercedes-Benz E-Class

the C-class) and the larger S-class, body choices on early models include convertible, coupe, wagon and sedan. Only the sedan is available for 1996 and 1997. All E-class models have a driver's airbag (dual airbags are optional in 1989, standard in 1993) and ABS.

The E-class has offered a diesel 5-cylinder, several in-line 6-cylinders, roughly 3-liters in size, and the V8-powered 400E, 420E, and

	1992	1993	1994	1995	1996
Size Class	Large	Large	Large	Large	Large
Drive	Rear	Rear	Rear	Rear	Rear
Crash Test	N/A	N/A	N/A	N/A	N/A
Airbags	Driver#	Dual	Dual	Dual	Dual
ABS	4-Whl	4-Whl	4-Whl	4-Whl	4-Whl
Parts Cost	Average	Vry. High	Vry. High	Vry. High	Vry. High
Complaints	Vry. Gd.	Average	Average	Poor	Average
Insurance	Discount	Discount	Discount	Discount	Discount
Fuel Econ.	20	20	18	20	28
Theft Rating	High	High	Vry. High	Vry. High	Vry. High
Bumpers					
Recalls	0	1	1	1	1
Trn. Cir. (ft.)	36.7	37	37	37	37.1
Weight (lbs.)	3330	3390	3525	3525	3538
Whlbase (in.)	110.2	110.2	110.2	110.2	111.5
Price	17-19,000	18-20,000	20-22,000	25-27,000	28-30,000
OVERALL~					

#Passenger Side Optional; **Estimate; ~Cars without crash tests do not receive an overall rating.

2001 Mercedes-Benz E-Class

500E. The basic 6 is certainly satisfactory. A few early E-class sedans have a 5-speed manual; most have automatic overdrive. Sudden acceleration was a widely reported problem on the E-class through 1989. Since the V8 models cost nearly as much as three or four compact cars, most E-class buyers concentrate on the 300 level E-class sedan or wagon. The front seats are outstanding - firm, yet relaxing on long drives. The rear seats are nearly as good. Thoughtful attention to safety and detail abound.

	1997	1998	1999	2000	2001
Size Class	Large	Large	Large	Large	Large
Drive	Rear	Rear	Rear	Rear	Rear
Crash Test	N/A	N/A	N/A	N/A	N/A
Airbags	Dual	Dual/Side	Dual/Side	Dual/Side	Dual/Side
ABS	4-Whl	4-Whl	4-Whl	4-Whl	4-Whl
Parts Cost	Vry. High	Vry. High	Vry. High	Vry. High	Very High
Complaints	Poor	Poor	Vry. Gd.	Vry. Gd.	Vry. Gd.
Insurance	Discount	Discount	Discount	Discount	Discount
Fuel Econ.	26	21	21	21	20
Theft Rating	Vry. High	Vry. High**	Vry. High**	Vry. High**	Vry. High**
Bumpers			Weak	Weak	Weak
Recalls	0	0	2	2	0
Trn. Cir. (ft.)	37.1	37.1	37.1	37.1	37.1
Weight (lbs.)	3538	3460	3525	3525	3525
Whlbase (in.)	111.5	111.5	111.5	111.5	111.5
Price	>30,000	>30,000	>30,000	>30,000	>30,000
OVERALL~					

Mercury Cougar 1992-2001

The Cougar was a twin of the Ford Thunderbird and, in many respects, a cut-rate version of the expensive Lincoln Mark Series. The 1996 edition received some minor sheet metal work, which helped

1996 Mercury Cougar

freshen up the front and rear end styling. The 1989-93 Cougars have motorized front shoulder belts and manual lap belts; 1994 models got dual airbags and conventional belts. ABS is optional from 1992 and standard from 1999.

Newer Cougars have a regular or supercharged V6 or a V8. On these cars, the standard 6 is adequate; the other engines are roughly equal in

	1992	1993	1994	1995	1996
Size Class	Large	Large	Large	Large	Large
Drive	Rear	Rear	Rear	Rear	Rear
Crash Test	Vry. Gd.	Vry. Gd.	Vry. Gd.	Vry. Gd.	Vry. Gd.
Airbags	None	None	Dual	Dual	Dual
ABS	4-Whl*	4-Whl*	4-Whl*	4-Whl*	4-Whl*
Parts Cost	Low	Low	Low	Low	Average
Complaints	Average	Poor	Average	Average	Good
Insurance	Discount	Discount	Discount	Discount	Discount
Fuel Econ.	17	17	19	19	19
Theft Rating	Average	Low	Low	Average	Average
Bumpers					
Recalls	2	2	0	0	2
Trn. Cir. (ft.)	37.5	36.6	36.6	36.6	36.6
Weight (lbs.)	3587	3512	3564	3533	3559
Whlbase (in.)	113	113	113	113	113
Price	4-6,000	5-7,000	6-8,000	7-9,000	9-11,000
OVERALL~	Good	Good	BEST BET	BEST BET	Vry. Gd.

*Optional; **Estimate; ~Cars without a crash test do not receive an overall rating.

244

2001 Mercury Cougar

power. With the 1999 redesign, a 2.0-liter 4-cylinder engine or 2.5-liter V6 are available. In general, the ride is comfortable, but the handling of base Cougars is less than crisp, which is improved by V8s with the special handling package. The 1992-98 Cougar, like the T-bird, has enough room for four plus luggage. The gauges have nicely designed dials, but avoid the electronic panel. The Cougar was considerably downsized in 1999.

	1997	1998	1999	2000	2001
Size Class	Large	Large	Compact	Compact	Compact
Drive	Rear	Rear	Rear	Rear	Rear
Crash Test	Vry. Gd.	Vry. Gd.	N/A	N/A	N/A
Airbags	Dual	Dual	Dual	Dual	Dual
ABS	4-Whl*	4-Whl*	4-Whl	4-Whl	4-Whl
Parts Cost	High	High	High	High	High
Complaints	Average	Vry. Gd.	Vry. Pr.	Vry. Pr.	Vry. Pr.
Insurance	Regular	Regular	Surcharge	Surcharge	Surcharge
Fuel Econ.	18	18	23	23	23
Theft Rating	Low	Low	Low	Low	Low**
Bumpers					
Recalls	0	0	0	0	0
Trn. Cir. (ft.)	36.5	36.5	37	37	37
Weight (lbs.)	3536	3536	2892	2892	2892
Whlbase (in.)	113	113	106.4	106.4	106.4
Price	11-13,000	12-14,000	14-16,000	15-17,000	17-19,000
OVERALL~	Good	Vry. Gd.			

Mercury Sable 1992-2001

This twin of the popular Taurus emphasizes luxury, even in base GS form. The Taurus and Sable, available as either a 4-door sedan or wagon, popularized aerodynamic car design, and both be-

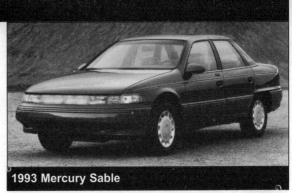

1993 Mercury Sable

came Ford's savior from financial disaster. Though widely imitated, these cars have held their own against tough competition; a redesign for the 1996 model year only strengthened that position. Models starting in 1990 have a driver's airbag; a passenger airbag became optional in 1992 and standard in 1993. ABS is optional beginning in 1991.

From 1989 on, all Sables have a 140 hp 3.0 V6 or the optional 3.8-

	1992	1993	1994	1995	1996
Size Class	Intermd.	Intermd.	Intermd.	Intermd.	Intermd.
Drive	Front	Front	Front	Front	Front
Crash Test	Good[1]	Good[1]	Good	Good	Vry. Gd.
Airbags	Driver#	Dual	Dual	Dual	Dual
ABS	4-Whl*	4-Whl*	4-Whl*	4-Whl*	4-Whl*
Parts Cost	Low	Low	Low	Low	Low
Complaints	Vry. Pr.	Vry. Pr.	Poor	Poor	Poor
Insurance	Discount	Discount	Discount	Discount	Discount
Fuel Econ.	20	21	20	20	20
Theft Rating	Low	Vry. Low	Vry. Low	Vry. Low	Vry. Low
Bumpers	Strong	Weak	Weak	Weak	Strong
Recalls	5	8	4	3	5
Trn. Cir. (ft.)	38.6	38.6	38.6	38.6	38
Weight (lbs.)	3147	3122	3275	3144	3388
Whlbase (in.)	106	106	106	106	108.5
Price	3-5,000	4-6,000	5-7,000	6-8,000	9-11,000
OVERALL	Average	Good	Good	Good	Vry. Gd.

[1]Data given for sedan. Crash test for wagon is Vry. Good; *Optional; #Passenger Side Optional; **Estimate

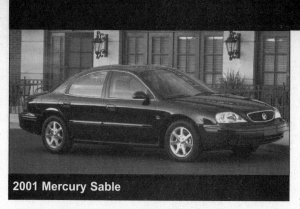

2001 Mercury Sable

liter V6, also 140 hp. The base engine is peppy; the 3.8-liter offers more torque for towing or heavy loads. With standard suspension, Sable rides smoother but corners less precisely than the Taurus. The optional suspension improves handling but makes the ride stiffer. Replace the General tires with ones better suited for handling. Inside, Sable's dashboard is easy to read, and four adults will have ample room and comfort.

	1997	1998	1999	2000	2001
Size Class	Intermd.	Intermd.	Intermd.	Intermd.	Intermd.
Drive	Front	Front	Front	Front	Front
Crash Test	Vry. Gd.	Vry. Gd.	Vry. Gd.	Vry. Gd.	Vry. Gd.
Airbags	Dual	Dual	Dual	Dual	Dual
ABS	4-Whl*	4-Whl*	4-Whl*	4-Whl*	4-Whl*
Parts Cost	Low	Average	Vry. Low	Vry. Low	Vry. Low
Complaints	Good	Average	Average	Average	Average
Insurance	Discount	Discount	Discount	Discount	Discount
Fuel Econ.	20	20	20	20	20
Theft Rating	Vry. Low	Vry. Low**	Vry. Low**	Vry. Low**	Vry. Low**
Bumpers	Strong		Strong	Strong	
Recalls	3	2	3	1	0
Trn. Cir. (ft.)	38	38	38	39.8	39.8
Weight (lbs.)	3388	3299	3302	3302	3302
Whlbase (in.)	108.5	108.5	108.5	108.5	108.5
Price	10-12,000	11-13,000	12-14,000	16-18,000	17-19,000
OVERALL	BEST BET	BEST BET	BEST BET	BEST BET	BEST BET

Mercury Tracer 1992-1999

In the winter of 1990, Ford replaced the Escort with a Mazda Protégé-based car for 1991, and Mercury's version of the new Escort took the name Tracer. Finally, in 1997, the Tracer was once again all-new, this time following the Escort's lead. 1994 models have a driver's airbag, and 1995 models have dual airbags. You can order ABS only on the 1994-97 LTS.

1993 Mercury Tracer

Acceleration is strong with the 1.8-liter engine, adequate with the other engines. The handling on all Tracers can become skittish in highway-speed cornering; the newer Tracer's suspension helped. The stan-

	1992	1993	1994	1995	1996
Size Class	Subcomp.	Subcomp.	Subcomp.	Subcomp.	Subcomp.
Drive	Front	Front	Front	Front	Front
Crash Test	Vry. Gd.	Vry. Gd.	Good	Average	Average
Airbags	None	None	Driver	Dual	Dual
ABS	None	None	4-Whl*	4-Whl*	4-Whl*
Parts Cost	Low	Low	Low	Low	Low
Complaints	Vry. Gd.	Poor	Good	Good	Vry. Gd.
Insurance	Surchg.	Surchg.	Surchg.	Surchg.	Surchg.
Fuel Econ.	26	25	25	30	23
Theft Rating	Low	Low	Vry. Low	Vry. Low	Vry. Low
Bumpers					
Recalls	2	1	1	3	0
Trn. Cir. (ft.)	31.5	31.5	31.5	31.5	31.5
Weight (lbs.)	2356	2348	2393	2418	2409
Whlbase (in.)	98.4	98.4	98.4	98.4	98.4
Price	<3,000	2-4,000	3-5,000	4-6,000	5-7,000
OVERALL	Good	Poor	Good	Average	Good

*Optional; **Estimate

1998 Mercury Tracer

dard five-speed shifts adequately; automatic transmissions on 1991-later Tracers have an overdrive gear that helps gas mileage. The room and comfort is good in front, average for subcompacts in the rear, with a spacious trunk. Instruments and controls are adequate. Tracers are good cars, especially the more recent models.

	1997	1998	1999	2000	2001
Size Class	Subcomp.	Subcomp.	Subcomp.		
Drive	Front	Front	Front		
Crash Test	Average	Average	Average		
Airbags	Dual	Dual	Dual		
ABS	4-Whl*	4-Whl*	4-Whl*		
Parts Cost	Vry. Low	Vry. Low	Vry. Low		
Complaints	Poor	Good	Vry. Gd.		
Insurance	Surchg.	Surchg.	Surchg.		
Fuel Econ.	28	28	28		
Theft Rating	Vry. Low	Vry. Low	Vry. Low**		
Bumpers	Weak	Weak			
Recalls	0	0	0		
Trn. Cir. (ft.)	31.5	31.5	31.5		
Weight (lbs.)	2457	2469	2469		
Whlbase (in.)	98.4	98.4	98.4		
Price	6-8,000	8-10,000	9-11,000		
OVERALL	Good	Vry. Gd.	BEST BET		

No Model Produced

Mercury Villager/Nissan Quest 1993-2001

1993 Mercury Villager

The Villager differs from its near-twin, the Nissan Quest, only in standard equipment. Ford turned the design work over to Nissan, and Ford builds them in Ohio. Though they were all-new for 1993, Nissan designed the Villager and Quest with no airbags in 1993 and only one airbag in 1994. The awkward motorized shoulder belts with separate lap belts were standard through 1995. The Villager and Quest kept the same protection through 1995 - a tremendous disadvantage in this competitive market. Finally, in 1996, dual airbags were added. The 4-wheel ABS, standard on all Villagers, is optional on the

	1992	1993	1994	1995	1996
Size Class	No Model Produced	Minivan	Minivan	Minivan	Minivan
Drive		Front	Front	Front	Front
Crash Test		Vry. Gd.	Average	Average	Good
Airbags		Driver	Driver	Driver	Dual
ABS		4-Whl[1]	4-Whl[1]	4-Whl[1]	4-Whl[1]
Parts Cost		Low	Low	Low	Average
Complaints		Vry. Pr.	Poor	Vry. Pr.	Poor
Insurance		Discount	Discount	Discount	Discount
Fuel Econ.		17	17	17	17
Theft Rating		Low	Vry. Low	Vry. Low	Vry. Low
Bumpers		Weak	Weak	Weak	Weak
Recalls			8	2	5
Trn. Cir. (ft.)		38.7	38.7	38.7	38.7
Weight (lbs.)		3015	3015	3015	2876
Whlbase (in.)		112.2	112.2	112.2	112.2
Price		6-8,000	7-9,000	8-10,000	11-13,000
OVERALL		Poor	Average	Average	Good

[1]Data given for Villager. ABS is optional on the Quest; **Estimate

2001 Mercury Villager

Quest.

Both vehicles have an adequate 151 hp, 3-liter V6 that gets overwhelmed with too much towing, but the optional towing package helps. The handling is only average. However, it can be firmed up with the optional "handling package" suspension; you'll find these minivans ride remarkably like passenger cars. They were crash tested this year and did extremely well.

	1997	1998	1999	2000	2001
Size Class	Minivan	Minivan	Minivan	Minivan	Minivan
Drive	Front	Front	Front	Front	Front
Crash Test	Good	Good	Good	Average	Vry. Gd.
Airbags	Dual	Dual	Dual	Dual	Dual
ABS	4-Whl[1]	4-Whl[1]	4-Whl[1]	4-Whl[1]	4-Whl[1]
Parts Cost	High	Average	High	High	High
Complaints	Good	Poor	Vry. Pr.	Good	Vry. Pr.
Insurance	Discount	Discount	Discount	Discount	Discount
Fuel Econ.	17	17	17	17	17
Theft Rating	Vry. Low	Vry. Low	Vry. Low**	Vry. Low**	Vry. Low**
Bumpers	Weak	Weak			
Recalls	4	2	1	1	1
Trn. Cir. (ft.)	38.7	38.7	38.7	38.7	38.7
Weight (lbs.)	2865	3865	3830	3847	3997
Whlbase (in.)	112.2	112.2	112.2	112.2	112.2
Price	13-15,000	15-17,000	18-20,000	23-25,000	24-26,000
OVERALL	Vry. Gd.	Good	Good	BEST BET	Good

251

Mitsubishi Diamante 1992-2001

The Mitsubishi Diamante was introduced in 1992 and was targeted at the sports sedan buyer who wants lots of technical gadgetry. A lower-level wagon is available through 1995; Mitsubishi

1992 Mitsubishi Diamante

dropped the LS and wagon in 1996 and refocused on the luxury sedan market. In an effort to increase sales, Mitsubishi revamped the 1997 Diamante, increasing interior room and rounding out the edges. Inn 1999, it was reduced to only one trim level. A driver airbag was added in 1993, a second airbag in 1994. Four-wheel ABS has been available since the Diamante's introduction.

	1992	1993	1994	1995	1996
Size Class	Large	Large	Large	Large	Large
Drive	Front	Front	Front	Front	Front
Crash Test	Good	Good	Good	Good	Good
Airbags	Driver	Driver	Dual	Dual	Dual
ABS	4-Whl*	4-Whl*	4-Whl*	4-Whl*	4-Whl*
Parts Cost	Vry. High	Vry. High	Vry. High	Vry. High	Vry. High
Complaints	Poor	Average	Average	Good	Vry. Gd.
Insurance	Regular	Regular	Regular	Regular	Regular
Fuel Econ.	18	18	18	18	18
Theft Rating	Vry. High	Vry. High	Vry. High	High	Vry. High
Bumpers					
Recalls	3	4	3	1	0
Trn. Cir. (ft.)	36.7	36.7	36.7	36.7	36.7
Weight (lbs.)	3428	3483	3483	3505	3483
Whlbase (in.)	107.1	107.1	107.1	107.1	107.1
Price	5-7,000	6-8,000	7-9,000	9-11,000	10-12,000
OVERALL~	Vry. Pr.	Vry. Pr.	Poor	Average	Good

*Optional; **Estimate; ~Cars without crash tests do not receive an overall rating.

2001 Mitsubishi Diamante

The 3-liter V6 is powerful enough, especially at higher speeds. Fuel economy is average for a car this size, but still not good. The Diamante handles, rides, accelerates, and brakes adequately, though none of these items surpass other cars in its class. The trunk is spacious and easy to access. The up-level LS competes with BMW and Lexus models. While only slightly larger than the Ford Taurus, Honda Accord and Toyota Camry, pay the extra money and you'll get a somewhat more sophisticated car with lots of computer wizardry.

	1997	1998	1999	2000	2001
Size Class	Large	Large	Large	Large	Large
Drive	Front	Front	Front	Front	Front
Crash Test	N/A	N/A	N/A	N/A	N/A
Airbags	Dual	Dual	Dual	Dual	Dual
ABS	4-Whl*	4-Whl	4-Whl	4-Whl	4-Whl
Parts Cost	Vry. High	Vry. High	Vry. High	Vry. High	Vry. High
Complaints	Poor	Average	Vry. Gd.	Average	Good
Insurance	Regular	Regular	Regular	Regular	Regular
Fuel Econ.	18	18	18	18	18
Theft Rating	Vry. High	Vry. High**	Vry. High**	Vry. High**	Vry. High**
Bumpers			Strong	Strong	Strong
Recalls	0	0	1	1	0
Trn. Cir. (ft.)	36.7	36.7	36.7	36.7	36.7
Weight (lbs.)	3363	3417	3417	3417	3417
Whlbase (in.)	107.1	107.1	107.1	107.1	107.1
Price	16-18,000	17-19,000	20-22,000	24-26,000	25-27,000
OVERALL~					

Mitsubishi Galant 1992-2001

The Galant competes with Toyota's Camry and Cressida /Avalon, the Honda Accord and the Nissan MaximaCsome tough competition. The 1989 model came with a 4-cylinder engine. The Galant was

1992 Mitsubishi Galant

again redesigned in 1994, adding a V6 midway through the 1995 model year. In 1999, it received a complete remake. Galants from 1989-93 have motorized front shoulder belts and manual lap belts, and the Galant picked up dual airbags and conventional belts with the 1994 redesign. ABS was optional from 1989 on.

The 2.0 and 2.4-liter 4-cylinder engines are adequately powerful and

	1992	1993	1994	1995	1996
Size Class	Compact	Compact	Compact	Compact	Compact
Drive	Front	Front	Front	Front	Front
Crash Test	Poor	Poor	Good	Good	Good
Airbags	None	None	Dual	Dual	Dual
ABS	4-Whl*	4-Whl*	4-Whl*	4-Whl*	4-Whl*
Parts Cost	Vry. High	Vry. High	Vry. High	High	High
Complaints	Average	Vry. Gd.	Vry. Gd.	Poor	Average
Insurance	Regular	Regular	Regular	Regular	Surchg.
Fuel Econ.	19	21	22	22	23
Theft Rating	Low	Vry. Low	Average	Vry. High	Low
Bumpers	Strong	Strong	Weak	Weak	Weak
Recalls	2	0	2	2	1
Trn. Cir. (ft.)	34.8	34.8	34.8	34.8	34.8
Weight (lbs.)	2667	2712	2755	2866	2755
Whlbase (in.)	102.4	102.4	103.7	103.7	103.7
Price	4-6,000	5-7,000	6-8,000	8-10,000	8-10,000
OVERALL	Vry. Pr.	Average	Good	Poor	Poor

*Optional; **Estimate

2001 Mitsubishi Galant

generally economical; the turbo in the 4-wheel drive VR-4 is faster but thirstier. The Galant Sigma's V6 and later V6 models also consume a lot more gas. The Galant's ride tends to be firm. The handling is decent, typical of mid-size Japanese sedans; the new GS's sport-tuned suspension should be better. The roominess in the rear seat shrinks on the 1994 and later models and is tight for adults.

	1997	1998	1999	2000	2001
Size Class	Compact	Compact	Compact	Compact	Compact
Drive	Front	Front	Front	Front	Front
Crash Test	Good	Good	Vry. Gd.	Vry. Gd.	Vry. Gd.
Airbags	Dual	Dual	Dual	Dual	Dual
ABS	4-Whl*	4-Whl*	4-Whl	4-Whl	4-Whl
Parts Cost	Low	Low	Vry. Low	Vry. Low	Vry. Low
Complaints	Good	Good	Vry. Pr.	Vry. Gd.	Vry. Pr.
Insurance	Surchg.	Surchg.	Surchg.	Surchg.	Surchg.
Fuel Econ.	23	23	23	23	23
Theft Rating	High	High**	High**	Vry. High	Vry. High
Bumpers	Weak	Weak		Strong	Strong
Recalls	1	1	2	6	3
Trn. Cir. (ft.)	34.8	34.8	34.8	34.8	34.8
Weight (lbs.)	2777	2778	2835	2835	2835
Whlbase (in.)	103.7	103.7	103.7	103.7	103.7
Price	10-12,000	11-13,000	14-16,000	15-17,000	17-19,000
OVERALL	Good	Good	Good	BEST BET	Average

Mitsubishi Mirage 1992-2001

The Mirage was restyled for 1993, and finally, in 1997, the Mirage received yet another facelift. From 1989 until 1993, Mirages have motorized shoulder belts with separate lap belts. In 1994, the Mirage got a driver

1992 Mitsubishi Mirage

airbag and regular seat belt, but the right front seat kept a motorized belt and separate lap belt until 1995 when a passenger airbag was added. ABS became available in 1993, but only on top-line sedans. For the 1995 and 1996 models, ABS is not offered, since sedans were relegated to fleet status at the end of 1994.

The Mirage's performance with the standard 4-cylinder (1.5 or 1.6-

	1992	1993	1994	1995	1996
Size Class	Subcomp.	Subcomp.	Subcomp.	Subcomp.	Subcomp.
Drive	Front	Front	Front	Front	Front
Crash Test	N/A	Good[1]	Good[1]	Good[1]	Good[1]
Airbags	None	None	Driver	Dual	Dual
ABS	None	4-Whl*	4-Whl*	None	None
Parts Cost	Vry. High	Average	Average	High	Vry. High
Complaints	Poor	Poor	Average	Average	Good
Insurance	Surchg.	Regular	Surchg.	Surchg.	Surchg.
Fuel Econ.	21	27	28	28	32
Theft Rating	Low	Vry. Low	Vry. Low	Vry. Low	Vry. Low
Bumpers	Fair				
Recalls	2	4	0	0	0
Trn. Cir. (ft.)	30.2	32.8	32.8	32.8	32.8
Weight (lbs.)	2205	2085	2085	2085	2085
Whlbase (in.)	93.9	96.1	96.1	96.1	96.1
Price	<3000	2-4,000	3-5,000	4-6,000	5-7,000
OVERALL~		Poor	Average	Good	Good

[1]Data given for sedan. Crash test for coupe is Average; *Optional; **Estimate; ~Cars without crash tests do not receive an

2001 Mitsubishi Mirage

liter) is fine, but all models do better with the 1.8-liter 4-cylinder engine. Gas mileage is good. The 5-speed is a better match than the 3-speed automatic for these engines. Handling is good through 1992, especially on turbo models; however, it tends to be imprecise but still safe on newer base models. The interior is fairly comfortable for four from 1989 onward, and the instrument panel layout is good.

	1997	1998	1999	2000	2001
Size Class	Subcomp.	Subcomp.	Subcomp.	Subcomp.	Subcomp.
Drive	Front	Front	Front	Front	Front
Crash Test	N/A	N/A	N/A	N/A	N/A
Airbags	Dual	Dual	Dual	Dual	Dual
ABS	4-Whl*	4-Whl*	4-Whl*	4-Whl*	4-Whl*
Parts Cost	High	Average	Average	Average	Average
Complaints	Average	Good	Good	Vry. Gd.	Good
Insurance	Surchg.	Surchg.	Surchg.	Surchg.	Surchg.
Fuel Econ.	33	33	33	33	33
Theft Rating	Vry. Low	Low**	Low**	Low**	Low**
Bumpers	Weak	Weak			
Recalls	1	3	0	0	0
Trn. Cir. (ft.)	32.8	32.8	32.8	32.8	32.8
Weight (lbs.)	2127	2125	2125	2125	2125
Whlbase (in.)	96.1	95.1	95.1	95.1	95.1
Price	6-8,000	7-9,000	8-10,000	11-13,000	13-15,000
OVERALL~					

overall rating.

Mitsubishi Montero 1992-2001

The Montero, designed to be a mid-sized sport utility vehicle that attracts a wealthy customer, has been holding its own in this growing market. Its first re-design since its inception in 1984 oc-

1992 Mitsubishi Montero

curred in 1992 going from a square look to the more rounded model you see in showrooms today. In terms of safety, airbags were not available until 1994, when a driver airbag became standard; dual airbags became standard in 1996. Look for 4-wheel ABS, available on certain Monteros beginning in 1992. Side airbags became standard for 2001 as well as ABS.

	1992	1993	1994	1995	1996
Size Class	Sp. Util.	Sp. Util.	Sp. Util.	Sp. Util.	Sp. Util.
Drive	2WD/4WD	2WD/4WD	2WD/4WD	2WD/4WD	2WD/4WD
Crash Test	Good	Good	Vry. Gd.	Vry. Gd.	Average
Airbags	None	None	Driver	Driver	Dual
ABS	4-Whl*	4-Whl*	4-Whl*	4-Whl*	4-Whl*
Parts Cost	Average	Average	Average	Average	High
Complaints	Average	Vry. Gd.	Good	Poor	Average
Insurance	Surchg.	Surchg.	Surchg.	Surchg.	Surchg.
Fuel Econ.	15	15	15	15	15
Theft Rating	Average	Vry. High	Vry. High	Vry. High	Vry. High
Bumpers					
Recalls	4	3	3	1	1
Trn. Cir. (ft.)	38.7	38.7	38.7	38.7	38.7
Weight (lbs.)	4130	4130	4175	4265	4290
Whlbase (in.)	107.3	107.3	107.3	107.3	107.3
Price	9-11,000	10-12,000	11-13,000	13-15,000	16-18,000
OVERALL	Vry. Pr.	Poor	Poor	Poor	Vry. Pr.

*Optional; **Estimate

2001 Mitsubishi Montero

The 1990-97 models have a much more powerful 3-liter V6 on base and LS models. Also, a standard 3.5-liter V6 is on the SR model, which puts out a peppy 214 hp. Though you'll be happier with the power on the later models, fuel economy with any of these engines is poor. The ride is much more car-like than other sport utilities, but the handling is still rather clumsy. Inside, passenger comfort is good, but cargo space is minimal. All of these improve thought with the all new 2001 version, which has a longer wheelbase, wider track and lower height as well as a smaller turning radius.

	1997	1998	1999	2000	2001
Size Class	Sp. Util.	Sp. Util.	Sp. Util.	Sp. Util.	Sp. Util.
Drive	2WD/4WD	2WD/4WD	2WD/4WD	2WD/4WD	2WD/4WD
Crash Test	Average	Average	Average	Average	Average
Airbags	Dual	Dual	Dual	Dual	Dual
ABS	4-Whl*	4-Whl*	4-Whl	4-Whl	4-Whl
Parts Cost	Vry. High	High	Vry. High	Vry. High	Vry. High
Complaints	Vry. Pr.	Vry. Pr.	Average	Vry. Gd.	Average
Insurance	Surchg.	Surchg.	Surchg.	Surchg.	Surchg.
Fuel Econ.	16	16	16	16	16
Theft Rating	Vry. High	Vry. High	Vry. High**	Vry. High**	Vry. High**
Bumpers					
Recalls	2	2	0	0	0
Trn. Cir. (ft.)	38.7	38.7	38.7	38.7	38.7
Weight (lbs.)	4385	4431	4431	4431	4431
Whlbase (in.)	107.3	107.3	107.3	107.3	107.3
Price	17-19,000	19-21,000	20-22,000	>30,000	>30,000
OVERALL	Vry. Pr.	Vry. Pr.	Poor	Poor	Vry. Pr.

Nissan 240SX 1992-98

Nissan added a convertible in 1992, which, in 1994, became the only 240SX model offered. In '95, a lower and wider 240SX with standard dual airbags and a hardtop was introduced. Minor changes can be found

1992 Nissan 240SX

on the 1997 model. All 240SX coupes and hatchbacks have motorized front shoulder belts and separate lap belts. Unlike most of its competitors, the 240SX convertible has no airbags before 1995, just door-mounted belts. Dual airbags are standard on 1995-97 models. ABS is optional on the 240SX from 1989 on.

The 240SX comes with a 2.4-liter 4-cylinder engine that's amply

	1992	1993	1994	1995	1996
Size Class	Compact	Compact	Compact	Compact	Compact
Drive	Rear	Rear	Rear	Rear	Rear
Crash Test	Vry. Gd.	Vry. Gd.	Vry. Gd.	Average	Average
Airbags	None	None	None	Dual	Dual
ABS	4-Whl*	4-Whl*	4-Whl*	4-Whl*	4-Whl*
Parts Cost	High	High	Average	Average	Low
Complaints	Vry. Gd.	Vry. Gd.	Vry. Gd.	Vry. Pr.	Vry. Gd.
Insurance	Surchg.	Surchg.	Surchg.	Surchg.	Surchg.
Fuel Econ.	22	22	21	22	21
Theft Rating	Average	Average	Vry. High	Vry. High	Vry. High
Bumpers	Strong	Strong	Strong		
Recalls	0	0	0	1	0
Trn. Cir. (ft.)	30.8	30.8	30.8	31.5	34.1
Weight (lbs.)	2699	2730	2869	2760	2753
Whlbase (in.)	97.4	97.4	97.4	99.4	99.4
Price	5-7,000	6-8,000	7-9,000	7-9,000	10-12,000
OVERALL	Good	Good	Good	Vry. Pr.	Good

*Optional; **Estimate

1998 Nissan 240SX

powerful with inferior gas mileage. The 1994 convertibles come only with an automatic overdrive. The ride, as you might expect, is firm. The handling is generally good, but not up to the best sporty cars. Up front, comfort is good; the rear seat is too small for adults, and trunk space is minimal.

	1997	1998	1999	2000	2001
Size Class	Compact	Compact			
Drive	Rear	Rear			
Crash Test	Average	Average			
Airbags	Dual	Dual			
ABS	4-Whl*	4-Whl*			
Parts Cost	Vry. High	Vry. High			
Complaints	Vry. Gd.	Poor			
Insurance	Surchg.	Surchg.	No Model Produced		
Fuel Econ.	22	22			
Theft Rating	Vry. High	Vry. High**			
Bumpers					
Recalls	0	0			
Trn. Cir. (ft.)	31.5	31.5			
Weight (lbs.)	2800	2800			
Whlbase (in.)	99.4	99.4			
Price	13-15,000	14-16,000			
OVERALL	Poor	Vry. Pr.			

Nissan 300ZX 1992-96

Nissan likes people to think the ZX is more refined than other sports cars, and in some ways it is. Door-mounted lap-shoulder belts are standard from 1989-93. A driver's airbag was optional in 1991, standard in 1992, and

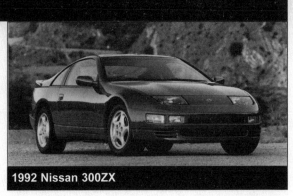

1992 Nissan 300ZX

a passenger airbag was added in 1995. ABS was optional in 1989 and standard beginning in 1991.

All ZX models have a 3-liter 6-cylinder engine, which provides excellent handling. In 1989, the ZX got a new styling aimed directly at traditional sports cars like the Chevrolet Corvette, with an emphasis on high technology. The Turbo coupe, with added goodies, is equipped

	1992	1993	1994	1995	1996
Size Class	Intermd.	Intermd.	Intermd.	Intermd.	Intermd.
Drive	Rear	Rear	Rear	Rear	Rear
Crash Test	N/A	N/A	N/A	N/A	N/A
Airbags	Driver	Driver	Driver	Dual	Dual
ABS	4-Whl	4-Whl	4-Whl	4-Whl	4-Whl
Parts Cost	High	Vry. High	High	Average	Average
Complaints	Vry. Gd.	Poor	Good	Good	Average
Insurance	Surchg.	Surchg.	Surchg.	Surchg.	Surchg.
Fuel Econ.	18	18	18	24	24
Theft Rating	High	High	High	High	Vry. High
Bumpers					
Recalls	0	0	0	0	0
Trn. Cir. (ft.)	34.1	34.1	34.1	34.1	34.1
Weight (lbs.)	3186	3186	3432	3518	3287
Whlbase (in.)	96.5	96.5	96.5	96.5	96.5
Price	13-15,000	14-16,000	15-17,000	17-19,000	21-23,000
OVERALL~					

~Cars without crash tests do not receive an overall rating.

1996 Nissan 300ZX

much like the hot Dodge Stealth or Mitsubishi 3000G with turbo-charged V6, 4-wheel steering with driver-adjustable suspension.

Considering the handling and the ZX character, the ride on later models isn't bad. Inside, the rear seat on earlier models is a joke, and the controls could stand improvement. For this much money, don't settle for a ZX without dual airbags and conventional seat belts.8

	1997	1998	1999	2000	2001
Size Class					
Drive					
Crash Test					
Airbags					
ABS					
Parts Cost					
Complaints					
Insurance					
Fuel Econ.					
Theft Rating		No Model Produced			
Bumpers					
Recalls					
Trn. Cir. (ft.)					
Weight (lbs.)					
Whlbase (in.)					
Price					
OVERALL~					

Nissan Maxima 1992-2001

The Maxima is the most expensive sedan model sold under the Nissan name. A redesign in 1995 brought more interior room and a more powerful engine. The 1989-94 Maximas have motorized shoulder belts and separate lap belts; 1992-94 models supplement these belts with a driver's airbag, though it is only standard from 1993 on. For 1995, dual airbags and conventional belts were added. ABS is a common option on 1989-97 models. Side and head airbags became optional with the new redesign in 2000.

1992 Nissan Maxima

The Maxima uses a tamer version of Nissan's 300ZX engine, which

	1992	1993	1994	1995	1996
Size Class	Intermd.	Intermd.	Intermd.	Intermd.	Intermd.
Drive	Front	Front	Front	Front	Front
Crash Test	Average	Average	Average	Average	Average
Airbags	Driver*	Driver	Driver	Dual	Dual
ABS	4-Whl*	4-Whl*	4-Whl*	4-Whl*	4-Whl*
Parts Cost	Average	High	High	Average	Average
Complaints	Average	Good	Vry. Gd.	Good	Vry. Gd.
Insurance	Discount	Discount	Regular	Regular	Surchrg.
Fuel Econ.	19	19	19	21	21
Theft Rating	High	Vry. High	Vry. High	Vry. High	Vry. High
Bumpers				Weak	Weak
Recalls	2	3	2	0	0
Trn. Cir. (ft.)	36.7	36.7	36.7	34.8	34.8
Weight (lbs.)	3129	3139	3165	3010	3001
Whlbase (in.)	104.3	104.3	104.3	106.3	106.3
Price	6-8,000	7-9,000	8-10,000	10-12,000	12-14,000
OVERALL	Average	Average	Poor	Good	Average

*Optional; **Estimate

264

2001 Nissan Maxima

provides ample performance; you won't need the 1993-94 SE's additional 30 horsepower. Maxima's handling is good, particularly on 1989 and later models, and the ride is on the firm side. The rear seat has enough room for two adults, and the trunk can accommodate luggage for four and the new 200 model has even more space. The gauges can be difficult to read in the daytime - at night, they're fine. A good mid-size car, marred by the unavoidable automatic belt system on earlier models.

	1997	1998	1999	2000	2001
Size Class	Intermd.	Intermd.	Intermd.	Intermd.	Intermd.
Drive	Front	Front	Front	Front	Front
Crash Test	Average	Good	Good	Good	Good
Airbags	Dual	Dual/Side*	Dual/Side*	Dual/Side*	Dual/Side*
ABS	4-Whl*	4-Whl*	4-Whl*	4-Whl*	4-Whl*
Parts Cost	Vry. High	Vry. High	Vry. High	Vry. High	Vry. High
Complaints	Vry. Gd.	Good	Vry. Gd.	Average	Average
Insurance	Regular	Regular	Surcharge	Surcharge	Surcharge
Fuel Econ.	22	22	22	22	22
Theft Rating	Vry. High	Vry. High	Vry. High**	Vry. High**	Vry. High**
Bumpers	Weak	Weak	Strong	Weak	Weak
Recalls	0	0	0	0	0
Trn. Cir. (ft.)	34.8	34.8	34.8	34.8	34.8
Weight (lbs.)	3001	3012	3012	3012	3012
Whlbase (in.)	106.3	106.3	106.3	106.3	106.3
Price	14-16,000	16-18,000	17-19,000	20-22,000	21-23,000
OVERALL	Average	Good	Good	Poor	Poor

Nissan Pathfinder 1992-2001

The Pathfinder came in two trim levels, XE and the fancy SE. All-new in 1996, the Pathfinder is complete with dual airbags, unlike any previous model year. Since 1991, ABS has been standard on rear wheels

1993 Nissan Pathfinder

only but moved to all four wheels in 1997.

A 3-liter V6 is the only engine choice on the Pathfinder between '89 and '95; a larger V6 is optional in 1996 and 1997. Both engines could be ordered with 5-speed manual or automatic overdrive. Handling, like the Jeep Cherokee's, is about as good as it gets for a sport utility vehicle, but it's still short of the mark set by better cars. The ride is forgiv-

	1992	1993	1994	1995	1996
Size Class	Sp. Util.	Sp. Util.	Sp. Util.	Sp. Util.	Sp. Util.
Drive	Rear/4	Rear/4	Rear/4	Rear/4	Rear/4
Crash Test	Poor	Poor	Poor	Poor	Poor
Airbags	None	None	None	None	Dual
ABS	2-Whl	2-Whl	2-Whl	2-Whl	2-Whl
Parts Cost	Low	Low	Low	Low	Low
Complaints	Good	Good	Average	Vry. Gd.	Good
Insurance	Regular	Surchg.	Surchg.	Surchg.	Discount
Fuel Econ.	15	17	15	15	17
Theft Rating	High	Vry. High	Vry. High	Vry. High	Vry. High
Bumpers					
Recalls	0	0	1	0	2
Trn. Cir. (ft.)	35.5	35.5	35.4	35.5	35.4
Weight (lbs.)	3520	3520	3885	4090	3815
Whlbase (in.)	104.3	104.3	104.3	104.3	104.3
Price	7-9,000	8-10,000	9-11,000	10-12,000	14-16,000
OVERALL	Poor	Vry. Pr.	Vry. Pr.	Poor	Good

**Estimate

2001 Nissan Pathfinder

ing, better than most utility vehicles. Interior room in 1989-95 models is a bit tight and not too comfortable in back; the new 1996 has an larger wheelbase which provides more room. As in the pickup, major controls and gauges are good. Cargo area is on the small side. With the addition of airbags and other safety features, the Pathfinder has moved up near the top of this class.

	1997	1998	1999	2000	2001
Size Class	Sp. Util.	Sp. Util.	Sp. Util.	Sp. Util.	Sp. Util.
Drive	Rear/4	Rear/4	Rear/4	Rear/4	Rear/4
Crash Test	Poor	Poor	Poor	Vry. Gd.	Vry. Gd.
Airbags	Dual	Dual	Dual	Dual	Dual
ABS	4-Whl	4-Whl	4-Whl	4-Whl	4-Whl
Parts Cost	High	Vry. High	Vry. High	High	High
Complaints	Good	Good	Vry. Gd.	Vry. Gd.	Vry. Gd.
Insurance	Surchg.	Surchg.	Regular	Regular	Regular
Fuel Econ.	16	16	16	15	15
Theft Rating	Vry. High	Vry. High	Vry. High	Vry. High**	Vry. High**
Bumpers					
Recalls	0	0	0	0	0
Trn. Cir. (ft.)	37.4	37.4	37.4	37.4	37.4
Weight (lbs.)	3675	3675	3675	3675	3675
Whlbase (in.)	106.3	106.3	106.3	106.3	106.3
Price	17-19,000	18-20,000	21-23,000	27-29,000	28-30,000
OVERALL	Vry. Pr.	Vry. Pr.	Average	Good	Good

Nissan Sentra 1992-2001

The Sentra has been transformed four times since its birth in 1982. The original 1986 model was replaced in mid-year by the 1987 model, whose European styling resembled the late-1970's Audi Fox.

1992 Nissan Sentra

The 1991-94 Sentra looks like its predecessor with rounder edges. The 1995 Sentra comes only as a 4-door (2-door version is renamed as the 200SX) with even rounder edges to compete with the Toyota Tercel, Saturn SL and Neon sedans. The 2000 model got a facelift with new headlights and grille. The 1990 Sentras have door-mounted shoulder belts with manual lap belts; from 1991 on, you get awful door-mount-

	1992	1993	1994	1995	1996
Size Class	Subcomp.	Subcomp.	Subcomp.	Subcomp.	Subcomp.
Drive	Front	Front	Front	Front	Front
Crash Test	Good	Good	Good	Good	Good
Airbags	None	Driver*	Driver*	Driver*	Dual
ABS	4-Whl*	4-Whl*	4-Whl*	4-Whl*	4-Whl*
Parts Cost	Average	Average	Average	Average	Low
Complaints	Vry. Gd.	Vry. Gd.	Vry. Gd.	Good	Good
Insurance	Surchg.	Surchg.	Surchg.	Surchg.	Surchg.
Fuel Econ.	27	27	26	26	30
Theft Rating	Low	Average	Vry. Low	Vry. Low	Vry. Low
Bumpers	Weak	Weak	Weak		
Recalls	0	0	0	2	3
Trn. Cir. (ft.)	30.2	30.2	30.2	30.2	34.1
Weight (lbs.)	2288	2346	2324	2324	2315
Whlbase (in.)	95.7	95.7	95.7	95.7	99.8
Price	2-4,000	3-5,000	4-6,000	5-7,000	6-8,000
OVERALL	Good	Good	Good	Average	Good

*Optional; **Estimate

2001 Nissan Sentra

ed lap-shoulder belts or motorized shoulder belts with separate lap belts. Driver airbags became available in 1993, but automatic belts remained; the late 1995 models have standard dual airbags. ABS was available beginning in 1991.

The base engine is peppy with either a 5-speed or an automatic transmission with overdrive. The SE-R comes with a hotter engine and a 5-speed. The Sentra is fun to drive in SE-R form, but other models don't handle as well. The ride is fairly good on lesser models. The front seat is adequate, but the rear seat is cramped.

	1997	1998	1999	2000	2001
Size Class	Subcomp.	Subcomp.	Subcomp.	Subcomp.	Subcomp.
Drive	Front	Front	Front	Front	Front
Crash Test	Good	Average	Average	N/A	N/A
Airbags	Dual	Dual	Dual	Dual	Dual
ABS	4-Whl*	4-Whl*	4-Whl*	4-Whl*	4-Whl*
Parts Cost	Average	Average	Average	Average	Average
Complaints	Vry. Gd.	Vry. Gd.	Vry. Gd.	Vry. Gd.	Average
Insurance	Surchg.	Surchg.	Surchg.	Surchg.	Reg
Fuel Econ.	29	30	29	29	27
Theft Rating	Vry. Low	Low	Low**	Low**	Average
Bumpers		Weak	Strong	Weak	Weak
Recalls	4	1	0	0	0
Trn. Cir. (ft.)	34.1	34.1	34.1	34.1	34.1
Weight (lbs.)	2315	2315	2617	2617	2617
Whlbase (in.)	99.8	99.8	99.8	99.8	99.8
Price	7-9,000	8-10,000	10-12,000	12-14,000	13-15,000
OVERALL	Good	Good	Vry. Gd.	Vry. Gd.	Vry. Gd.

Nissan Stanza 1992, Altima 1993-2001

By 1985, Nissan had dropped the original Stanza 3-door hatchback and included a 4-door notchback sedan, as well as a minivan-wagon hybrid. The restyled 1987 Stanza became a cut-rate Maxima. Wagons,

1992 Nissan Stanza

with the old sheet metal, lasted through 1988. Nissan restyled the Stanza for 1990 and, for 1993, Nissan renamed its compact the Altima. Its styling deliberately mimics the Infiniti J30 sedan, a much more expensive model. The 2000 model received new front and rear fascias and noise filtering was improved. All 1990-93 models have motorized front shoulder belts and manual lap belts; the Altima also has a driver's

	1992	1993	1994	1995	1996
Size Class	Compact	Compact	Compact	Compact	Intermd.
Drive	Front	Front	Front	Front	Front
Crash Test	Poor	Vry. Gd.	Average	Average	Average
Airbags	None	Driver	Dual	Dual	Dual
ABS	4-Whl*	4-Whl*	4-Whl*	4-Whl*	4-Whl*
Parts Cost	Low	Average	Average	Average	Average
Complaints	Vry. Gd.	Average	Vry. Gd.	Vry. Gd.	Vry. Gd.
Insurance	Surchg.	Regular	Regular	Regular	Surchg.
Fuel Econ.	21	21	21	21	24
Theft Rating	Average	Low	Average	Average	Average
Bumpers	Weak	Weak	Weak	Weak	Weak
Recalls	1	1	1	2	0
Trn. Cir. (ft.)	35.4	37.4	37.4	37.4	37.4
Weight (lbs.)	2788	2829	2829	2908	2853
Whlbase (in.)	100.4	103.1	103.1	103.1	103.1
Price	3-5,000	5-7,000	6-8,000	7-9,000	8-10,000
OVERALL	Poor	Good	Good	Good	Good

*Optional; **Estimate

2001 Nissan Altima

airbag. For 1994, the Altima got conventional belts and dual airbags. ABS first became optional in 1990.

Engines in 1989 Stanza sedans don't perform well, and, as a result, gas mileage suffers. The 140 hp 4-cylinder used since 1990 offers better performance. Front seats are fine for two, but the back is uncomfortable for large adults. There are four Altima trim levels out there: XE, GXE, SE, and GLEC- so make sure you buy only what you want. On the dash, gauges and controls are easy to use. From 1993 on, this is a good, solid choice.

	1997	1998	1999	2000	2001
Size Class	Intermd.	Intermd.	Intermd.	Intermd.	Intermd.
Drive	Front	Front	Front	Front	Front
Crash Test	Average	Poor	Poor	Vry. Gd.	Vry. Gd.
Airbags	Dual	Dual	Dual	Dual	Dual
ABS	4-Whl*	4-Whl*	4-Whl*	4-Whl*	4-Whl*
Parts Cost	Average	Average	Average	Average	Average
Complaints	Vry. Gd.	Good	Vry. Gd.	Vry. Gd.	Vry. Gd.
Insurance	Surchg.	Surchg.	Surchg.	Surchg.	Surchg.
Fuel Econ.	24	24	24	24	24
Theft Rating	Average	High	High**	High**	High**
Bumpers	Weak				
Recalls	1	0	0	0	0
Trn. Cir. (ft.)	37.4	37.4	37.4	37.4	37.4
Weight (lbs.)	2853	2859	2859	2859	2859
Whlbase (in.)	103.1	103.1	103.1	103.1	103.1
Price	9-11,000	12-14,000	13-15,000	15-17,000	17-19,000
OVERALL	Average	Poor	Good	Vry. Gd.	Vry. Gd.

Oldsmobile 88 1992-99

Like the Buick LeSabre and the Pontiac Bonneville, the 88 has undergone many changes in the past 10 years. The Delta name vanished for 1989, and the 88s got a new body for 1992 but kept the

1992 Oldsmobile 88

same chassis. In '96, Oldsmobile dropped the highest trim level, renamed it the LSS, and marketed it as a different car; but don't be fooled —it's still based on the 88. During 1987, 88s got door-mounted front belts; unfortunately, these stayed through 1991. Some 1989-91 88s have an optional driver's airbag and regular front belts. In 1992, all 88s received a driver's airbag and conventional belts; the 1994 models

	1992	1993	1994	1995	1996
Size Class	Large	Large	Large	Large	Large
Drive	Front	Front	Front	Front	Front
Crash Test	Good	Good	Good	Good	Good
Airbags	Driver	Driver	Dual	Dual	Dual
ABS	4-Whl*	4-Whl	4-Whl	4-Whl	4-Whl
Parts Cost	Low	Average	Low	Average	Average
Complaints	Average	Average	Good	Average	Vry. Gd.
Insurance	Discount	Discount	Discount	Discount	Discount
Fuel Econ.	18	19	19	19	18
Theft Rating	Low	Vry. Low	Vry. Low	Vry. Low	Vry. Low
Bumpers					
Recalls	2	2	1	1	2
Trn. Cir. (ft.)	39.4	39.4	40.7	40.7	40.7
Weight (lbs.)	3404	3404	3439	3400	3455
Whlbase (in.)	110.8	110.8	110.8	110.8	110.8
Price	4-6,000	5-7,000	6-8,000	8-10,000	10-12,000
OVERALL	Good	Good	BEST BET	Vry. Gd.	BEST BET

*Optional; **Estimate

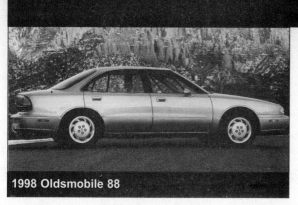

1998 Oldsmobile 88

added a passenger airbag. ABS was optional in 1989; it's standard on the 1992 LS and on all 1993 and later models.

For the past 10 years, Oldsmobile has offered only one engine choice, a 3.8-liter 6-cylinder which should provide plenty of power. Early transmissions have a reliability problem so have it checked out before you buy. The 88 with standard suspension gives a mushy ride at the expense of good handling. There's room for five and trunk space is generous. If you like the car but are turned off by the gauges and controls, consider a Bonneville.

	1997	1998	1999	2000	2001
Size Class	Large	Large	Large		
Drive	Front	Front	Front		
Crash Test	Good	Good	Good		
Airbags	Dual	Dual	Dual		
ABS	4-Whl	4-Whl	4-Whl		
Parts Cost	Average	Low	Low		
Complaints	Good	Good	Vry. Gd.		
Insurance	Discount	Discount	Discount		
Fuel Econ.	19	19	19		
Theft Rating	Vry. Low	Vry. Low**	Vry. Low**		
Bumpers				No Model Produced	
Recalls	0	0	0		
Trn. Cir. (ft.)	40.7	40.7	40.7		
Weight (lbs.)	3465	3455	3455		
Whlbase (in.)	110.8	110.8	110.8		
Price	11-13,000	13-15,000	14-16,000		
OVERALL	BEST BET	BEST BET	BEST BET		

Oldsmobile 98 1992-96

Starting in 1986, the Oldsmobile 98, Buick Electra/Park Avenue and Cadillac DeVille/Fleetwood shared a new, smaller front-wheel drive chassis. The 98 stayed the same until 1991, when, like the Park Av-

1992 Oldsmobile 98

enue, the 98 got a new, less popular body and has not changed since. Airbags were optional, but sparsely available. The 1991 models changed to regular belts with a driver airbag; 1994 models added a second airbag for the front passenger. ABS was standard on the 1989-90 Touring Sedan, optional on other 98s. It became standard on all 98s for 1991.

	1992	1993	1994	1995	1996
Size Class	Large	Large	Large	Large	Large
Drive	Front	Front	Front	Front	Front
Crash Test	N/A	N/A	N/A	N/A	N/A
Airbags	Driver	Driver	Dual	Dual	Dual
ABS	4-Whl	4-Whl	4-Whl	4-Whl	4-Whl
Parts Cost	Low	Low	Low	High	Average
Complaints	Good	Vry. Gd.	Good	Average	Vry. Gd.
Insurance	Discount	Discount	Discount	Discount	Discount
Fuel Econ.	17	19	19	19	19
Theft Rating	Low	Vry. Low	Vry. Low	Vry. Low	Vry. Low
Bumpers					
Recalls	2	2	1	2	2
Trn. Cir. (ft.)	39.4	39.4	39.4	40	39.4
Weight (lbs.)	3593	3512	3509	3515	3515
Whlbase (in.)	110.8	110.8	110.8	110.8	110.8
Price	6-8,000	7-9,000	8-10,000	10-12,000	12-14,000
OVERALL~					

~Cars without a crash test do not receive an overall rating.

1996 Oldsmobile 98

Most 98s have a 3.8-liter V6, with an optional supercharger between 1992 and 1995. Nearly all 98s have a soft, smooth big-car ride, at the cost of mediocre handling. The Touring Sedan or touring suspension option makes driving more enjoyable, with little deterioration in ride. There's room for six and a generous trunk. The 98s from 1991-93 (especially the Touring Sedan) are possible, cheaper alternatives to the Park Avenue/Ultra but hard to recommend without crash tests.

	1997	1998	1999	2000	2001
Size Class					
Drive					
Crash Test					
Airbags					
ABS					
Parts Cost					
Complaints					
Insurance					
Fuel Econ.					
Theft Rating		No Model Produced			
Bumpers					
Recalls					
Trn. Cir. (ft.)					
Weight (lbs.)					
Whlbase (in.)					
Price					
OVERALL					

Oldsmobile Achieva 1992-98

In 1992, the Olds Achieva replaced the Olds Calais. It kept the old chassis but gained nine inches in length. A new interior highlighted the changes for '96, and there were no major changes

1992 Oldsmobile Achieva

for '97. These cars pioneered the use of GM's notorious door-mounted belts midway through 1987. The Achieva got a driver's airbag for 1994, but it kept the door-mounted belts through '95. Finally in 1996, the Achieva received dual airbags, and the door mounted belts disappeared. ABS is standard on all Achievas.

The Quad 4 is quick but rough and unreliable; the V6 is smoother but

	1992	1993	1994	1995	1996
Size Class	Compact	Compact	Compact	Compact	Compact
Drive	Front	Front	Front	Front	Front
Crash Test	Vry. Pr.	Vry. Pr.[1]	Average	Average	Vry. Gd.[1]
Airbags	None	None	Driver	Driver	Dual
ABS	4-Whl	4-Whl	4-Whl	4-Whl	4-Whl
Parts Cost	Vry. Low	Low	Low	Low	Low
Complaints	Average	Good	Good	Average	Average
Insurance	Regular	Regular	Regular	Regular	Regular
Fuel Econ.	19	22	22	22	23
Theft Rating	Low	Vry. Low	Vry. Low	Vry. Low	Vry. Low
Bumpers					
Recalls	0	1	1	0	6
Trn. Cir. (ft.)	35.3	35.3	35.3	35.3	35.3
Weight (lbs.)	2778	2779	2769	2717	2751
Whlbase (in.)	103.4	103.4	103.4	103.4	103.4
Price	2-4,000	3-5,000	4-6,000	5-7,000	6-8,000
OVERALL	Poor	Poor[2]	Good	Good	Good[2]

[1]Data given for coupe. Crash test for sedan in 1993 is Poor; 1996-98 is Good; [2]Data given for coupe. Overall rating for

1997 Oldsmobile Achieva

uses more gas. Automatics on all models (except 1994) have only 3-speeds; hence, performance and economy suffer. The Achieva lacks rear seat room, despite its mid-size exterior length.

	1997	1998	1999	2000	2001
Size Class	Compact	Compact			
Drive	Front	Front			
Crash Test	Vry. Gd.[1]	Vry. Gd.[1]			
Airbags	Dual	Dual			
ABS	4-Whl	4-Whl			
Parts Cost	Average	High			
Complaints	Good	Vry. Pr.			
Insurance	Regular	Regular			
Fuel Econ.	23	22			
Theft Rating	Vry. Low	Vry. Low		No Model Produced	
Bumpers					
Recalls	1	0			
Trn. Cir. (ft.)	35.3	35.3			
Weight (lbs.)	2917	2917			
Whlbase (in.)	103.4	103.4			
Price	7-9,000	8-10,000			
OVERALL	Vry. Gd.[2]	Average			

sedan may vary based on footnotes.

Oldsmobile Aurora 1995-2001

Olds stepped into the 21st century in 1995 by introducing the Aurora—called the Aurora by Oldsmobile, not Oldsmobile Aurora, which represents Oldsmobile's effort to distance themselves from

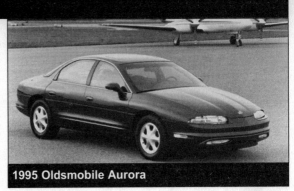
1995 Oldsmobile Aurora

the past. Instead of big, heavy, and boxy cars, the Aurora introduces Oldsmobile's new line of big, heavy, and curved cars. The powerfully built Aurora comes with dual airbags, ABS, traction control, speed-variable power steering, and a host of other items, which are all standard. Oldsmobile tried to add as many bells and whistles as they could. It performed only average in government crash testing during its early

	1992	1993	1994	1995	1996
Size Class				Large	Large
Drive				Front	Front
Crash Test				Average	Average
Airbags				Dual	Dual
ABS				4-Whl	4-Whl
Parts Cost				Low	Low
Complaints				Vry. Pr.	Vry. Pr.
Insurance				Discount	Discount
Fuel Econ.				17	17
Theft Rating				Vry. Low	Vry. Low
Bumpers		No Model Produced			
Recalls				0	1
Trn. Cir. (ft.)				41	41
Weight (lbs.)				3967	3967
Whlbase (in.)				113.8	113.8
Price				11-13,000	14-16,000
OVERALL				Good	Good

**Estimate

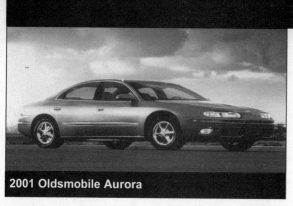
2001 Oldsmobile Aurora

years but in later years, did very well. Its safety features also make it a good buy.

The Aurora benefits greatly from a very rigid structure and rides well for a car its size. However, like many large cars, the Aurora wallows in turns. The 4-liter V8, Aurora's large engine, is more powerful than any competitor's, and its fuel economy, though not notable by any means, holds its own against the competition.

	1997	1998	1999	2000	2001
Size Class	Large	Large	Large	Large	Large
Drive	Front	Front	Front	Front	Front
Crash Test	Average	Average	Average	Average	Vry. Gd.
Airbags	Dual	Dual	Dual	Dual	Dual
ABS	4-Whl	4-Whl	4-Whl	4-Whl	4-Whl
Parts Cost	High	High	Average	Average	Average
Complaints			Average	Good	Good
Insurance	Discount	Discount	Discount	Discount	Discount
Fuel Econ.	17	17	17	17	17
Theft Rating	Vry. Low	Vry. Low**	Vry. Low**	Vry. Low**	Vry. Low**
Bumpers					
Recalls	0	0	0	0	0
Trn. Cir. (ft.)	41.9	41.9	41	41	41
Weight (lbs.)	3967	3967	3967	3967	3967
Whlbase (in.)	113.8	113.8	113.8	113.8	113.8
Price	16-18,000	19-21,000	23-25,000	28-30,000	>30,000
OVERALL	Good	Good	Vry. Gd.	Vry. Gd.	BEST BET

Oldsmobile Cutlass Ciera 1992-96, Cutlass 1997-2000

A very dramatic change took place at Oldsmobile, as the Ciera was finally replaced in 1997 with the all-new Cutlass. The 1997 Cutlass is now the twin of the all-new Chevrolet Malibu. Over the years,

1993 Oldsmobile Cutlass Ciera

Cieras have come in several trim levels including some sport packages. Starting in 1990, all models got GM's horrible, door-mounted seat belts. For 1993, models offered an optional airbag and ABS, which both became standard in 1994, though the Ciera kept the door-mounted belts in front. For 1997 on, the door mounted belts are gone and dual airbags are standard; ABS is optional.

	1992	1993	1994	1995	1996
Size Class	Intermd.	Intermd.	Intermd.	Intermd.	Intermd.
Drive	Front	Front	Front	Front	Front
Crash Test	Average	Good	Good	Good	Good
Airbags	None	Driver*	Driver	Driver	Driver
ABS	None	4-Whl*	4-Whl	4-Whl	4-Whl
Parts Cost	Vry. Low	Vry. Low	Low	Vry. Low	Vry. Low
Complaints	Average	Average	Vry. Gd.	Vry. Gd.	Average
Insurance	Discount	Discount	Discount	Discount	Regular
Fuel Econ.	19	20	19	25	24
Theft Rating	Low	Low	Low	Vry. Low	Average
Bumpers	Weak	Weak	Weak	Weak	Weak
Recalls	2	2	4	1	1
Trn. Cir. (ft.)	38.1	38.1	38.1	38.1	38.1
Weight (lbs.)	2886	2886	2833	2931	2924
Whlbase (in.)	104.9	104.9	104.9	104.9	104.9
Price	3-5,000	4-6,000	5-7,000	6-8,000	7-9,000
OVERALL	Average	Vry. Gd.	Vry. Gd.	BEST BET	Good

*Optional; **Estimate

1997 Oldsmobile Cutlass

Like the Century, the Ciera offers a good ride on smooth roads, but look elsewhere for responsive handling. The Cutlass provides a better ride. Skip the 4-cylinder engine in the Ciera wagonCit's a slug. Get the base V6 with automatic overdrive for both the Ciera and the new Cutlass. Some earlier models offer the big 3.8-liter V6 that comes in GM's full-size models; it's plenty powerful, but gas mileage is second-rate for a mid-sized car. Room inside and comfort for four are adequate.

	1997	1998	1999	2000	2001
Size Class	Intermd.	Intermd.	Intermd.	Intermd.	
Drive	Front	Front	Front	Front	
Crash Test	Good	Good	Good	Good	
Airbags	Dual	Dual	Dual	Dual	
ABS	4-Whl*	4-Whl	4-Whl	4-Whl	
Parts Cost	Low	Low	Low	Low	
Complaints	Poor	Poor	Vry. Gd.	Vry. Gd.	
Insurance	Regular	Regular	Regular	Regular	
Fuel Econ.	20	20	22	22	
Theft Rating	Vry. Low	Vry. Low	Vry. Low**	Vry. Low**	
Bumpers					
Recalls	0	0	0	0	
Trn. Cir. (ft.)	36.1	36.1	36.3	36.3	
Weight (lbs.)	2982	3102	3102	3102	
Whlbase (in.)	107	107	107	107	
Price	10-12,000	11-13,000	12-14,000	13-15,000	
OVERALL	Good	Good	BEST BET	BEST BET	

No Model Produced

Oldsmobile Cutlass Supreme 1992-97

During its time, the Cutlass was one of the most popular vehicles on the road, so you'll find plenty to choose from. With the exception of some trim and color changes, the Cutlass remained essentially the same

1992 Oldsmobile Cutlass Supreme

from '92-'97. Beware, as a popular fleet car, make sure the odometer reading is correct because fleet cars generally have more than the average number of miles. Model-wise, you'll find coupe, sedan, and convertible versions in the market. All 1989-94 Cutlasses have GM's lamentable door-mounted front belts; 1994 models supplement these belts with a driver's airbag, and 1995 models add a passenger airbag. ABS

	1992	1993	1994	1995	1996
Size Class	Intermd.	Intermd.	Intermd.	Intermd.	Intermd.
Drive	Front	Front	Front	Front	Front
Crash Test	Good	Good	Vry. Pr.	Average	Average
Airbags	None	None	Driver	Dual	Dual
ABS	4-Whl*	4-Whl*	4-Whl	4-Whl	4-Whl
Parts Cost	Vry. Low	Low	Low	Average	Average
Complaints	Vry. Gd.	Vry. Gd.	Vry. Gd.	Vry. Gd.	Vry. Gd.
Insurance	Discount	Discount	Discount	Discount	Regular
Fuel Econ.	19	19	19	19	20
Theft Rating	Low	Low	Vry. Low	Vry. Low	Vry. Low
Bumpers					
Recalls	1	2	4	3	0
Trn. Cir. (ft.)	37.5	37.5	39	37.5	37.5
Weight (lbs.)	3375	3354	3405	3286	3283
Whlbase (in.)	107.5	107.5	107.5	107.5	107.5
Price	4-6,000	5-7,000	6-8,000	7-9,000	9-11,000
OVERALL	BEST BET	Vry. Gd.	Good	Vry. Gd.	Vry. Gd.

*Optional

1995 Oldsmobile Cutlass Supreme Convertible

first became optional for 1989, standard for 1994.

Earlier Cutlass Supremes come with a 2.8-liter V6 that provides only adequate power in this heavy car. A larger 3.1-liter V6 can be found in later models, and it performs better. For the best balance of ride and cornering, look for cars with the FE-3 suspension. Skip cars with digital instruments. While the room inside is reasonable, comfort is no better than average. Trunk space is ample.

	1997	1998	1999	2000	2001
Size Class	Intermd.				
Drive	Front				
Crash Test	Average				
Airbags	Dual				
ABS	4-Whl				
Parts Cost	High				
Complaints	Vry. Gd.				
Insurance	Discount				
Fuel Econ.	17				
Theft Rating	Vry. Low				
Bumpers					
Recalls	0				
Trn. Cir. (ft.)	39				
Weight (lbs.)	3388				
Whlbase (in.)	107.5				
Price	10-12,000				
OVERALL	Vry. Gd.				

No Model Produced

Pontiac Bonneville 1992-2001

The Bonneville changed drastically in the 1980s. For 1987, Pontiac borrowed the Olds Delta 88/Buick LeSabre front-wheel drive chassis and made the more expensive Bonnevilles into large sports sedans.

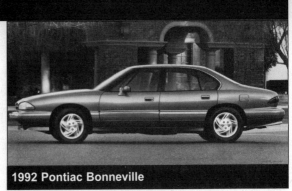

1992 Pontiac Bonneville

These models (SSE and SSEi) dominated the lineup after the Bonneville got a new body for 1992. They offer the best balance of performance, ride, and handling in GM's big cars. Beware of door-mounted belts from 1989-91. From 1992 on, Pontiac uses airbags (dual standard on SSEi and all 1994-97 models, optional on 1992-93 SSE; driver's only on 1992-93 SE). ABS was optional in 1989, standard in

	1992	1993	1994	1995	1996
Size Class	Large	Large	Large	Large	Large
Drive	Front	Front	Front	Front	Front
Crash Test	Good	Good	Good	Good	Good
Airbags	Driver#	Driver#	Dual	Dual	Dual
ABS	4-Whl*	4-Whl	4-Whl	4-Whl	4-Whl
Parts Cost	Low	Average	Low	Average	Average
Complaints	Poor	Average	Good	Average	Vry. Gd.
Insurance	Discount	Discount	Discount	Discount	Discount
Fuel Econ.	19	16	19	19	19
Theft Rating	Low	Vry. Low	Vry. Low	Vry. Low	Vry. Low
Bumpers					
Recalls	4	2	0	1	2
Trn. Cir. (ft.)	39.4	39.4	39.4	40.5	40.5
Weight (lbs.)	3446	3362	3446	3587	3446
Whlbase (in.)	110.8	110.8	110.8	110.8	110.8
Price	4-6,000	5-7,000	6-8,000	8-10,000	10-12,000
OVERALL	Average	Good	BEST BET	Vry. Gd.	BEST BET

*Optional; #Passenger Side Optional; **Estimate

284

2001 Pontiac Bonneville

1993.

The base 3.8-liter V6 engine found on most models is powerful enough; the optional supercharged V6 only adds a little more power and more repair complexity. The SSE is a pleasure to drive, but its ride is firm. Room for four is ample, as is trunk space. Look for optional gauges but avoid the silly head-up speedometer. The 1992-94 dashboard is thoughtfully designed. The 1992-97 Bonneville is GM's best product and a very competent automobile.

	1997	1998	1999	2000	2001
Size Class	Large	Large	Large	Large	Large
Drive	Front	Front	Front	Front	Front
Crash Test	Good	Good	Good	Vry. Gd.	Vry. Gd.
Airbags	Dual	Dual	Dual	Dual	Dual
ABS	4-Whl	4-Whl	4-Whl	4-Whl	4-Whl
Parts Cost	Average	Low	Vry. Low	Vry. Low	Vry. Low
Complaints	Good	Average	Poor	Vry. Gd.	Average
Insurance	Discount	Discount	Discount	Discount	Discount
Fuel Econ.	19	19	19	19	19
Theft Rating	Vry. Low	Vry. Low	Vry. Low**	Vry. Low**	Vry. Low**
Bumpers			Strong	Strong	Strong
Recalls	1	0	0	1	0
Trn. Cir. (ft.)	40.5	40.5	40.5	40.5	40.5
Weight (lbs.)	3446	3446	3446	3590	3590
Whlbase (in.)	110.8	110.8	110.8	112.2	112.2
Price	12-14,000	14-16,000	16-18,000	22-24,000	25-27,000
OVERALL	Vry. Gd.	BEST BET	BEST BET	BEST BET	BEST BET

Pontiac Firebird 1992-2001

The Pontiac Firebird, similar to the Chevrolet Camaro, is a vestige of the American pony cars (Mustang clones) of the late 1960s. Firebirds have undergone two major changes since 1970. The

1993 Pontiac Firebird

first was for 1982, when the Firebird got a lighter chassis, flip-up headlights, and a hatchback. However, these cars had reliability problems, particularly in the engine and transmission. The second major update occurred for 1993, with a new body featuring many plastic body panels and a revised chassis. A convertible is available from 1991-92 and again from 1994-97. Firebirds since 1990 have driver's airbags; a pas-

	1992	1993	1994	1995	1996
Size Class	Intermd.	Intermd.	Intermd.	Intermd.	Intermd.
Drive	Rear	Rear	Rear	Rear	Rear
Crash Test	Vry. Gd.	Vry. Gd.	Vry. Gd.	Vry. Gd.	Vry. Gd.
Airbags	Driver	Dual	Dual	Dual	Dual
ABS	None	4-Whl	4-Whl	4-Whl	4-Whl
Parts Cost	Low	Low	Average	Average	Average
Complaints	Poor	Poor	Poor	Poor	Average
Insurance	Surchg.	Surchg.	Surchg.	Surchg.	Surchg.
Fuel Econ.	16	19	19	19	19
Theft Rating	Average	Vry. High	Low	Average	Average
Bumpers					
Recalls	2	1	1	1	0
Trn. Cir. (ft.)	38.5	37.9	37.9	37.9	37.9
Weight (lbs.)	3146	3241	3232	3230	3311
Whlbase (in.)	101	101.1	101.1	101.1	101.1
Price	6-8,000	7-9,000	8-10,000	10-12,000	12-14,000
OVERALL	Poor	Average	Average	Poor	Average

**Estimate

1999 Pontiac Firebird

senger airbag became standard on the 1993 models. All 1993-97 Firebirds have ABS and remain excellent crash test performers.

The 2.8-, 3.1-, or 3.4-liter V6 engines that can be found on the Firebirds are all good choices. The Formula and Trans Am come with strong V8s. For 1993, chassis and suspension changes made the Firebird feel more solid than previous models. Ride is typical of large sporty cars, and handling is responsive. The Firebird is mid-sized outside but really fits only two inside because the back seat is a real squeeze, even for kids.

	1997	1998	1999	2000	2001
Size Class	Intermd.	Intermd.	Intermd.	Intermd.	Intermd.
Drive	Rear	Rear	Rear	Rear	Rear
Crash Test	Vry. Gd.	Vry. Gd.	Vry. Gd.	Vry. Gd.	Vry. Gd.
Airbags	Dual	Dual	Dual	Dual	Dual
ABS	4-Whl	4-Whl	4-Whl	4-Whl	4-Whl
Parts Cost	High	High	Average	Average	Average
Complaints	Average	Vry. Pr.	Average	Poor	Average
Insurance	Surchg.	Surchg.	Surchg.	Surchg.	Surchg.
Fuel Econ.	19	19	19	19	19
Theft Rating	Average	Average	Average**	Average**	Average**
Bumpers					
Recalls	2	0	0	0	0
Trn. Cir. (ft.)	37.9	37.9	37.9	37.9	37.9
Weight (lbs.)	3311	3477	3341	3341	3341
Whlbase (in.)	101.1	101.1	101.1	101.1	101.1
Price	15-17,000	16-18,000	18-20,000	19-21,000	20-22,000
OVERALL	Poor	Poor	Average	Average	Average

Pontiac Grand Am 1992-2001

The Grand Am got a new body and grew nearly ten inches in length for 1992 but kept the old chassis. In '96, Pontiac redesigned the interior and exterior slightly, giving the Grand Am a new hood, new

1992 Pontiac Grand Am

fenders, and a new instrument panel. All Grand Ams between 1989 and 1995 have GM's notorious door-mounted belts as standard equipment, though the 1994 adds a standard driver's airbag. For 1996, Grand Ams come with standard dual airbags and conventional belts. The 1991 Grand Am SE and all Grand Ams since 1992 have ABS. The Grand Am also received and overhaul for 1999 with a new cockpit design, re-

	1992	1993	1994	1995	1996
Size Class	Compact	Compact	Compact	Compact	Compact
Drive	Front	Front	Front	Front	Front
Crash Test	Vry. Pr.[1]	Vry. Pr.[1]	Average[1]	Average[1]	Vry. Gd.[1]
Airbags	None	None	Driver	Driver	Dual
ABS	4-Whl	4-Whl	4-Whl	4-Whl	4-Whl
Parts Cost	Vry. Low	Low	Low	Low	Low
Complaints	Good	Good	Good	Good	Average
Insurance	Surchg.	Regular	Surchg.	Surchg.	Regular
Fuel Econ.	19	22	22	22	23
Theft Rating	Low	Vry. Low	Vry. Low	Vry. Low	Vry. Low
Bumpers	Weak	Weak	Weak	Weak	Weak
Recalls	3	1	1	0	4
Trn. Cir. (ft.)	34.1	34.1	36.4	35.3	35.3
Weight (lbs.)	2727	2728	2793	2888	2881
Whlbase (in.)	103.4	103.4	103.4	103.4	103.4
Price	3-5,000	4-6,000	5-7,000	6-8,000	7-9,000
OVERALL	Vry. Pr.	Poor	Average	Average	Vry. Gd.

[1]Data given for coupe. Crash test for sedan for 1992-95 is Poor; 1996-97 is Good; **Estimate

2001 Pontiac Grand Am

designed bucket seats, four-wheel independent suspension, enhanced traction system, and fog lamps.

The basic 4 performs adequately; the Quad 4 is quick, but rough and possibly unreliable. The V6 is smoother but uses more fuel. Automatics on all Grand Ams through 1993 have only 3-speedsCperformance and economy suffer. All 1994 models have automatic overdrive. Handling is very good on base models. It improves with sport suspension, but the ride suffers. The back seat is a very tight fit, which didn't improve with the 1992 restyle. You'll find a well-laid-out dashboard.

	1997	1998	1999	2000	2001
Size Class	Compact	Compact	Compact	Compact	Compact
Drive	Front	Front	Front	Front	Front
Crash Test	Vry. Gd.[1]	Vry. Gd.	Vry. Gd.	Vry. Gd.	Vry. Gd.
Airbags	Dual	Dual	Dual	Dual	Dual
ABS	4-Whl	4-Whl	4-Whl	4-Whl	4-Whl
Parts Cost	Average	High	Average	High	Average
Complaints	Good	Good	Poor	Vry. Gd.	Vry. Pr.
Insurance	Regular	Regular	Regular	Regular	Surcharge
Fuel Econ.	23	23	22	22	21
Theft Rating	Vry. Low	Vry. Low	Average	Vry. Low**	Average
Bumpers	Weak	Weak		Strong	Strong
Recalls	1	0	0	1	0
Trn. Cir. (ft.)	35.3	35.3	37.7	37.7	37.7
Weight (lbs.)	2835	2877	3066	3066	3066
Whlbase (in.)	103.4	103.4	107	107	107
Price	8-10,000	10-12,000	12-14,000	14-16,000	17-19,000
OVERALL	Vry. Gd.	Vry. Gd.	Good	BEST BET	Average

Pontiac Grand Prix 1992-2001

A 4-door Grand Prix sedan joined the line in 1990, available as an all-wheel drive STE model that had previously been part of the Pontiac 6000 series. Changes for 1997 include a wider stance and a

1992 Pontiac Grand Prix

lower roof-line, which give the Grand Prix a sportier look. Every Grand Prix from 1989-93 has GM's awful door-mounted front belts; from 1994-96, only the coupes have them. They are not present in the 1997 version. For 1994-97, models have standard dual airbags. ABS first became optional in 1989. A theft deterrent system and Onstar communications are some of the options now offered.

	1992	1993	1994	1995	1996
Size Class	Intermd.	Intermd.	Intermd.	Intermd.	Intermd.
Drive	Front	Front	Front	Front	Front
Crash Test	Good	Good	Average	Average	Average
Airbags	None	None	Dual	Dual	Dual
ABS	4-Whl*	4-Whl*	4-Whl*	4-Whl*	4-Whl*
Parts Cost	Vry. Low	Low	Low	Average	Average
Complaints	Average	Good	Average	Good	Vry. Gd.
Insurance	Discount	Discount	Discount	Discount	Discount
Fuel Econ.	17	19	19	19	20
Theft Rating	Low[1]	Vry. Low	Vry. Low	Vry. Low	Vry. Low
Bumpers					
Recalls	1	1	1	3	0
Trn. Cir. (ft.)	36.7	36.7	39	36.7	36.7
Weight (lbs.)	3303	3312	3370	3318	3243
Whlbase (in.)	107.5	107.5	107.5	107.5	107.5
Price	3-5,000	4-6,000	5-7,000	7-9,000	8-10,000
OVERALL	Good	Vry. Gd.	Vry. Gd.	Good	BEST BET

[1]Data given for sedan. Theft rating for coupe is Average.; Optional; **Estimate

2001 Pontiac Grand Prix

Earlier models have a 2.8-liter V6, which provides adequate power in this heavy car. The Quad 4 is quick but noisy. Later V6 models have more power, and the GTP's 3.4 V6 is as quick as a V8. The early Grand Prix focuses on ride, not agility. From 1989 on, the Grand Prix became more of a driver's car. The dashboard is busy and inefficient until 1994. Room inside is reasonable, but comfort is average. Trunk space is generous. From 1990 on, Grand Prix models have improved each consecutive year.

	1997	1998	1999	2000	2001
Size Class	Intermd.	Intermd.	Intermd.	Intermd.	Intermd.
Drive	Front	Front	Front	Front	Front
Crash Test	Good	Good	Good	Good	Good
Airbags	Dual	Dual	Dual	Dual	Dual
ABS	4-Whl	4-Whl	4-Whl	4-Whl	4-Whl
Parts Cost	High	Low	Low	Low	Very Low
Complaints	Poor	Poor	Good	Vry. Gd.	Average
Insurance	Discount	Discount	Discount	Discount	Discount
Fuel Econ.	20	20	20	20	20
Theft Rating	Vry. Low	Vry. Low	Vry. Low**	Average	Average
Bumpers	Weak		Strong	Strong	Strong
Recalls	0	0	0	2	1
Trn. Cir. (ft.)	36.9	36.9	36.9	36.9	36.9
Weight (lbs.)	3396	3396	3414	3414	3414
Whlbase (in.)	110.5	110.5	110.5	110.5	110.5
Price	10-14,000	13-15,000	15-17,000	16-18,000	22-24,000
OVERALL	Good	BEST BET	BEST BET	BEST BET	BEST BET

Pontiac Sunbird 1992-94, Sunfire 1995-2001

The Sunbird, like its twin the Cavalier, goes back a long way. Over the years, Sunbirds have come in a wide range of body styles. By 1994, these were reduced to a convertible, 2-door coupe, and 4-door sedan.

1992 Pontiac Sunbird

The Sunbird was replaced in 1995 by the Sunfire. For 1990-94, Sunbirds have door-mounted front belts. ABS is standard on all models starting in 1992, but airbags were not offered until the 1995 redesign, which brought dual airbags.

The Sunbird's 4-cylinder engines perform adequately at best. A V6 option first became available in 1985, but it's almost too powerful. The

	1992	1993	1994	1995	1996
Size Class	Compact	Compact	Compact	Compact	Compact
Drive	Front	Front	Front	Front	Front
Crash Test	Good	Good	Good	Good	Good
Airbags	None	None	None	Dual	Dual
ABS	4-Whl	4-Whl	4-Whl	4-Whl	4-Whl
Parts Cost	Vry. Low	Low	Low	Low	Low
Complaints	Poor	Poor	Poor	Good	Average
Insurance	Surchg.	Regular	Surchg.	Regular	Surchg.
Fuel Econ.	23	20	23	24	25
Theft Rating	Low	Vry. Low	Vry. Low	Vry. Low	Vry. Low
Bumpers	Weak	Weak	Weak	Weak	Weak
Recalls	3	2	1	4	5
Trn. Cir. (ft.)	34.3	34.3	35.3	37.2	37.2
Weight (lbs.)	2537	2537	2502	2679	2679
Whlbase (in.)	101.3	101.3	101.3	104.1	104.1
Price	2-4,000	3-5,000	4-6,000	5-7,000	7-9,000
OVERALL	Poor	Average	Poor	Vry. Gd.	Average

**Estimate

GT has a turbocharged 4. If you want an automatic, you're stuck with a 3-speed, which means inferior gas mileage. A 4-speed automatic is available starting in 1996. The 5-speed transmission isn't too

2001 Pontiac Sunfire

smooth or precise, but later ones are better. The seats are very low; it's almost like you're sitting right on the floor. The ride isn't up to the standard for compacts, but handling is responsive, especially on the GT. Controls improved dramatically on the Sunfire. Accommodations are fine for two, tight for four.

	1997	1998	1999	2000	2001
Size Class	Compact	Compact	Compact	Compact	Compact
Drive	Front	Front	Front	Front	Front
Crash Test	Good	Good	Good	Good	Good
Airbags	Dual	Dual	Dual	Dual	Dual
ABS	4-Whl	4-Whl	4-Whl	4-Whl	4-Whl
Parts Cost	High	Average	Low	Low	Low
Complaints	Good	Good	Good	Average	Good
Insurance	Surchg.	Surchg.	Surchg.	Surchg.	Surchg.
Fuel Econ.	25	25	24	24	24
Theft Rating	Vry. Low	Vry. Low	Vry. Low**	Vry. Low**	Vry. Low**
Bumpers	Weak	Weak			
Recalls	3	1	0	0	0
Trn. Cir. (ft.)	37.2	37.2	35.6	35.6	35.6
Weight (lbs.)	2627	2670	2630	2630	2630
Whlbase (in.)	104.1	104.1	104.1	104.1	104.1
Price	8-10,000	9-11,000	10-12,000	12-14,000	14-16,000
OVERALL	Average	Good	Vry. Gd.	Good	Vry. Gd.

Saab 900 1992-98, 9-3 1999-2001

The Saab 900 is a close relative of the 1969 Saab 99; the 900 arrived ten years later. The 900 comes as a 3-door hatchback or 4-door sedan, and a convertible joined the lineup for 1987. Models in-

1992 Saab 900

cluded the plain 900, the fancier 900S, the 900 Turbo, and the SPG (Special Performance Group). The 1994 900 got a complete redesign, resembling the old 900, but it's a bit more conventional. Some 1989 models have motorized front shoulder belts and separate lap belts. Since 1990, all models have ABS, regular belts, and a driver's airbag. The 1994 900 (except convertible) and later models have dual airbags.

	1992	1993	1994	1995	1996
Size Class	Compact	Compact	Intermd.	Intermd.	Intermd.
Drive	Front	Front	Front	Front	Front
Crash Test	N/A	N/A	Good	Good	Good
Airbags	Driver	Driver	Dual	Dual	Dual
ABS	4-Whl	4-Whl	4-Whl	4-Whl	4-Whl
Parts Cost	High	Average	High	Vry. High	Average
Complaints	Poor	Average	Vry. Pr.	Vry. Pr.	Average
Insurance	Surchg.	Surchg.	Surchg.	Regular	Discount
Fuel Econ.	21	19	19	19	19
Theft Rating	High	High	High	High	High
Bumpers	Weak	Weak	Strong	Strong	Strong
Recalls	0	0	8	6	3
Trn. Cir. (ft.)	33.8	33.8	35.4	35.4	34.4
Weight (lbs.)	2776	2770	2950	3120	2990
Whlbase (in.)	99.1	99.1	102.4	102.4	102.4
Price	7-9,000	8-10,000	10-12,000	12-14,000	14-16,000
OVERALL~			Vry. Pr.	Poor	Vry. Gd.

**Estimate; ~Cars without crash tests do not receive an overall rating.

294

In 1999, the Saab 9-3 replaced the 900 but it is basically a name change.

All pre-1994 900 engines have 4 cylinders: single-cam, twin-cam, or twin-cam turbo. A 2.5-liter V6 is optional for 1994.

2001 Saab 9-3

Avoid older, used turbos. They're likely to require expensive repairs. The 900 was extensively re-engineered in 1999 and called the 9-3 Series. Models included a 5-dr., convertible, and 3-dr. coupe. The 900 has room for four to sit in comfort, plus plenty of luggage space. It's a versatile, roomy cargo carrier. A standard child booster seat was added in 1994.

	1997	1998	1999	2000	2001
Size Class	Intermd.	Intermd.	Intermd.	Intermd.	Intermd.
Drive	Front	Front	Front	Front	Front
Crash Test	Good	Good	N/A	N/A	N/A
Airbags	Dual	Dual	Dual	Dual	Dual
ABS	4-Whl	4-Whl	4-Whl	4-Whl	4-Whl
Parts Cost	Vry. High	Vry. High	Vry. High	Vry. High	Vry. High
Complaints	Good	Average	Poor	Vry. Pr.	Vry. Pr.
Insurance	Discount	Discount	Regular	Regular	Regular
Fuel Econ.	21	22	20	20	20
Theft Rating	Vry. Low	Vry. Low	Vry. Low**	Vry. Low**	Vry. Low**
Bumpers	Strong	Strong		Strong	Strong
Recalls	3	2	1	1	0
Trn. Cir. (ft.)	34.3	34.3	34.4	34.4	34.4
Weight (lbs.)	2940	2990	2990	2990	2990
Whlbase (in.)	102.4	102.4	111.3	111.3	111.3
Price	16-18,000	17-19,000	26-28,000	29-31,000	>30,000
OVERALL~	Vry. Gd.	Vry. Gd.			

Saab 9000 1992-98, 9-5 1999-2001

The Saab 9000 has helped Saab compete with more expensive Volvos and new competitors like Acura and Lexus. The car has not changed much since 1986. Saab is one of the last automakers to offer a

1992 Saab 9000

hatchback car; most automakers and consumers have gone to traditional sedans. The 9000 CD and CDE are notchback sedans with separate trunks, and the CS and CSE are hatchbacks. For 1996, Saab dropped the sedan models and concentrated solely on the hatchback. Most of the changes to the 9000 have been minor in nature or additions to standard safety equipment. The 1989 CD has a standard driver's airbag, which

	1992	1993	1994	1995	1996
Size Class	Intermd.	Intermd.	Intermd.	Intermd.	Intermd.
Drive	Front	Front	Front	Front	Front
Crash Test	Vry. Gd.	Good	Good	Good	Good
Airbags	Driver	Driver	Dual	Dual	Dual
ABS	4-Whl	4-Whl	4-Whl	4-Whl	4-Whl
Parts Cost	High	Average	Vry. High	High	High
Complaints	Vry. Pr.	Average	Average	Average	Vry. Gd.
Insurance	Discount	Discount	Discount	Discount	Discount
Fuel Econ.	17	18	18	20	20
Theft Rating	Average	Vry. Low	Average	Average	Average
Bumpers					
Recalls	3	4	3	0	0
Trn. Cir. (ft.)	35.8	35.8	35.8	35.8	35.8
Weight (lbs.)	3089	3110	3210	3260	3110
Whlbase (in.)	105.2	105.2	105.2	105.2	105.2
Price	9-11,000	10-12,000	11-13,000	13-15,000	15-17,000
OVERALL	Average	Average	Average	Good	Vry. Gd.

**Estimate

2001 Saab 9-5

spread to the rest of the line for 1990. For 1994, Saab added a standard passenger airbag. ABS is optional on the 9000 in 1989 and standard from 1990 on. The 9000 became the Saab 9-5 in 1999, along with the 900/9-3. In 1999 the redesigned version of the 9000 became the 9-5.

Saab's standard engine provides enough power. The turbo delivers even more, but you don't need it. Handling is good, better on turbos, but the ride is more harsh. All of these models provide plenty of space for five and generous room for luggage. For the earlier models, stick to the standard CS and CD; they're better values than the E or Aero.

	1997	1998	1999	2000	2001
Size Class	Intermd.	Intermd.	Intermd.	Intermd.	Intermd.
Drive	Front	Front	Front	Front	Front
Crash Test	Good	Good	N/A	N/A	N/A
Airbags	Dual	Dual	Dual	Dual	Dual
ABS	4-Whl	4-Whl	4-Whl	4-Whl	4-Whl
Parts Cost	Vry. High	Vry. High	Vry. High	Vry. High	Vry. High
Complaints	Vry. Gd.	Vry. Gd.	Vry. Gd.	Poor	Vry. Gd.
Insurance	Regular	Regular	Regular	Regular	Regular
Fuel Econ.	20	21	21	21	21
Theft Rating	Vry. Low	Vry. Low	Vry. Low**	Vry. Low**	Vry. Low**
Bumpers					
Recalls	1	1	1	1	0
Trn. Cir. (ft.)	35.8	35.7	35.4	35.4	35.4
Weight (lbs.)	3130	3250	3280	3280	3280
Whlbase (in.)	105.2	105.2	106.4	106.4	106.4
Price	17-19,000	21-23,000	20-22,000	>30,000	>30,000
OVERALL	Good	Good			

Saturn SC/SL 1992-2001, SW 1993-2001

The newest division of General Motors, Saturn represents the company's most serious effort to please subcompact car buyers. The first SC coupes were equivalent in trim to the fancy SL2 sedans, and

1993 Saturn SL

when sales didn't meet expectations, Saturn introduced a base model SC1 for 1993. The SW wagon joined the line in 1993. The SL and SW models were all-new for '96 and the SC was all-new in '97. All Saturns through 1994 have motorized front shoulder belts with separate lap belts. Saturn added an optional driver's airbag during 1992, which became standard in 1993; dual airbags and manual belts became standard

	1992	1993	1994	1995	1996
Size Class	Subcomp.	Subcomp.	Subcomp.	Subcomp.	Subcomp.
Drive	Front	Front	Front	Front	Front
Crash Test	Average	Average	Average	Vry. Gd.	Vry. Gd.[1]
Airbags	Driver*	Driver	Driver	Dual	Dual
ABS	4-Whl*	4-Whl*	4-Whl*	4-Whl*	4-Whl*
Parts Cost	High	Vry. Low	Vry. Low	Vry. Low	Vry. Low
Complaints	Average	Average	Average	Average	Average
Insurance	Regular	Regular	Regular	Regular	Regular
Fuel Econ.	26	23	25	28	25
Theft Rating	Low	Low	Low	Vry. Low	Vry. Low
Bumpers	Weak	Weak	Weak	Weak	Weak
Recalls	2	2	0	2	1
Trn. Cir. (ft.)	37.1	37.1	37.1	37.1	37.1
Weight (lbs.)	2313	2320	2314	2325	2282
Whlbase (in.)	102.4[2]	102.4[2]	102.4[2]	102.4[2]	102.4[2]
Price	2-4,000	3-5,000	4-6,000	5-7,000	6-8,000
OVERALL	Poor	Average	Good	BEST BET	BEST BET

[1]Data given for SL/SW. SC has not been tested; [2]Data given for SL/SW. Wheelbase for SC is 99.2; *Optional; **Estimate

2001 Saturn SC

in 1995. ABS is optional beginning in 1992.

The twin-cam engine on the SC, SC1, SL2, and SW2 is quicker than the base models' standard 4-cylinder, yet almost as economical. Both engines can be noisy. The 5-speed is more pleasant than the automatic and a better choice with the base engine. Handling is generally very good. Ride is decent, but you'll feel the bumps. Front seat comfort is fairly good, but in back it's cramped and uncomfortable for adults. The sedan and wagon have excellent crash tests.

	1997	1998	1999	2000	2001
Size Class	Subcomp.	Subcomp.	Subcomp.	Subcomp.	Subcomp.
Drive	Front	Front	Front	Front	Front
Crash Test	Vry. Gd.[1]	Vry. Gd.[1]	Vry. Gd.[1]	Vry. Gd.[1]	Vry. Gd.[1]
Airbags	Dual	Dual	Dual	Dual	Dual
ABS	4-Whl*	4-Whl*	4-Whl*	4-Whl*	4-Whl*
Parts Cost	Vry. Low	Vry. Low	Vry. Low	Vry. Low	Vry. Low
Complaints	Average	Average	Average	Average	Good
Insurance	Discount	Discount	Discount	Discount	Discount
Fuel Econ.	28	28	29	29	29
Theft Rating	Vry. Low	Vry. Low**	Vry. Low**	Vry. Low**	Vry. Low**
Bumpers	Weak	Weak			Strong
Recalls	3	0	0	7	2
Trn. Cir. (ft.)	37.1	37.1	37.1	37.1	37.1
Weight (lbs.)	2321	2326	2320	2320	2320
Whlbase (in.)	102.4[2]	102.4[2]	102.4[2]	102.4[2]	102.4[2]
Price	8-10,000	8-10,000	9-11,000	10-12,000	13-15,000
OVERALL	BEST BET	BEST BET	BEST BET	BEST BET	BEST BET

Subaru Impreza 1993-2001

The Subaru Impreza, originally produced in 1993 and the replacement for the Loyale in 1995, is Subaru's entrant in the crowded subcompact market. Its base price is slightly higher than most subcompacts, and

1995 Subaru Impreza

it comes with a dizzying array of options, so expect to pay more. The sedan and coupe come in base, L or LX versions, and the wagon comes in L, LX or Outback. A driver's airbag was standard in 1993, a passenger's airbag was optional in 1994, and dual airbags became standard in 1995. ABS has been optional since its introduction.

The base model's engine is a 1.8-liter 4-cylinder that is adequate,

	1992	1993	1994	1995	1996
Size Class		Subcomp.	Subcomp.	Subcomp.	Subcomp.
Drive		Front/All	Front/All	Front/All	Front/All
Crash Test		Good	Good	Good	Good
Airbags		Driver#	Driver#	Dual	Dual
ABS		4-Whl*	4-Whl*	4-Whl*	4-Whl*
Parts Cost	No Model Produced	Average	Average	Average	Average
Complaints		Good	Vry. Gd.	Average	Good
Insurance		Regular	Regular	Regular	Surchg.
Fuel Econ.		24	24	24	25
Theft Rating		Vry. Low	Vry. Low	Vry. Low	Vry. Low
Bumpers					
Recalls		1	0	0	0
Trn. Cir. (ft.)		33.5	33.5	33.5	33.5
Weight (lbs.)		2325	2325	2400	2565
Whlbase (in.)		99.2	99.2	99.2	99.2
Price		4-6,000	5-7,000	6-8,000	8-10,000
OVERALL		Good	Vry. Gd.	Good	Good

*Optional; #Passenger Side Optional; **Estimate

2001 Subaru Impreza

though a more powerful 2.2-liter 4-cylinder is standard on the LX and optional on the L and Outback models. Fuel economy falls below other subcompacts, especially with the larger engine. Base models are front-wheel drive, while LX models are all-wheel drive, and L and Outback models can be either. Handling and ride are typical of subcompacts - quite average. Front seats are comfortable; the back seat is the typical subcompact squeeze, and truck space is small. The best choice is the LX, with its rear stabilizer bar; it out handles the cheaper models and has ABS.

	1997	1998	1999	2000	2001
Size Class	Subcomp.	Subcomp.	Subcomp.	Subcomp.	Subcomp.
Drive	Front/All	Front/All	Front/All	Front/All	Front/All
Crash Test	Good	Good	Good	Good	Good
Airbags	Dual	Dual	Dual	Dual	Dual
ABS	4-Whl*	4-Whl	4-Whl	4-Whl	4-Whl
Parts Cost	Average	Average	Average	Average	Average
Complaints	Vry. Gd.	Vry. Gd.	Good	Average	Vry. Gd.
Insurance	Surchg.	Surchg.	Surchg.	Surchg.	Surchg.
Fuel Econ.	23	23	22	22	22
Theft Rating	Vry. Low	Vry. Low	Vry. Low**	Vry. Low**	Vry. Gd.
Bumpers					
Recalls	0	0	0	0	0
Trn. Cir. (ft.)	33.5	33.5	33.5	33.5	33.5
Weight (lbs.)	2720	2720	2730	2730	2730
Whlbase (in.)	99.2	99.2	99.2	99.2	99.2
Price	9-11,000	12-14,000	14-16,000	16-18,000	17-19,000
OVERALL	Good	Vry. Gd.	Good	Good	Vry. Gd.

Subaru Legacy 1992-2001

For many years, the Legacy has been Subaru's best-selling vehicle, although it was not a truly good vehicle until 1993. The Legacy first came out in mid-1989 and received a significant redesign

1992 Subaru Legacy

with more interior room for 1995. The 1990-94 Legacy has motorized shoulder belts and separate lap belts. An airbag for the driver became optional in 1992, standard in 1993, and a second airbag was added in 1995. Getting ABS is tricky—it's more likely found on the more expensive models, such as the LSi and Touring; however, it's standard on 1996 and 1997 models.

	1992	1993	1994	1995	1996
Size Class	Compact	Compact	Compact	Compact	Compact
Drive	Front/All	Front/All	Front/All	Front/All	Front/All
Crash Test	Average	Good	Good	Vry. Gd.	Vry. Gd.
Airbags	Driver*	Driver	Driver	Dual	Dual
ABS	4-Whl*	4-Whl*	4-Whl*	4-Whl*	4-Whl
Parts Cost	High	High	High	High	Average
Complaints	Good	Good	Good	Poor	Good
Insurance	Regular	Regular	Regular	Regular	Discount
Fuel Econ.	21	22	21	24	24
Theft Rating	Low	Vry. Low	Vry. Low	Vry. Low	Vry. Low
Bumpers	Weak	Weak	Weak	Weak	Weak
Recalls	2	1	0	0	1
Trn. Cir. (ft.)	33.5	33.6	33.5	34.8	36.7
Weight (lbs.)	2740	2800	2825	2655	3080
Whlbase (in.)	101.6	101.6	101.6	103.5	103.5
Price	5-7,000	6-8,000	7-9,000	8-10,000	12-14,000
OVERALL	Poor	Average	Good	Good	BEST BET

*Optional; *Estimate

2001 Subaru Legacy

The Legacy's model lineup ended up like something out of Detroit circa 1965. There are as many as seven trim levels: Base, GT, L, LS, LSi, Sport and Touring. The 2.2-liter 4-cylinder engine is average for compacts in power and mileage. Starting in 1996, models come with an optional 2.5-liter 4-cylinder engine that offers more power with only a slight loss in gas mileage. A turbo was standard on Sport and Touring models, and full-time 4-wheel drive is a Subaru exclusive on low-priced cars.

	1997	1998	1999	2000	2001
Size Class	Compact	Compact	Compact	Compact	Compact
Drive	Front/All	Front/All	Front/All	Front/All	Front/All
Crash Test	Vry. Gd.	Good	Good	Good	Good
Airbags	Dual	Dual	Dual	Dual	Dual
ABS	4-Whl	4-Whl	4-Whl	4-Whl	4-Whl
Parts Cost	Average	Average	Average	Average	Average
Complaints	Good	Average	Average	Average	Average
Insurance	Regular	Regular	Regular	Regular	Regular
Fuel Econ.	23	23	22	22	22
Theft Rating	Vry. Low	Vry. Low	Vry. Low**	Vry. Low**	Vry. Low**
Bumpers	Weak	Weak	Strong	Strong	Strong
Recalls	4	2	1	1	0
Trn. Cir. (ft.)	34.8	34.8	34.8	34.8	34.8
Weight (lbs.)	2885	2885	2885	2885	2885
Whlbase (in.)	103.5	103.5	103.5	103.5	103.5
Price	13-15,000	14-16,000	16-18,000	20-22,000	21-23,000
OVERALL	Vry. Gd.	Good	Vry. Gd.	BEST BET	BEST BET

303

Subaru SVX 1992-97

The original XT was loaded with 4-wheel drive, electronic instruments, and optional turbocharger. Sales were minuscule, and Subaru gradually stripped the base XT so that by 1990 it had the Loyale's engine

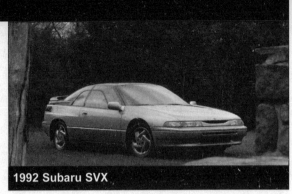
1992 Subaru SVX

and 2-wheel drive. For 1992, Subaru replaced the XT with the all-new SVX. Its styling was even more outlandish than the XT's. Like the XT, the SVX has sold slowly. The 1992-93 SVX has motorized shoulder belts and manual lap belts; the SVX adds a driver's airbag. The SVX offers dual airbags and normal belts on the higher LS and LSi 1994 models and on all later models. ABS is standard on all SVXs.

	1992	1993	1994	1995	1996
Size Class	Large	Large	Large	Large	Large
Drive	Front/All	Front/All	Front/All	Front/All	Front/All
Crash Test	N/A	N/A	N/A	N/A	N/A
Airbags	Driver	Driver	Driver#	Dual	Dual
ABS	4-Whl	4-Whl	4-Whl	4-Whl	4-Whl
Parts Cost	High	Vry. High	Vry. High	High	Average
Complaints	Vry. Pr.	Good	Vry. Pr.	Vry. Pr.	Vry. Pr.
Insurance	Regular	Regular	Regular	Regular	Surchg.
Fuel Econ.	17	18	18	17	17
Theft Rating	Average	Average	Average	Average	High
Bumpers					
Recalls	0	0	0	0	0
Trn. Cir. (ft.)	35.4	35.4	35.4	35.4	35.4
Weight (lbs.)	3525	3525	3430	3430	3525
Whlbase (in.)	102.8	102.8	102.8	102.8	102.8
Price	6-8,000	7-9,000	8-10,000	10-12,000	13-15,000
OVERALL~					

#Passenger Side Optional; ~Cars without crash tests do not receive an overall rating.

1996 Subaru SVX

The XT and SVX move well with the XT's turbo 4- or the 6-cylinder engine, but gas mileage suffers. The SVX's side windows take some getting used to—only part of each window rolls down. The handling is fine on both, but the SVX emphasizes ride a bit more than cornering. Room and comfort for two are good, but the back seat is useless for adults. The early XT's electronic instrument panel, with 4-wheel drive graphics, is more irritating and unreliable than useful.

	1997	1998	1999	2000	2001
Size Class	Large				
Drive	Front/All				
Crash Test	N/A				
Airbags	Dual				
ABS	4-Whl				
Parts Cost	High				
Complaints	Poor				
Insurance	Regular				
Fuel Econ.	17				
Theft Rating	Average				
Bumpers					
Recalls	0		No Model Produced		
Trn. Cir. (ft.)	35.4				
Weight (lbs.)	3525				
Whlbase (in.)	102.8				
Price	15-17,000				
OVERALL~					

Suzuki Esteem 1996-2001

The Esteem, the larger of Suzuki's two models, is their first entry into the compact sedan market, a competitive and crowded market. The base model comes with dual airbags and optional ABS; the

1996 Suzuki Esteem

upgraded GLX has added features. It was revamped in 1999 and received new sheet metal work, grille, fenders, and headlights.

The standard 1.6 liter 4 cylinder engine offers poor power and little excitement, a sacrifice for good gas mileage. Be sure to check out the larger 1.8-liter engine. The interior is small, if not tight, and trunk space is likewise. Pack lightly. Noise levels are minimal. Though the price is

	1992	1993	1994	1995	1996
Size Class					Subcomp.
Drive					Front
Crash Test					N/A
Airbags					Dual
ABS					4-Whl*
Parts Cost					Vry. High
Complaints					Vry. Gd.
Insurance					Surchg.
Fuel Econ.					30
Theft Rating					Average
Bumpers		No Model Produced			
Recalls					0
Trn. Cir. (ft.)					32.2
Weight (lbs.)					2227
Whlbase (in.)					97.6
Price					4-6,000
OVERALL~					

*Optional; **Estimate; ~Cars without a crash test do not receive an overall rating.

2001 Suzuki Esteem

as small as the car, your money would be well spent elsewhere.

	1997	1998	1999	2000	2001
Size Class	Subcomp.	Subcomp.	Subcomp.	Subcomp.	Subcomp.
Drive	Front	Front	Front	Front	Front
Crash Test	N/A	N/A	N/A	N/A	N/A
Airbags	Dual	Dual	Dual	Dual	Dual
ABS	4-Whl*	4-Whl*	4-Whl*	4-Whl*	4-Whl*
Parts Cost	Vry. High	Vry. High	Vry. High	Vry. High	Vry. High
Complaints	Vry. Gd.	Poor	Average	Good	Good
Insurance	Surchg.	Surchg.	Surchg.	Surchg.	Surchg.
Fuel Econ.	30	30	30	30	30
Theft Rating	Average	Average	Average	Average**	Average**
Bumpers			Weak		
Recalls	0	0	0	0	0
Trn. Cir. (ft.)	32.2	32.2	32.2	32.2	32.2
Weight (lbs.)	2227	2227	2227	2227	2227
Whlbase (in.)	97.6	97.6	97.6	97.6	97.6
Price	5-7,000	7-9,000	8-10,000	9-11,000	14-16,000
OVERALL~					

Toyota 4Runner 1992-2001

The 4Runner, a thinly disguised Toyota compact pickup, underwent moderate changes in 1990 at the same time the pickup was updated. Before 1996, the 4Runner trailed the pack with respect to safety; this sport utility

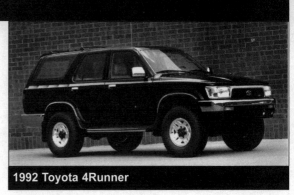

1992 Toyota 4Runner

never offered its occupants an airbag, and ABS was only offered on rear wheels. All this changed in '96 as the 4Runner got a standard driver airbag and optional 4-wheel ABS. Dual airbags were standard in 1997. The later model crash tests have improved vastly from those on the early 90's 4Runner.

4Runners used to have a standard 2.4-liter 4-cylinder, engine which

	1992	1993	1994	1995	1996
Size Class	Sp. Util.	Sp. Util.	Sp. Util.	Sp. Util.	Sp. Util.
Drive	Rear/4	Rear/4	Rear/4	Rear/4	Rear/4
Crash Test	Poor	Poor	Poor	Poor	Average
Airbags	None	None	None	None	Driver
ABS	2-Whl*	2-Whl*	2-Whl*	2-Whl*	2-Whl[1]
Parts Cost	Low	Average	Average	Average	Average
Complaints	Vry. Gd.	Vry. Gd.	Good	Vry. Gd.	Vry. Gd.
Insurance	Surchg.	Surchg.	Surchg.	Surchg.	Surchg.
Fuel Econ.	15	18	17	19	19
Theft Rating	High	High	Vry. High	Vry. High	Vry. High
Bumpers					Weak
Recalls	0	0	0	0	1
Trn. Cir. (ft.)	37.4	37.4	37.4	37.4	37.4
Weight (lbs.)	4050	3800	3820	3825	3825
Whlbase (in.)	103.3	103.3	103.3	103.3	103.3
Price	9-11,000	10-12,000	11-13,000	13-15,000	15-17,000
OVERALL	Poor	Vry. Pr.	Vry. Pr.	Vry. Pr.	Poor

[1]Optional 4-Wheel ABS; *Optional; **Estimate

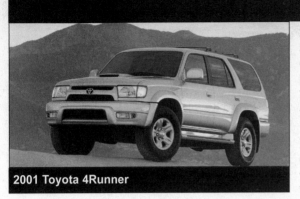

2001 Toyota 4Runner

resulted in a barely adequate 116 hp. Optional was a 3-liter V6 which boosts output to a more satisfying 150 hp. They now have a 4 or 6-liter engine which provide more power. Until 1990, the 4Runner was only available as a 2-door model, with either 2- or 4-wheel drive. With the 1990 redesign, a 4-door model was added, and 4-wheel drive was dropped as an option on the 2-door model. Ride, handling, rear-seat room and comfort have all improved over the years, but don't expect it to ride and feel like a car. Head- and legroom are still cramped, although for 1996 these improve slightly.

	1997	1998	1999	2000	2001
Size Class	Sp. Util.	Sp. Util.	Sp. Util.	Sp. Util.	Sp. Util.
Drive	Rear/4	Rear/4	Rear/4	Rear/4	Rear/4
Crash Test	Average	Average	Average	Vry. Gd.	Vry. Gd.
Airbags	Dual	Dual	Dual	Dual	Dual
ABS	4-Whl*	4-Whl*	4-Whl*	4-Whl*	4-Whl*
Parts Cost	High	Vry. High	High	High	High
Complaints	Vry. Gd.	Average	Good	Average	Vry. Gd.
Insurance	Surchg.	Surchg.	Surchg.	Surchg.	Surchg.
Fuel Econ.	16	17	17	17	17
Theft Rating	Vry. High	Vry. High	Vry. High**	Vry. High**	Vry. High**
Bumpers	Weak	Weak			
Recalls	0	0	0	0	0
Trn. Cir. (ft.)	37.4	37.4	37.4	37.4	37.4
Weight (lbs.)	3440	3440	3440	3440	3440
Whlbase (in.)	105.3	105.3	105.3	105.3	105.3
Price	17-19,000	19-21,000	23-25,000	28-30,000	29-31,000
OVERALL	Poor	Vry. Pr.	Poor	Average	Vry. Gd.

Toyota Camry 1992-2001

For 1992, Toyota increased the Camry's length to match mid-size cars, and, in 1994, a coupe joined the line. Finally, an all-new version was available for 1997 with a new, conservative look. The 1989-91

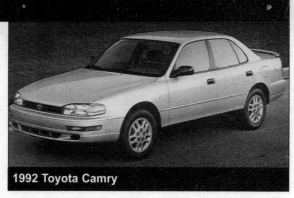

1992 Toyota Camry

Camry has motorized shoulder belts and separate lap belts. The 1992-93 Camrys have a driver's airbag and regular belts; 1994 models add a passenger airbag. ABS was optional in 1989 but was not widely available until 1991.

The 1989-97 Camry 4-cylinder engine has a lively twin cam. You can choose an optional V6 engine, which is quite powerful. You can choose

	1992	1993	1994	1995	1996
Size Class	Intermd.	Intermd.	Intermd.	Intermd.	Intermd.
Drive	Front	Front	Front	Front	Front
Crash Test	Vry. Gd.	Vry. Gd.	Good	Good	Good[1]
Airbags	Driver	Driver	Dual	Dual	Dual
ABS	4-Whl*	4-Whl*	4-Whl*	4-Whl*	4-Whl*
Parts Cost	High	Vry. High	High	High	High
Complaints	Poor	Good	Good	Good	Vry. Gd.
Insurance	Discount	Discount	Discount	Discount	Regular
Fuel Econ.	21	21	21	21	23
Theft Rating	Average	Average	High	Vry. High	Average
Bumpers	Weak	Weak	Weak	Weak	Weak
Recalls	0	0	1	0	2
Trn. Cir. (ft.)	35.4	35.4	35.4	35.4	35.4
Weight (lbs.)	2943	2943	2932	3086	2932
Whlbase (in.)	103.1	103.1	103.1	103.1	103.1
Price	6-8,000	7-9,000	8-10,000	9-11,000	11-13,000
OVERALL	Good	Vry. Gd.	Vry. Gd.	Vry. Gd.	Good

[1]Data given for sedan. Crash test rating for coupe is Vry. Good; *Optional; **Estimate

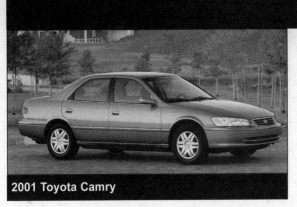
2001 Toyota Camry

between power and better ride with the V6 and economy and better handling with the 4. The bumper system on 1992-97 models was incredibly weak, but improved in 1997. The interior is spacious and comfortable for four, and the truck is nicely shaped. Options, packages, and other choices abound, so make sure you look around. It faces stiff competition with the Accord and Taurus but has been a best seller. It has a history of good crash tests as well.

	1997	1998	1999	2000	2001
Size Class	Intermd.	Intermd.	Intermd.	Intermd.	Intermd.
Drive	Front	Front	Front	Front	Front
Crash Test	Good	Vry. Gd.	Vry. Gd.	Vry. Gd.	Vry. Gd.
Airbags	Dual	Dual/Side*	Dual/Side*	Dual/Side*	Dual/Side*
ABS	4-Whl*	4-Whl*	4-Whl*	4-Whl*	4-Whl*
Parts Cost	High	Vry. High	Vry. High	High	Average
Complaints	Average	Average	Good	Good	Average
Insurance	Regular	Regular	Regular	Regular	Regular
Fuel Econ.	23	23	23	23	24
Theft Rating	High	Vry High	Vry. High**	Vry. High**	Average
Bumpers	Weak	Strong	Strong	Strong	Strong
Recalls	2	2	2	2	1
Trn. Cir. (ft.)	35.4	35.4	35.4	35.4	35.4
Weight (lbs.)	2976	2998	2998	2998	2998
Whlbase (in.)	105.2	105.2	105.2	105.2	105.2
Price	13-15,000	14-16,000	15-17,000	17-19,000	21-23,000
OVERALL	Average	Average	Vry. Gd.	Vry. Gd.	Vry. Gd.

Toyota Celica 1992-2001

The 1990 Celica looked much like earlier models, but with rounded rather than linear edges. A 4-wheel drive All-Trac model was offered from 1989-93. The Celica received new styling for 1994, and the

1992 Toyota Celica

ST and All-Trac disappeared. The 1990-93 models have a driver's airbag and regular belts; 1994 models have dual airbags. ABS became optional in 1988.The Celica was reinvented for 2000 with a shorter length, longer wheelbase, and some serious new styling. Side airbags also became optional with this model.

The base engine is fairly powerful; on the highway, it's reasonably

	1992	1993	1994	1995	1996
Size Class	Compact	Compact	Compact	Compact	Compact
Drive	Front/All	Front/All	Front	Front	Front
Crash Test	Good	Good	N/A	N/A	N/A
Airbags	Driver	Driver	Dual	Dual	Dual
ABS	4-Whl*	4-Whl*	4-Whl*	4-Whl*	4-Whl*
Parts Cost	High	Vry. High	High	Vry. High	Vry. Low
Complaints	Good	Vry. Gd.	Good	Good	Vry. Gd.
Insurance	Surchg.	Surchg.	Regular	Surchg.	Surchg.
Fuel Econ.	22	21	23	22	22
Theft Rating	Average	Average	Average	Low	Vry. Low
Bumpers	Weak	Weak			
Recalls	0	0	0	0	1
Trn. Cir. (ft.)	36.1	36.1	34.2	34.1	34.1
Weight (lbs.)	2646	2646	2415	2560	2415
Whlbase (in.)	99.4	99.4	99.9	99.9	99.9
Price	6-8,000	7-9,000	8-10,000	10-12,000	13-15,000
OVERALL~	Poor	Average			

*Optional; **Estimate; ~Cars without crash tests do not receive an overall rating.

2001 Toyota Celica

economical. Buyers can get a turbocharged 4-cylinder engine on the GT-S, which will provide more power with only a slight loss in fuel economy. The 5-speed and automatic are good performers. The standard suspension handles capably, but the GT-S is even better. On all models, the ride is decent and, at times, noisy. The dashboard is typically functional and intelligently laid out. The interior has room for two, but the rear seat is an afterthought.

	1997	1998	1999	2000	2001
Size Class	Compact	Compact	Compact	Compact	Compact
Drive	Front	Front	Front	Front	Front
Crash Test	N/A	N/A	N/A	N/A	N/A
Airbags	Dual	Dual	Dual	Dual/Side*	Dual/Side*
ABS	4-Whl*	4-Whl*	4-Whl*	4-Whl*	4-Whl*
Parts Cost	High	High	High	High	Average
Complaints	Vry. Gd.	Vry. Gd.	Vry. Gd.	Poor	Average
Insurance	Surchg.	Surchg.	Surchg.	Surchg.	Surchg.
Fuel Econ.	22	22	22	28	28
Theft Rating	Average	Average	Average	Average**	Average**
Bumpers			Strong	Strong	Strong
Recalls	0	0	0	0	0
Trn. Cir. (ft.)	34.2	34.2	34.2	36.1	36.1
Weight (lbs.)	2415	2415	2580	2425	2425
Whlbase (in.)	99.9	99.9	99.9	102.3	102.4
Price	14-16,000	17-19,000	18-20,000	18-20,000	19-21,000
OVERALL~					

Toyota Corolla 1992-2001

Toyota's major entry in the compact market, the Corolla has performed very well over the past 15 years and is still one of Toyota's best-selling models. For 1990-92, Corollas have door-mounted

1992 Toyota Corolla

ed shoulder belts and manual lap belts. In 1993, Toyota added a driver's airbag and regular belts. The 1994 Corollas have dual airbags. ABS became optional in 1993. Side airbags became an option in 1998.

The single-cam 1.6-liter engine provides adequate power but is noisy with the 3-speed automatic. The twin-cam 1.6-liter or 1.8-liter 4-cylinder is quicker, and fuel economy remains good. For 2001, the 1.8-liter

	1992	1993	1994	1995	1996
Size Class	Subcomp.	Compact	Compact	Compact	Compact
Drive	Front	Front	Front	Front	Front
Crash Test	Average	Average	Good	Good	Good
Airbags	None	Driver	Dual	Dual	Dual
ABS	None	4-Whl*	4-Whl*	4-Whl*	4-Whl*
Parts Cost	High	High	High	Vry. High	Average
Complaints	Vry. Gd.	Good	Good	Vry. Gd.	Vry. Gd.
Insurance	Surchg.	Regular	Regular	Regular	Surchg.
Fuel Econ.	26	26	26	28	31
Theft Rating	Low	Low	Average	Average	Average
Bumpers	Strong				
Recalls	1	2	4	3	1
Trn. Cir. (ft.)	31.5	32.2	32.2	32.2	32.2
Weight (lbs.)	2253	2304	2315	2381	2315
Whlbase (in.)	95.7	97	97	97	97
Price	3-5,000	4-6,000	5-7,000	6-8,000	7-9,000
OVERALL	Poor	Average	Average	Good	Vry. Gd.

*Optional; **Estimate

2001 Toyota Corolla

became the standard and with 125 horses, this engine shows a lot of pep. The handling is good, but tricky at higher speeds. The Corolla can transport four people in modest comfort with room for luggage. Typical of Toyotas, controls are logical and easy to use. The Corolla is an outstanding compact, but be wary of models with average to poor crash test scores. In the past, the Prizm could save you money but now, you can get a base Corolla for less.

	1997	1998	1999	2000	2001
Size Class	Compact	Compact	Compact	Compact	Compact
Drive	Front	Front	Front	Front	Front
Crash Test	Good	Good	Good	Good	Good
Airbags	Dual	Dual/Side*	Dual/Side*	Dual/Side*	Dual/Side*
ABS	4-Whl*	4-Whl*	4-Whl*	4-Whl*	4-Whl*
Parts Cost	High	High	High	High	High
Complaints	Vry. Gd.	Good	Vry. Gd.	Vry. Gd.	Vry. Gd.
Insurance	Surchg.	Surchg.	Surchg.	Surchg.	Surchg.
Fuel Econ.	31	31	31	31	21
Theft Rating	Average	Average	Average**	Average**	Average
Bumpers		Weak	Strong	Strong	Strong
Recalls	2	0	0	0	0
Trn. Cir. (ft.)	32.2	32.2	32.2	32.2	32.2
Weight (lbs.)	2337	2414	2414	2414	2414
Whlbase (in.)	97	97	97	97	97
Price	9-11,000	10-12,000	11-13,000	12-14,000	13-15,000
OVERALL	Good	Good	Vry. Gd.	Vry. Gd.	Good

Toyota Cressida 1992, Avalon 1995-2001

Toyota's plushest model, the Cressida, has gone through many changes over the years, including being discontinued and renamed. By 1992, the Cressida had been squeezed out of the model gap between the

1992 Toyota Cressida

Toyota Camry and the base Lexus ES, and the Cressida was discontinued. However, in 1995, Toyota brought the car back—this time as the Avalon. The 1981 Cressida was the first car sold in the U.S. with motorized shoulder belts and manual lap belts, a design later used by dozens of manufacturers. Not surprisingly, all Cressidas right up through 1992 kept the motorized belts. ABS became available in 1989,

	1992	1993	1994	1995	1996
Size Class	Large			Intermd.	Intermd.
Drive	Rear			Front	Front
Crash Test	Good			Vry. Gd.	Vry. Gd.
Airbags	None			Dual	Dual
ABS	4-Whl*			4-Whl*	4-Whl*
Parts Cost	Average			High	High
Complaints	Vry. Gd.			Good	Average
Insurance	Discount			Regular	Discount
Fuel Econ.	19			20	20
Theft Rating	High			Vry. Low	Vry. Low
Bumpers		No Model Produced		Weak	Weak
Recalls	0			0	0
Trn. Cir. (ft.)	32.8			37.6	37.6
Weight (lbs.)	3439			3263	3263
Whlbase (in.)	105.5			107.1	107.1
Price	8-10,000			12-14,000	13-15,000
OVERALL	Vry. Gd.			Vry. Gd.	Vry. Gd.

*Optional; **Estimate

316

2001 Toyota Avalon

though airbags were never offered. The Avalon comes standard with dual airbags and optional 4-wheel ABS until 1999, when it became standard. In 1998, side airbags also became standard.

The Cressidas have a 3.0-liter 6-cylinder engine from 1989 on. The Avalon also offers only one engine choice, a revamped 3.0-liter V6 similar to the one found in the Cressida. Both are spirited but consume quite a bit of fuel. The balance between ride and handling tips slightly toward ride. The interior is comfortable, and the trunk is nicely shaped.

	1997	1998	1999	2000	2001
Size Class	Intermd.	Intermd.	Intermd.	Intermd.	Intermd.
Drive	Front	Front	Front	Front	Front
Crash Test	Vry. Gd.	Vry. Gd.	Good	Good	Good
Airbags	Dual	Dual/Side	Dual/Side	Dual/Side	Dual/Side
ABS	4-Whl*	4-Whl*	4-Whl	4-Whl	4-Whl
Parts Cost	High	High	High	High	High
Complaints	Average	Poor	Average	Good	Average
Insurance	Discount	Discount	Discount	Discount	Discount
Fuel Econ.	21	21	21	21	21
Theft Rating	Vry. Low	Average	Average**	Average**	Average**
Bumpers	Weak	Weak			
Recalls	1	1	1	1	0
Trn. Cir. (ft.)	37.6	37.6	37.6	37.6	37.6
Weight (lbs.)	3263	3340	3340	3340	3340
Whlbase (in.)	107.1	107.1	107.1	107.1	107.1
Price	15-17,000	17-19,000	20-22,000	25-27,000	26-28,000
OVERALL	Vry. Gd.	Vry. Gd.	Vry. Gd.	BEST BET	Vry. Gd.

Toyota Paseo 1992-98

Paseo, which, in Spanish, means "promenade", was introduced in 1992 and received major revisions in 1996 and a convertible version in 1997. It is a two-seater with room for four in a pinch, but don't

1992 Toyota Paseo

plan on putting much more than groceries in the back. The Paseo is basically a sporty version of the Tercel coupe. While Toyota's least expensive sports car, the Paseo offers the same safety features as the more expensive ones. Starting in 1993, ABS was optional and a driver's airbag was standard. In 1996, dual airbags became standard.

Since its introduction, the Paseo has offered a 1.5-liter 4-cylinder en-

	1992	1993	1994	1995	1996
Size Class	Subcomp.	Subcomp.	Subcomp.	Subcomp.	Subcomp.
Drive	Front	Front	Front	Front	Front
Crash Test	Average	Average	Good	Good	Good
Airbags	Driver	Driver	Driver	Driver	Dual
ABS	4-Whl*	4-Whl*	4-Whl*	4-Whl*	4-Whl*
Parts Cost	High	High	High	High	High
Complaints	Vry. Gd.	Vry. Gd.	Vry. Gd.	Vry. Gd.	Vry. Gd.
Insurance	Regular	Regular	Regular	Surchg.	Surchg.
Fuel Econ.	28	28	26	29	30
Theft Rating	Low	Low	Vry. Low	Average	Low
Bumpers	Weak	Weak	Weak	Weak	Weak
Recalls	0	0	0	0	0
Trn. Cir. (ft.)	32.5	32.5	32.5	32.5	32.2
Weight (lbs.)	2070	2070	2070	2070	2025
Whlbase (in.)	93.7	93.7	93.7	93.7	93.7
Price	4-6,000	5-7,000	6-8,000	8-10,000	9-11,000
OVERALL	Poor	Good	Good	Average	Good

*Optional

1997 Toyota Paseo

gine that produces 20-25% more power than the Toyota Tercel. However, the power was slightly reduced in 1996 as Toyota tried to meet emissions requirements. Both the standard manual or optional automatic transmissions are fairly fuel efficient. The ride and handling don't live up to the sporty styling, and sound insulation is on the skimpy side.

	1997	1998	1999	2000	2001
Size Class	Subcomp.	Subcomp.			
Drive	Front	Front			
Crash Test	Good	Good			
Airbags	Dual	Dual			
ABS	4-Whl*	4-Whl*			
Parts Cost	High	High			
Complaints	Vry. Gd.	Vry. Gd.			
Insurance	Surchg.	Surchg.			
Fuel Econ.	31	31			
Theft Rating	Vry. Low	Vry. Low		No Model Produced	
Bumpers	Weak	Weak			
Recalls	0	0			
Trn. Cir. (ft.)	32.2	32.2			
Weight (lbs.)	2025	2025			
Whlbase (in.)	93.7	93.7			
Price	10-12,000	10-12,000			
OVERALL	Good	Vry. Gd.			

Toyota Previa 1992-97

1992 Toyota Previa

The Toyota Van arrived here in 1984, just as Chrysler started caching in on the minivan market. With its rear-wheel drive and forward control design, the Toyota Van had more in common with the outdated vans of the 1960s than the modern minivans. In 1991, Toyota scrapped the van and introduced the Previa. The Previa retained the rear-wheel drive, but the layout of the interior and the exterior styling were very modern.

The 4-cylinder engine is adequate, and four-wheel drive is available. The interior is comfortable and roomy. The ride and handling are great-

	1992	1993	1994	1995	1996
Size Class	Minivan	Minivan	Minivan	Minivan	Minivan
Drive	Rear/All	Rear/All	Rear/All	Rear/All	Rear/All
Crash Test	Average	Average	Average	Average	Average
Airbags	Driver	Driver	Dual	Dual	Dual
ABS	4-Whl*	4-Whl*	4-Whl*	4-Whl*	4-Whl*
Parts Cost	High	High	High	Average	Average
Complaints	Average	Good	Good	Good	Average
Insurance	Regular	Regular	Discount	Discount	Discount
Fuel Econ.	17	17	17	17	18
Theft Rating	Average	Average	Average	Average	Average
Bumpers			Weak	Weak	Weak
Recalls	0	0	0	0	0
Trn. Cir. (ft.)	37.4	37.4	37.4	37.4	37.4
Weight (lbs.)	3765	3765	3610	3615	3755
Whlbase (in.)	112.8	112.8	112.8	112.8	112.8
Price	8-10,000	9-11,000	10-12,000	12-14,000	14-16,000
OVERALL	Poor	Poor	Good	Vry. Gd.	Good

*Optional

1997 Toyota Previa

ly improved on the Previa, especially compared to the old Toyota Van. The Previa finally gave Toyota a viable competitor in the hot minivan market.

	1997	1998	1999	2000	2001
Size Class	Minivan				
Drive	Rear/All				
Crash Test	Average				
Airbags	Dual				
ABS	4-Whl*				
Parts Cost	Vry. High				
Complaints	Average				
Insurance	Discount				
Fuel Econ.	18				
Theft Rating	Average				
Bumpers	Weak				
Recalls	1				
Trn. Cir. (ft.)	37.4				
Weight (lbs.)	3755				
Whlbase (in.)	112.8				
Price	16-18,000				
OVERALL	Average				

No Model Produced

Toyota RAV4 1996-2001

The Toyota RAV4 (Recreational Active Vehicle with 4WD) is designed to be a light, off-road vehicle that seats five. Toyota has equipped this new vehicle well, with standard dual airbags and option-

1996 Toyota RAV4

al 4-wheel ABS. All the power options are available on the base model and standard on the L version.

The RAV4 is powered by an average 2-liter 4-cylinder engine, which can beat out many sporty coupes and sedans but is unable to compete with some of the other small sport utilities. It has a wide stance, which gives it decent room inside for four. You have your choice between a 2-

	1992	1993	1994	1995	1996
Size Class					Sp. Util.
Drive					2WD/4WD
Crash Test					Average
Airbags					Dual
ABS					4-Whl*
Parts Cost					High
Complaints					Vry. Gd.
Insurance					Regular
Fuel Econ.					22
Theft Rating					Average
Bumpers		No Model Produced			
Recalls					0
Trn. Cir. (ft.)					33.5
Weight (lbs.)					2789
Whlbase (in.)					86.6
Price					9-11,000
OVERALL~					Good

*Optional; **Estimate; ~Cars without crash tests do not receive an overall rating.

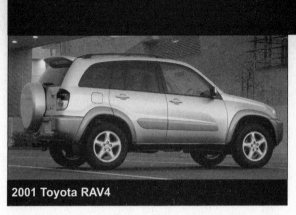

2001 Toyota RAV4

and 4-door model, and from many different appearance packages. The RAV4 is all-new for 2001. You'll find a bit more cargo space that the first generation model as well as adjustable front cup holders and a foot rest for the passenger.

	1997	1998	1999	2000	2001
Size Class	Sp. Util.	Sp. Util.	Sp. Util.	Sp. Util.	Sp. Util.
Drive	2WD/4WD	2WD/4WD	2WD/4WD	2WD/4WD	2WD/4WD
Crash Test	Average	Average	Average	Average	Good
Airbags	Dual	Dual	Dual	Dual	Dual
ABS	4-Whl*	4-Whl*	4-Whl*	4-Whl*	4-Whl*
Parts Cost	High	High	High	Very High	Average
Complaints	Vry. Gd.	Good	Good	Vry. Gd.	Average
Insurance	Regular	Regular	Regular	Regular	Surchg.
Fuel Econ.	22	24	24	24	25
Theft Rating	Average	Average	Average	Low	Average**
Bumpers					
Recalls	0	2	2	0	0
Trn. Cir. (ft.)	36.1	36.1	36.1	33.5	35.4
Weight (lbs.)	2789	2701	2701	2701	2711
Whlbase (in.)	94.9	94.9	94.9	94.9	98
Price	12-14,000	13-15,000	15-17,000	16-18,000	17-19,000
OVERALL~	Good	Average	Average	Good	Good

Toyota Supra 1992-97

The Supra started off in 1979 as a Celica with a 6-cylinder engine instead of a 4. The last model to be based on the Celica was in 1985; it shared the Celica's chassis, but the Supra had distinctive front-end styling. With a complete restyling for 1986, the Supra kept its rear-wheel drive layout (Celicas went to front-wheel drive that year) and moved into the Camaro/Firebird class in power and weight. The Supra looked the same until 1993, when Toyota brought out a totally new Supra that was unmistakably a sports car, competitive with the Nissan 300ZX and Chevrolet Corvette. For 1990-92, models have

1992 Toyota Supra

	1992	1993	1994	1995	1996
Size Class	Large	Intermd.	Intermd.	Intermd.	Intermd.
Drive	Rear	Rear	Rear	Rear	Rear
Crash Test	N/A	N/A	N/A	N/A	N/A
Airbags	Driver	Dual	Dual	Dual	Dual
ABS	4-Whl*	4-Whl	4-Whl	4-Whl	4-Whl
Parts Cost	Average	Average	Average	Average	Average
Complaints	Vry. Gd.	Good	Good	Vry. Gd.	Vry. Gd.
Insurance	Surchg.	Surchg.	Surchg.	Surchg.	Surchg.
Fuel Econ.	18	18	17	17	17
Theft Rating	Average	Average	Average	Average	Average
Bumpers					
Recalls	0	0	0	0	0
Trn. Cir. (ft.)	35.4	35.4	35.8	35.8	35.8
Weight (lbs.)	3463	3215	3215	3210	3210
Whlbase (in.)	102.2	100.4	100.4	100.4	100.4
Price	13-15,000	14-16,000	16-18,000	18-20,000	20-22,000
OVERALL~					

*Optional; ~Cars without crash tests do not receive an overall rating.

1996 Toyota Supra

a driver's airbag and regular belts; dual airbags became standard in 1993. ABS was optional in 1989, standard in 1993.

The standard 6-cylinder engine is powerful, but the 1989-92 Supra responds a little slowly because of its excess weight, though the turbo helps. The engines in the newest Supras are more responsive, or, at least, they seem that way because the newer Supra is a couple hundred pounds lighter than the older model. The handling is very good on pre-1993 Supras, excellent after that. The dashboard emphasizes function. The interior has enough room for two.

	1997	1998	1999	2000	2001
Size Class	Intermd.				
Drive	Rear				
Crash Test	N/A				
Airbags	Dual				
ABS	4-Whl				
Parts Cost	Average				
Complaints	Vry. Gd.				
Insurance	Surchg.				
Fuel Econ.	17				
Theft Rating	Average				
Bumpers					
Recalls	0				
Trn. Cir. (ft.)	35.8				
Weight (lbs.)	3210				
Whlbase (in.)	100.4				
Price	24-26,000				
OVERALL~					

No Model Produced

Toyota Tercel 1992-98

Toyota's cheapest car, the Tercel, offers more than most competitive subcompacts. The 1987 Tercel got new styling, and a notchback coupe joined the line. The old Tercel wagons carried over into

1992 Toyota Tercel

1987, and the 4-wheel drive wagon was replaced by the Corolla All-Trac wagon in 1988. The redesigned 1991 models kept the original Tercel's chassis, but rounded the edges. The all-new 1995 model did not look much different from the previous generation. From 1990-92, and on the passenger side of the 1993-94 Tercels, occupants have an automatic shoulder belt and a separate manual lap belt. Starting in 1993, Ter-

	1992	1993	1994	1995	1996
Size Class	Subcomp.	Subcomp.	Subcomp.	Subcomp.	Subcomp.
Drive	Front	Front	Front	Front	Front
Crash Test	Poor	Good	Good	Average	Average
Airbags	None	Driver	Driver	Dual	Dual
ABS	None	4-Whl*	4-Whl*	4-Whl*	4-Whl*
Parts Cost	Average	High	High	High	High
Complaints	Vry. Gd.	Vry. Gd.	Vry. Gd.	Vry. Gd.	Vry. Gd.
Insurance	Surchg.	Surchg.	Surchg.	Surchg.	Surchg.
Fuel Econ.	26	28	28	31	30
Theft Rating	Low	Vry. Low	Vry. Low	Vry. Low	Vry. Low
Bumpers	Weak	Weak	Weak		
Recalls	0	0	0	0	0
Trn. Cir. (ft.)	31.5	31.5	31.5	31.5	31.5
Weight (lbs.)	2005	2005	1950	2005	1950
Whlbase (in.)	93.7	93.7	93.7	93.7	93.7
Price	2-4,000	3-5,000	4-6,000	5-7,000	6-8,000
OVERALL	Poor	Good	Good	Good	Good

[1]Data given for Sedan. Crash test for the coupe is Good; *Optional; **Estimate

1997 Toyota Tercel

cels were equipped with a standard driver's airbag and optional ABS; dual airbags became standard with the 1995 redesign.

Tercels are certainly not sports cars. Early Base Tercels have a 4-speed manual transmission, minimal sound insulation, and few options. Find one with a 5-speed for best performance and gas mileage. The Tercel handles reasonably well, though response improves with power steering. The room inside is typical of subcompacts, tight, however, you'll find the controls and gauges are easy to use.

	1997	1998	1999	2000	2001
Size Class	Subcomp.	Subcomp.			
Drive	Front	Front			
Crash Test	Average[1]	Average[1]			
Airbags	Dual	Dual			
ABS	4-Whl*	4-Whl*			
Parts Cost	High	High			
Complaints	Average	Vry. Pr.			
Insurance	Surchg.	Surchg.			
Fuel Econ.	32	32			
Theft Rating	Vry. Low	Vry. Low**			
Bumpers					
Recalls	0	0			
Trn. Cir. (ft.)	31.5	31.5			
Weight (lbs.)	2010	2010			
Whlbase (in.)	93.7	93.7			
Price	8-10,000	9-11,000			
OVERALL	Average	Poor			

No Model Produced

Volkswagen Golf/Jetta 1992-2001

The Golf, introduced in 1985, was more rounded and aerodynamic than the long-running Rabbit series it replaced; the Jetta is essentially a Golf with a separate trunk. The Jetta comes in base, GL

1996 Volkswagen Jetta

and sporty GLI trim; the top-model Golf is the high-performance GTI. After a complete revision late in 1993, they were called Golf or Jetta III, but the new models look much like the old ones. Later Golfs kept the door-mounted belts and also added a lap belt. For 1994, a driver's airbag was standard and a passenger airbag was optional. Starting in 1995, dual airbags are standard. ABS is optional beginning in 1991.

	1992	1993	1994	1995	1996
Size Class	Subcomp.	Subcomp.	Compact	Compact	Compact
Drive	Front	Front	Front	Front	Front
Crash Test	Average	Average	Average	Average	Average
Airbags	None	None	Driver#	Dual	Dual
ABS	4-Whl*	4-Whl*	4-Whl*	4-Whl*	4-Whl*
Parts Cost	Low	Average	Average	Average	Average
Complaints	Average	Good	Poor	Poor	Average
Insurance	Surchg.	Surchg.	Regular	Surchg.	Surchg.
Fuel Econ.	25	24	21	24	22
Theft Rating	High	Low	Low	Low	Vry. Low
Bumpers	Weak	Weak	Weak	Weak	Weak
Recalls	2	5	6	5	1
Trn. Cir. (ft.)	34.4	32.6	32.6	32.6	32.6
Weight (lbs.)	2320	2320	2577	2577	2577
Whlbase (in.)	97.3	97.3	97.4	97.4	97.4
Price	4-6,000	5-7,000	6-8,000	8-10,000	11-13,000
OVERALL	Poor	Poor	Poor	Vry. Pr.	Average

[1]Side airbags standard for 1999-2001 Golf; [2]Theft rating for 2000 Jetta is Average; *Optional; #Passenger Side Optional;

2001 Volkswagen Golf

Golfs and Jettas share a 1.6-liter diesel engine and a gasoline-fueled 1.8- or 2-liter 4-cylinder; 1994 models offer a 2.8 narrow-angle V6 engine. The diesels are slow but economical. Otherwise, performance is lively, especially with the V6. Precise cornering and a firm, comfortable ride can be found-better on the Jetta than the Golf. The seats are supportive and there's enough room for four. A high number of complaints and high insurance costs bring the Golf and Jetta down. However, the recent crash tests have been excellent. The 2000 is a "Best Bet."

	1997	1998	1999	2000	2001
Size Class	Compact	Compact	Compact	Compact	Compact
Drive	Front	Front	Front	Front	Front
Crash Test	Average	Average	Vry. Gd.	Vry. Gd.	Vry. Gd.
Airbags	Dual	Dual/Side*	Dual/Side[1]	Dual/Side[1]	Dual/Side[1]
ABS	4-Whl*	4-Whl*	4-Whl*	4-Whl*	4-Whl*
Parts Cost	High	Average	Average	Average	High
Complaints	Good	Average	Poor	Average	Vry. Pr.
Insurance	Surchg.	Surchg.	Surchg.	Surchg.	Surchg.
Fuel Econ.	22	24	24	24	25
Theft Rating	Vry. Low	Vry. Low	Vry. Low	High[2]**	Low**
Bumpers	Weak	Weak	Weak	Strong	Strong
Recalls	0	0	0	0	0
Trn. Cir. (ft.)	32.8	32.8	32.8	32.8	32.8
Weight (lbs.)	2661	2729	2729	2729	2729
Whlbase (in.)	97.4	97.4	97.4	97.4	97.4
Price	13-15,000	14-16,000	15-17,000	16-18,000	17-19,000
OVERALL	Good	Average	Good	Vry. Gd.	Average

**Estimate

Volkswagen Passat 1992-2001

First introduced in 1990 as the replacement for the Dasher, the front-wheel drive Passat is marketed as a European luxury sedan/wagon without the luxury price tag. This model led a relatively quiet

1992 Volkswagen Passat

existence until the 1995 model year, when it was redesigned and VW finally paid some advertising attention to it. Airbags were not available until the 1995 redesign gave it two; before that, you were stuck with motorized shoulder belts and separate lap belts in the front seats. Four-wheel ABS, an option from 1990-92, became standard in 1993.

The 1990-93 models have a 2-liter 4-cylinder engine that puts out a

	1992	1993	1994	1995	1996
Size Class	Intermd.	Intermd.	Intermd.	Intermd.	Intermd.
Drive	Front	Front	Front	Front	Front
Crash Test	Poor	Poor	Poor	Good	Good
Airbags	None	None	None	Dual	Dual
ABS	4-Whl*	4-Whl	4-Whl	4-Whl	4-Whl
Parts Cost	High	High	Average	High	High
Complaints	Vry. Pr.	Vry. Pr.	Good	Vry. Pr.	Vry. Pr.
Insurance	Surchg.	Surchg.	Surchg.	Surchg.	Surchg.
Fuel Econ.	21	21	18	18	20
Theft Rating	Average	Vry. High	High	High	Vry. High
Bumpers				Weak	Weak
Recalls	1	3	1	1	0
Trn. Cir. (ft.)	35.1	35.1	38.4	38.4	38.4
Weight (lbs.)	2985	2985	3152	3140	3140
Whlbase (in.)	103.3	103.3	103.3	103.3	103.3
Price	5-7,000	6-8,000	7-9,000	8-10,000	11-13,000
OVERALL	Vry. Pr.	Vry. Pr.	Vry. Pr.	Vry. Pr.	Vry. Pr.

*Optional; **Estimate

2001 Volkswagen Passat

more than adequate 134 hp. The 2.8-liter V6 is available on 1993-97 GLX sedans as well as wagons. Though the Passat is VW's plushest model, a plush VW is nothing like a plush Buick. The Passat has a spacious, comfortable interior, but the ride can actually be a little too firm. Cargo space is generous, and passengers will be comfortable on long trips. The latest Passats are be a good choice for their excellent crash tests but are still plagued by high numbers of complaints.

	1997	1998	1999	2000	2001
Size Class	Intermd.	Intermd.	Intermd.	Intermd.	Intermd.
Drive	Front	Front	Front	Front	Front
Crash Test	Good	Vry Gd	Vry. Gd.	Vry. Gd.	Vry. Gd.
Airbags	Dual	Dual/Side	Dual/Side	Dual/Side	Dual/Side
ABS	4-Whl	4-Whl	4-Whl	4-Whl	4-Whl
Parts Cost	Vry. High	Average	High	High	High
Complaints	Poor	Vry. Pr.	Vry. Pr.	Vry. Gd.	Vry. Pr.
Insurance	Surchg.	Surchg.	Surchg.	Surchg.	Surchg.
Fuel Econ.	20	23	23	23	23
Theft Rating	Vry. High	Average	Average**	Average**	Average**
Bumpers	Weak		Strong	Strong	Strong
Recalls	0	1	0	1	0
Trn. Cir. (ft.)	38.4	37.4	37.4	37.4	37.4
Weight (lbs.)	3175	3120	3120	3120	3120
Whlbase (in.)	103.3	106.4	106.4	106.4	106.4
Price	13-15,000	17-19,000	19-21,000	23-25,000	25-27,000
OVERALL	Average	Average	Good	Vry. Gd.	Average

Volvo 850 1993-97, C70/S70/V70 1998-2001

Volvo has continued to revise its model line over the years and, with the departure of the 200 Series in 1993, Volvo introduced a new, smoother model, the 850. Over its five years, the Volvo 850 maintained

1994 Volvo 850

Volvo's reputation for safety, performing well in government crash tests and coming standard with dual airbags and 4-wheel ABS. New for 1996, Volvo once again led the industry by offering side impact airbags. The new driver and passenger side airbags can be found in the front doors. They are standard on the Turbo sedans, optional on the base and GLT sedans and wagons. The 850 became the 70 Series line in 1998.

	1992	1993	1994	1995	1996
Size Class		Intermd.	Intermd.	Intermd.	Intermd.
Drive		Front	Front	Front	Front
Crash Test		Good	Good	Good	Good
Airbags		Dual	Dual	Dual	Dual
ABS		4-Whl	4-Whl	4-Whl	4-Whl
Parts Cost		Average	Average	Average	Average
Complaints		Average	Poor	Poor	Average
Insurance		Discount	Discount	Discount	Discount
Fuel Econ.		20	20	20	20
Theft Rating		Vry. Low	Vry. Low	Vry. Low	Vry. Low
Bumpers		Weak	Weak	Weak	Weak
Recalls		1	2	2	1
Trn. Cir. (ft.)		33.5	33.5	33.5	33.5
Weight (lbs.)		3232	3232	3232	3232
Whlbase (in.)		104.9	104.9	104.9	104.9
Price		12-14,000	13-15,000	14-16,000	16-18,000
OVERALL		Good	Good	Good	Vry. Gd.

(1992 column: No Model Produced)

**Estimate

2001 Volvo V70

This is the first front-wheel drive vehicle Volvo has sold in the U.S., and it is powered by a 5-cylinder engine that is not only powerful but very smooth. There is a turbo option, but it is probably unnecessary. In 1998, Volvo began the transition to the "70" series with a restyled, more aerodynamic exterior. Inside, accommodations for four people are good; five may be a squeeze. A fold out booster seat for children is standard on wagons and optional on sedans - an excellent feature.

	1997	1998	1999	2000	2001
Size Class	Intermd.	Intermd.	Intermd.	Intermd.	Intermd.
Drive	Front	Front	Front	Front	Front
Crash Test	Good	Vry. Gd.	Vry. Gd.	Vry. Gd.	Vry. Gd.
Airbags	Dual	Dual/Side	Dual/Side	Dual/Side	Dual/Side
ABS	4-Whl	4-Whl	4-Whl	4-Whl	4-Whl
Parts Cost	High	Average	Average	Average	Average
Complaints	Average	Average	Average	Average	Average
Insurance	Discount	Discount	Discount	Discount	Discount
Fuel Econ.	20	20	20	20	20
Theft Rating	Vry. Low	Vry. Low	Vry. Low**	Vry. Low**	Vry. Low**
Bumpers	Weak			Strong	Strong
Recalls	1	1	1	0	0
Trn. Cir. (ft.)	33.5	33.5	38.4	38.4	38.4
Weight (lbs.)	3232	3152	3601	3601	3601
Whlbase (in.)	104.9	104.9	104.9	104.9	104.9
Price	18-20,000	28-30,000	29-31,000	>30,000	>30,000
OVERALL	Good	BEST BET	BEST BET	Vry. Gd.	BEST BET

Volvo 900 Series 1992-97, S90/V90 1998, S80 1999-2001

The Volvo 940 and 960 are direct descendants of the 700 Series that first came out in 1983. New for 1991, the 900 Series has styling similar to the 700 Series, but many of the sharp edges are smoothed

1993 Volvo 940

out. The 960 was Volvo's top-level model, with a six-cylinder engine, leather upholstery, and many options. All 900 Series cars have a driver's airbag. The 1993 960 got a standard passenger airbag, and Volvo added this to the 940 for 1994. In 1996, side-impact airbags came as standard equipment—a first in the industry. All 900 Series cars have ABS. The 90 Series took over in 1998 from the 900 Series and in 1999,

	1992	1993	1994	1995	1996
Size Class	Intermediate	Intermediate	Intermediate	Intermediate	Intermediate
Drive	Rear	Rear	Rear	Rear	Rear
Crash Test	N/A	Good	Good	Good	Good
Airbags	Driver#	Driver#	Dual	Dual	Dual
ABS	4-Whl	4-Whl	4-Whl	4-Whl	4-Whl
Parts Cost	Vry. High	Vry. High	Average	Average	Average
Complaints	Vry. High	Average	Average	Average	Poor
Insurance	Discount	Discount	Discount	Discount	Discount
Fuel Econ.	19	19	19	19	18
Theft Rating	Average	Average	Average	Average	Low
Bumpers					
Recalls	1	0	0	2	1
Trn. Cir. (ft.)	32.2	32.2	32.2	32.2	31.8
Weight (lbs.)	3067	3067	3205	3208	3461
Whlbase (in.)	109.1	109.1	109.1	109.1	109.1
Price	9-11,000	10-12,000	11-13,000	14-16,000	17-19,000
OVERALL~		Vry. Gd.	Vry. Gd.	Good	Good

#Passenger Side Optional; **Estimate; ~Cars without crash tests do not receive an overall rating.

334

2001 Volvo S80

became the S80.

The 940 comes with a twin-cam 4, regular or turbocharged; the 960 gets a Porsche-designed 6-cylinder engine. Acceleration on the 960 and 940 turbo is quick; gas mileage is average for its size, but you must use premium fuel. The base 940 will be slower, especially in wagon form, but more economical. The sleeker, more aerodynamic 90 series was introduced in 1998. The interior comfort and room for four are exceptional. There's a clever, fold-away child booster in the rear center seat. The wagon's cargo area is large, and the sedan's trunk is roomy.

	1997	1998	1999	2000	2001
Size Class	Intermediate	Intermediate	Intermediate	Intermediate	Intermediate
Drive	Rear	Rear	Front	Front	Front
Crash Test	Good	Good	Vry. Gd.	Vry. Gd.	Vry. Gd.
Airbags	Dual	Dual/Side	Dual/Side	Dual/Side	Dual/Side
ABS	4-Whl	4-Whl	4-Whl	4-Whl	4-Whl
Parts Cost	Average	Average	Average	High	High
Complaints	Poor	Vry. Gd.	Good	Average	Average
Insurance	Regular	Regular	Regular	Regular	Regular
Fuel Econ.	18	18	18	18	19
Theft Rating	Low	Low	Low**	Low**	Low**
Bumpers					
Recalls	1	0	0	0	0
Trn. Cir. (ft.)	31.8	31.8	35.8	37	37
Weight (lbs.)	3461	3461	3300	3602	3602
Whlbase (in.)	109.1	109.1	109.9	109.9	109.9
Price	19-21,000	19-21,000	29-31,000	>30,000	>30,000
OVERALL~	Vry. Gd.	Good	BEST BET	Good	BEST BET

Index